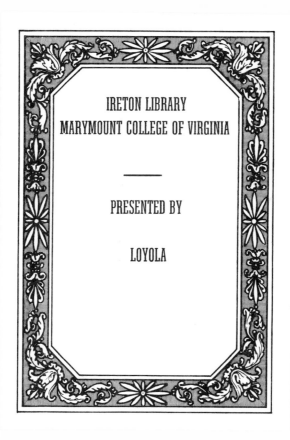

SENSATIONAL
DESIGNS
The Cultural Work of
American Fiction
1790-1860

SENSATIONAL DESIGNS

The Cultural Work of American Fiction 1790-1860

JANE TOMPKINS

New York • Oxford

OXFORD UNIVERSITY PRESS

1985

Oxford University Press

Oxford   London   New York   Toronto
Delhi   Bombay   Calcutta   Madras   Karachi
Kuala Lumpur   Singapore   Hong Kong   Tokyo
Nairobi   Dar es Salaam   Cape Town
Melbourne   Auckland

and associated companies in
Beirut   Berlin   Ibaden   Mexico City   Nicosia

Copyright © 1985 by Oxford University Press, Inc.

Published by Oxford University Press, Inc.,
200 Madison Avenue, New York, New York 10016

Library of Congress Cataloging in Publication Data
Tompkins, Jane P.
  Sensational designs.
  Includes index.
  1. American fiction—19th century—History and criticism.
2. American fiction—1783–1850–History and criticism.
3. Social problems in literature.
4. Literature and society—United States.
I. Title.
PS374.S7T66 1985   813′.2′09   85-4925
ISBN 0-19-503565-8

Printing (last digit): 9 8 7 6 5 4 3 2 1

Printed in the United States of America

For my parents
Henry Thomas Parry
Lucille Reilly Parry

Acknowledgments

The number of people to whom I have given parts of this book while I was writing it and from whom I have received criticism, encouragement, and advice is both embarrassingly and gratifyingly long. I am thankful to Michael Bell, Sacvan Bercovitch, William E. Cain, Sharon Cameron, Judith Fetterley, Jay Fliegelman, Michael Fried, Susan Getze, Jonathan Goldberg, Barbara Harman, Elisabeth Hansot, Elaine Hedges, William Hedges, Carolyn Karcher, David Levin, Walter Benn Michaels, Daniel O'Hara, Susan Stewart, Edward Tayler, and Michael Warner.

I would also like to thank those people whose professional support kept me going in various ways while I was working on the manuscript: Annette Kolodny, Frank Lentricchia, Richard Macksey, Alan Wilde, and Larzer Ziff. For help keeping going on the practical level of re-typing chapters and re-checking footnotes I would like to thank Michael Warner and, especially, Michael Moon.

I owe a special debt to Catherine Ingraham and Marilyn Sides, with whom I met every other week for fifteen months in a writing group that saved us from loneliness, despair, and bad rhetorical strategies, and provided me with essential insights and encouragement. And for the latter I also thank Mary Jane Lucas, R.N.

I am grateful to my parents, Henry T. Parry and Lucille Reilly Parry, who loaned me money while I took a year off to write, and to the Huntington Library for a summer fellowship to do research on the Susan Warner chapter. But beyond all others I am grateful to Stanley Fish, who supported me financially and in every other way. Who gave me tons of criticism and carloads of advice, ran zillions of errands, provided hundreds of dinners out, legislated vacations I would have been too stupid to take, shamed me into not giving up, fulminated, barked out orders, bought me presents, and washed the dishes. To him my debt is as deep as can be.

Earlier versions of the following chapters have appeared in the following publications: "Masterpiece Theater" in *American Quarterly* (Winter 1985); "No Apologies for the Iroquois" in *Criticism* (Winter 1981); "Sentimental Power" in *Glyph, 8* (1981); a much foreshortened version of "The Other American Renaissance" in *The American Renaissance Reconsidered*, ed. Donald E. Pease and Walter Benn Michaels (1985); part I of the same essay in *Genre* (Winter 1983); and a substantially different version of " 'But Is It Any Good?' " in the GRIP Report, volume 2.

I am grateful for permission to reprint.

Contents

Introduction: The Cultural Work of American Fiction

This book is the beginning of an attempt to move the study of American literature away from the small group of master texts that have dominated critical discussion for the last thirty years and into a more varied and fruitful area of investigation. It involves, in its most ambitious form, a redefinition of literature and literary study, for it sees literary texts not as works of art embodying enduring themes in complex forms, but as attempts to redefine the social order. In this view, novels and stories should be studied not because they manage to escape the limitations of their particular time and place, but because they offer powerful examples of the way a culture thinks about itself, articulating and proposing solutions for the problems that shape a particular historical moment. I believe that the works of fiction that this book examines were written not so that they could be enshrined in any literary hall of fame, but in order to win the belief and influence the behavior of the widest possible audience. These novelists have designs upon their audiences, in the sense of wanting to make people think and act in a particular way.

Consequently this book focuses primarily, though not exclusively, on works whose obvious impact on their readers has made them suspect from a modernist point of view, which tends to classify work that affects people's lives, or tries to, as merely sensational or propagandistic. *Uncle Tom's Cabin*, perhaps the most famous work of American fiction, has not until very recently drawn the attention of modern critics; Susan Warner's *The Wide, Wide World*, second only to Stowe's novel in its popular and critical success in the nineteenth century, has since dropped from sight completely; *The Last of the Mohicans*, also a best-seller in its own time, has retained critical visibility, but, like the novels by Warner and Stowe, has come to be thought of as more fit for children than for adults. Brockden Brown's novels, not at all popular when Brown was alive, subsequently gained a certain critical reputation but always with the proviso that they contained glaring artistic defects. In fact, what all of these texts share, from the perspective of modern criticism, is a certain set of defects that excludes them from the ranks of the great masterpieces: an absence of finely delineated characters, a lack of verisimilitude in the story line, an excessive reliance on plot, and a certain sensationalism in the events portrayed. None is thought to have a distinguished prose style or to reflect a concern with the unities and economies of formal construction that modern criticism seeks in great works of art. One purpose of this book is to ask why these works, many of which did not seem at all deficient to their original audiences, have come to seem deficient in the way I have just described. Another is to question the perspective from which these deficiencies spring to mind.

That perspective comes under fire in the opening chapter, which prepares the way for a consideration of non-canonical texts by investigating the processes through which canonical texts achieve their classic status. Using Hawthorne's reputation as a case in point, it argues that the reputation of a classic author arises not from the "intrinsic merit" of his or her work, but rather from the complex of circumstances that make texts visible initially and then maintain them in their preeminent position. When classic texts are seen not as the ineffable products of genius but as the bearers of a set of national, social, economic, institutional, and professional interests, then their domination of the critical scene seems less the result of their indisputable excellence than the product of historical contingencies. Through a close description of the reasons why Hawthorne's work has continued to compel our admiration, I attempt to loosen the hold his texts have exercised over American criticism, and thus to make possible the consideration of other texts, which the current canon has blotted from view.

In order to understand these neglected texts, that is, to see them, insofar as possible, as they were seen in the moment of their emergence, not as degraded attempts to pander to the prejudices of the multitude, but as providing men and women with a means of ordering the world they inhabited, one has to have a grasp of the cultural realities that made these novels meaningful. Thus, rather than asking how a given text handled the questions which have recently concerned modern critics—questions about the self, the body, the possibilities of knowledge, the limits of language— I have discussed the works of Brown, Cooper, Stowe, and Warner in relation to the religious beliefs, social practices, and economic and political circumstances that produced them. History is invoked here not, as in previous historical criticism, as a backdrop against which one can admire the artist's skill in transforming the raw materials of reality into art, but as the only way of accounting for the enormous impact of works whose force escapes the modern reader, unless he or she makes the effort to recapture the world view they sprang from and which they helped to shape. It is on this basis, that of a new kind of historical criticism, that I advance the claim that my approach yields more fruitful results than some more narrowly "literary" critical modes. Because I want to understand what gave these novels force for their initial readers, it seemed important to recreate, as sympathetically as possible, the context from which they sprang and the specific problems to which they were addressed. I have therefore not criticized the social and political attitudes that motivated these writers, but have tried instead to inhabit and make available to a modern audience the viewpoint from which their politics made sense.

This is not to say that my own attitude toward these texts is neutral or disinterested. Any reconstruction of "context" is as much determined by the attitudes and values of the interpreter as is the explication of literary works; my reading of the historical materials as well as the textual analyses I offer grow directly from the circumstances, interests, and aims that have constituted me as a literary critic. If I have from time to time accused other critics of a "presentist" bias, the same charge can be levelled against my own assumptions, which are of course no more free than theirs from the constraints of a particular historical situation. My claim is not that I am more neutral or disinterested than others, but rather that the readings I offer here provide a more satisfactory way of understanding the texts in question than the current critical consensus has.

To be specific about the interests that have motivated me: what lies behind this study is a growing awareness, on my part, of the extremely narrow confines of literary study as it is now practiced within the academy, and with that, a sense of the social implications of this exclusionary practice. Because I am a woman in a field dominated by male scholars, I have been particularly sensitive to the absence of women's writing from the standard American literature curriculum. I chose to discuss two works of domestic, or "sentimental," fiction because I wanted to demonstrate the power and ambition of novels written by women, and specifically by women whose work twentieth-century criticism has repeatedly denigrated.

Reading the scattered criticism of popular domestic novels led me to recognize—though I am certainly not the first to have done so—that the *popularity* of novels by women has been held against them almost as much as their preoccupation with "trivial" feminine concerns. And this led to the observation, again not original with me, that popular fiction, in general, at least since the middle of the nineteenth century, has been rigorously excluded from the ranks of "serious" literary works. That exclusion seems to me especially noteworthy in American literature, since the rhetoric of American criticism habitually invokes democratic values as a hallmark of greatness in American authors. When Melville calls upon that "great democratic God" and celebrates "meanest mariners, renegades, and castaways," it is cause for critical acclaim, but when the common man steps out of *Moby-Dick* or *Song of Myself* and walks into a bookstore, his taste in literature, or, as is more likely, hers, is held up to scorn. Because I think it is morally and politically objectionable, and intellectually obtuse, to have contempt for literary works that appeal to millions of people simply *because* they are popular, I chose to discuss three works of popular fiction in order to demonstrate the value of these texts: to explore the way that literature has power in the world, to see how it connects with the beliefs and attitudes of large masses of readers so as to impress or move them deeply.

I chose the texts I did because I wanted to find a way of opening up the canon not only to popular works and to works by women, but also to texts that are not usually thought to conform to a definition of imaginative literature—for example, the advice books, tract society reports, and hagiographic biographies discussed in the chapter on Susan Warner. These forms of non-fictional discourse, when set side by side with contemporary fiction, can be seen to construct the real world in the image of a set of ideals and beliefs in exactly the same way that novels and stories do. So much so that in certain instances, unless one already knows which is fiction and which fact, it is impossible to tell the difference. Finally, I have included chapters on two novels by Charles Brockden Brown because I wanted to show that texts already in the canon, which modern critics have considered artistically weak or defective, assume a quite different shape and significance when considered in light of the cultural "work" they were designed to do.

The critical perspective that has brought into focus the issues outlined here stems from the theoretical writings of structuralist and post-structuralist thinkers: Levi-Strauss, Derrida, and Foucault; Stanley Fish, Edward Said, and Barbara Herrnstein Smith. My debt to these writers is so pervasive that I have not, with one or two exceptions, cited their work at any particular point. But the way of thinking about literature that informs the book as a whole, as well as the kinds of arguments offered in individual chapters, springs directly from my study of their work. The perspective this work affords has not only determined many of the aims and values embodied here, but has also suggested some of the tactics that I have used in interpreting the texts under discussion.

Because I was trying to understand what gave these novels traction in their original setting (i.e., what made them popular, not what made them "art"), I have looked for continuities rather than ruptures, for the strands that connected a novel to other similar texts, rather than for the way in which the text might have been unique. I have not tried to emphasize the individuality or genius of the authors in question, to isolate the sensibility, modes of perception, or formal techniques that differentiate them from other authors or from one another. Rather I have seen them, in Foucault's phrase, as "nodes within a network," expressing what lay in the minds of many or most of their contemporaries. Therefore I do not argue for the value of these texts on the grounds of their *difference* from other texts, as is normally done in literary criticism, showing how they avoid the pieties of the age and shun what is stereotyped or clichéd. My aim rather has been to show what a text had *in common* with other texts. For a novel's impact on the culture at large depends not on its escape from the formulaic and derivative, but on its tapping into a storehouse of commonly held assumptions, reproducing what is already there in a typical and familiar form. The text that becomes exceptional in the sense of reaching an exceptionally large audience does so not because of its departure from the ordinary and conventional, but through its embrace of what is most widely shared.

My own embrace of the conventional led me to value everything that criticism had taught me to despise: the stereotyped character, the sensational plot, the trite expression. As I began to see the power of the copy as opposed to the original, I searched not for the individual but for the type. I saw that the presence of stereotyped characters, rather than constituting a defect in these novels, was what allowed them to operate as instruments of cultural self-definition. Stereotypes are the instantly recognizable representatives of overlapping racial, sexual, national, ethnic, economic, social, political, and religious categories; they convey enormous amounts of cultural information in an extremely condensed form. As the telegraphic expression of complex clusters of value, stereotyped characters are *essential* to popularly successful narrative. Figures like Stowe's little Eva, Cooper's Magua, and Warner's Ellen Montgomery operate as a cultural shorthand, and because of their multilayered representative function are the carriers of strong emotional associations. Their familiarity and typicality, rather than making them bankrupt or stale, are the basis of their effectiveness as integers in a social equation.

The more I thought about the structure of these novels, the more I came to see the solving or balancing of such equations as the purpose that rationalizes their often repetitive and improbable plots. The problems these plots delineate—problems concerning the relations among people of different sexes, races, social classes, ethnic groups, economic levels—require a narrative structure different from the plots of modern psychological novels, a structure that makes then seem sensational and contrived in comparison with texts like *The Ambassadors* or *The Scarlet Letter*. But the endlessly repeated rescue scenes in *Arthur Mervyn* and *The Last of the Mohicans*, the separation of families in *Uncle Tom*, and the Job-like trials of faith in *The Wide, Wide World*, while violating what seem to be self-evident norms of probability and formal economy, serve as a means of stating and proposing solutions for social and political predicaments. The benevolent rescuers of *Arthur Mervyn* and the sacrificial mothers of *Uncle Tom's Cabin* act out scenarios that teach readers what kinds of behavior to emulate or shun; because the function of these scenarios is heuristic and didactic rather than mimetic, they do not attempt to transcribe in detail a parabola of events as they "actually happen" in society; rather, they provide a basis for remaking the social and political order in which events take place. When read in the light of its original purpose, the design of a novel like *Wieland* is no less functional than that of *The Scarlet Letter*.

In arguing for the positive value of stereotyped characters and sensational, formulaic plots, I have self-consciously reversed the negative judgments that critics have passed on these features of popular fiction by re-describing them from the perspective of an altered conception of what literature is. When literary texts are conceived as agents of cultural formation rather than as objects of interpretation and appraisal, what counts as a "good" character or a logical sequence of events changes accordingly. When one sets aside modernist demands—for psychological complexity, moral ambiguity, epistemological sophistication, stylistic density, formal economy—and attends to the way a text offers a blueprint for survival under a specific set of political, economic, social, or religious conditions, an entirely new story begins to unfold, and one's sense of the formal exigencies of narrative alters accordingly, producing a different conception of what constitutes successful characters and plots. The text succeeds or fails on the basis of its "fit" with the features of its immediate context, on the degree to which it provokes the desired response, and not in relation to unchanging formal, psychological, or philosophical standards of complexity, or truth, or correctness.

Thus, the novel's literary style, no less than its characters and plot, will seem forceful and expressive to the degree that it adopts an idiom to which a contemporary audience can respond. When little Eva says to Topsy, " 'O, Topsy, poor child, *I* love you' . . . with a sudden burst of feeling, and laying her little thin, white hand on Topsy's shoulder; 'I love you because you haven't any father, or mother, or friends:—because you've been a poor, abused child! I love you, and I want you to be good,' " her style may seem saccharine or merely pathetic to us. But her language had power to move hundreds of thousands of readers in the nineteenth century because they believed in the spiritual elevation of a simple childlike idiom, in the spiritual efficacy of "sudden burst[s] of feeling," and in the efficacy of what is spiritual in general. And so when Eva ends her speech to Topsy by saying "it's only a little while I shall be with you," the comparison evoked between the doll-like Eva and the son of God does not seem absurd or contrived to Stowe's readers—it is not comparing great things with small, but affirming the potential of every person, man, woman, or child, to live and die as Christ did. Within the context of evangelical Christianity, one might say of Stowe what R. P. Blackmur said of Melville—that she habitually used words greatly.

This last point broaches, in summary fashion, an issue that goes to the heart of the present project, namely, the relationship between aesthetic value and the text's historical existence. Reconstituting the notion of value in literary works is an aim which all of these essays share. People who have read one or more of them in various forms, or heard me lecture over the last few years, almost invariably ask whether the works I am discussing are really literary or not—are they, someone always asks, really any *good*? This question, which raises theoretical issues central to my project, is the subject of the final chapter. I have postponed this discussion until the end, since any argument for changing the criteria by which we judge literary texts must depend not only on abstract reasons but on a discussion of individual cases as well.

SENSATIONAL DESIGNS
The Cultural Work of
American Fiction
1790-1860

I
Masterpiece Theater: The Politics of Hawthorne's Literary Reputation

The classic definition of a classic, as a work that has withstood the test of time, was formulated by Samuel Johnson in his *Preface to Shakespeare*. Where productions of genius are concerned, wrote Johnson, "of which the excellence is not absolute and definite, but gradual and comparative . . . no other test can be applied than length of duration and continuance of esteem." Once a great author has outlived his century, he continues, "whatever advantages he might once derive from personal allusions, local customs, or temporary opinions, have for many years been lost. . . . The effects of favor and competition are at an end; the tradition of his friendships and his enmities has perished; his works . . . , thus unassisted by interest or passion, . . . have past through variations of taste and changes of manners, and, as they devolved from one generation to another, have received new honors at every transmission."[1] The notion that literary greatness consists in the power of a work to transcend historical circumstance repeats itself in the nineteenth century, particularly in the work of Arnold and Shelley, and has been a commonplace of twentieth-century criticism.[2] T. S. Eliot and Frank Kermode, for instance, take it for granted that a classic does not depend for its appeal on any particular historical context and devote themselves to defining the criteria we should use to determine which works are classic, or to describing the characteristics of works already designated as such.[3] I propose here to question the accepted view that a classic work does not depend for its status on the circumstances in which it is read and will argue exactly the reverse: that a literary classic is a product of all those circumstances of which it has traditionally been supposed to be independent. My purpose is not to depreciate classic works but to reveal their mutability. In essence what I will be asserting is that the status of literary masterpieces is owing to arguments just like the one I am making here and that therefore the canon not only can but will change along with the circumstances within which critics argue.

I have chosen as a case in point the literary reputation of Nathaniel Hawthorne, a reputation so luminous and enduring that it would seem to defy the suggestion that it was based on anything other than the essential greatness of his novels and stories. Indeed, that assumption is so powerful that what follows may at times sound like a conspiracy theory of the way literary classics are made. As Hawthorne's success comes to seem, in my account, more and more dependent on the influence of his friends and associates, and then on the influence of their successors, it may appear that this description of the politics of Hawthorne's rise to prominence is being opposed, implicitly, to an ideal scenario in which the emergence of a classic author has nothing to do with power relations. But to see an account of the political and social processes by which a classic author is put in place as the account of a conspiracy is only possible if one assumes that classic status could be achieved independently of any political and social processes whatsoever. The argument that follows is not critical of the way literary reputations come into being, or of Hawthorne's reputation in particular. Its object, rather, is to suggest that a literary reputation could never be anything but a political matter. My assumption is not that "interest and passion" should be eliminated from literary evaluation—this is neither possible nor desirable—but that works that have attained the status of classic, and are therefore believed to embody universal values, are in fact embodying only the interests of whatever parties or factions are responsible for maintaining them in their preeminent position. Identifying the partisan processes that lead to the establishment of a classic author is not to revoke his or her claim to greatness, but simply to point out that that claim is open to challenge from other quarters, by other groups, representing equally partisan interests. It is to point out that the literary works that now make up the canon do so because the groups that have an investment in them are culturally the most influential. And finally, it is to suggest in particular that the casualties of Hawthorne's literary reputation—the writers who, by virtue of the same processes that led to his ascendancy, are now forgotten—need not remain forever obliterated by his success.

To question the standard definition of the classic, and thus the canon as it is presently constituted, is also to question the way of thinking about literature on which the canon is based. For the idea of the classic is virtually inseparable from the idea of literature itself. The following attempt to describe the man-made, historically produced nature of a single author's reputation, therefore, is likely to arouse a host of objections because it challenges, all at once, an entire range of assumptions on which literary criticism has traditionally operated. The strength of these assumptions does not stem from their being grounded in the truth about literature, however, but from the pervasiveness of one particular mode of constructing literature—namely, the one that assigns to literary greatness an ahistorical, transcendental ground. The overwhelming force of this conception lies in its seeming to have arisen not from any particular school of criticism or collection of interests, but naturally and inevitably, as a way of accounting for the ability of certain literary works to command the attention of educated readers generation after generation. That this theory is neither natural nor inevitable it will be the purpose of this chapter to show. "The effects of favor and competition," "the tradition of friendships," the "advantages" of "local customs," and "temporary opinions," far from being the irrelevant factors that Johnson considered them, are what originally created and subsequently sustained Hawthorne's reputation as a classic author. Hawthorne's work, from the very beginning, emerged into visibility, and was ignored or acclaimed, as a function of the circumstances in which it was read.

I

Between 1828 and 1836 Hawthorne published some of what are now regarded as his best short stories: "The Gentle Boy," "The Gray Champion," "Young Goodman Brown," "Roger Malvin's Burial," "The Minister's Black Veil," "The Maypole of Merrymount." But although these are among the most frequently anthologized American short stories, to Hawthorne's contemporaries they were indistinguishable from the surrounding mass of magazine fiction. Until the *Token* of 1836 appeared, says Bertha Faust, who wrote the best study of Hawthorne's early reception, "no one singled out one of Hawthorne's pieces by a single word."[4] This indifference to what we now regard as Hawthorne's finest tales requires an explanation. If an author's reputation really does depend upon the power of his art to draw attention to itself regardless of circumstances, then why did Hawthorne's first readers fail utterly to recognize his genius as we understand it, or as his contemporaries would later understand it? The reason, Faust says, is that Hawthorne's tales would not have stood out on the basis of their subject matter, since tales involving American colonial history or depicting a person dominated by a single obsession had many parallels in contemporary fiction. Moreover, since Hawthorne's stories, like most of what appeared in the gift book annuals, were published anonymously, there was no way of telling that they were the products of a single hand. Finally, since the annuals were rather lightly regarded at the time, critics had no expectation of finding anything of merit in them.[5]

This account of why Hawthorne's greatness went unrecognized initially argues that Hawthorne's readers could not have judged his tales accurately because of the misleading circumstances in which they were embedded. It implicitly assumes that the context acts as a kind of camouflage, making Hawthorne's tales look exactly like those of lesser writers, and that, under other circumstances, the tales would have been seen for what they "really" are. But what sorts of circumstances could these have been? If Hawthorne's tales had not appeared in the *Token*, they would have appeared in *Graham's Magazine*, or *Godey's Lady's Book*, or the

Southern Literary Messenger; in each case the context supplied by the periodical would have altered readers' perceptions of the tales themselves.[6] If the tales had not appeared anonymously, but under Hawthorne's name, then whatever associations readers attached to that name would have influenced their responses. Of course, it could be argued that while some circumstances get in the way of accurate perception, others merely reinforce qualities already present in the work, and so do not distort readers' perceptions of the work itself. But the difficulty with this argument is that since there is no way of knowing what a work is like exempted from all circumstances whatsoever, we can never know which circumstances distort and which reinforce the work "as it really is." Since pure perception is a practical impossibility, given that a text must always be perceived under some circumstances or other, one cannot use the notion of "misleading" vs. "reinforcing" circumstances to explain why Hawthorne's first readers did not see his tales the way we do.

Another way to explain the indifference to Hawthorne's work in the 1830s is to consider the possibility that the circumstances in which a text is read, far from *preventing* readers from seeing it "as it really is," are what make the text available to them in the first place. That is, circumstances define the work "as it really is"— under those circumstances. And they do this by giving readers the means of classifying a text in relation to what they already know. Thus, Hawthorne's first critics did not single out his tales for special commendation for the simple reason that they did not know anything about them beforehand. And that is why the stories they did single out—stories by John Neal, N. P. Willis, and Catherine Sedgewick—were written by well-published, widely-praised authors of whom they had already heard a great deal.[7] In praising *their* work, Hawthorne's contemporaries stood in exactly the same relation to it as modern critics stand in relation to Hawthorne's; that is, they were able to identify its merits because they already knew that it was good and were looking at it with certain expectations. Thus, when Samuel Goodrich, the editor of *The Token*, began telling other editors about Hawthorne's work, they began to pay attention to it for the first time; once the editors had a reason for seeing Hawthorne's work as exceptional, they began to see it that way. I am not suggesting that Goodrich had an especially keen eye for literary genius and so was able to point out to others what they had not been able to see for themselves, but that, as editor of the most prominent of the annuals, he was in a position to create a favorable climate for the reception of Hawthorne's work.[8] Until 1836 Hawthorne's tales not only seemed but *were* completely ordinary because the conditions necessary to their being perceived in any other way had not yet come into being.

I have been suggesting that "external circumstances," far from being irrelevant to the way a literary work is perceived, are what make it visible to its readers in the first place. But, one might ask, once "circumstances" had alerted readers to the existence of Hawthorne's fiction, from that point on wouldn't it stand or fall on its own merits? This would seem to be a plausible suggestion, but the particulars of Hawthorne's early reception point in a different direction. What they show is that circumstances not only brought Hawthorne's tales to the attention of critics; they also shaped critics' reactions to the tales themselves.

The first notice of any length to appear following the publication of *Twice-told Tales* in 1837 was an extremely laudatory piece by the editor of the *Salem Gazette*. This man, according to Faust, "was indebted to Hawthorne for a number of early contributions, all presumably unpaid, and . . . was about to increase his debt by reprinting . . . pieces from the volume in question."[9] Any one of a number of factors—local pride, a sense of financial obligation, personal gratitude, or an eye to future self-interest—positioned the editor of the *Salem Gazette* in relation to what he read. Circumstances, one might say, weighed heavily on this editor, and he found the *Twice-told Tales* quite spectacular as a result. What is important to note here is not that the laudatory review was the product of circumstances favorable to Hawthorne, but that this editor—like any reader—was *in a situation* when he read Hawthorne's work, and that that situation mediated his reading of it. His indebtedness to Hawthorne simply dramatizes the fact that every reader is embedded in some network of circumstances or other when he or she picks up a literary work. Thus it is never the case that a work stands or falls "on its own merits" since the merits—or demerits—that the reader perceives will always be a function of the situation in which he or she reads.

The other most laudatory review of the *Twice-told Tales*, the one that played the most decisive role in establishing Hawthorne's literary reputation, was a piece by Henry Wadsworth Longfellow published in the *North American Review*. Longfellow was no more neutral or disinterested a reader of *Twice-told Tales* than the editor of the *Salem Gazette*. He had been a classmate of Hawthorne's at Bowdoin College; they shared a common background and a common vocation. In the months preceding the publication of *Twice-told Tales* (which Hawthorne sent to Longfellow as soon as it appeared), Hawthorne had written Longfellow a series of letters suggesting that they collaborate on a volume of children's stories. Shortly before the review in question came out, he had written to Longfellow speaking of his reclusive existence, noctural habits, and unavailing efforts to "get back" into "the main current of life."[10] While none of these circumstances could guarantee that Longfellow would admire Hawthorne's collection of stories, they constituted a situation in which a negative response would have been embarrassing and difficult.

It is possible, of course, that Longfellow and the editor of the *Gazette* may have felt pressured into admiring Hawthorne's work for what we could call, broadly speaking, "political" reasons, and that their true opinion of Hawthorne may have been quite different from what they publically expressed. Longfellow, for instance, might have harbored a secret dislike for Hawthorne because of some prank he had played in college, or he might have thought the tale an inferior literary genre, or been bored by stories that used a historical setting, and therefore might have found Hawthorne's tales dull and trivial. But even if that had been the case, *that* set of circumstances would have been no more neutral or disinterested than any other. The circumstances within which a reader encounters a literary text are always, in this broad sense, political, since they always involve preferences, interests, tastes, and beliefs that are not universal but part of the particular reader's situation. If it seems that I have chosen to discuss only "special

political?

cases" in the reception of Hawthorne's early work, i.e., cases where special interests were involved, and have omitted examples in which the reviewer had no prior interests at stake, that is because readers are always situated, or circumstanced, in relation to a work—if not by their prior knowledge of it, then, as we have seen, by their ignorance. There is never a case in which circumstances do not affect the way people read and hence *what* they read—the text itself.

In the case of Longfellow's review, the circumstances in question had an extremely positive effect on Hawthorne's literary career. Longfellow was someone whose opinion carried weight in critical circles; he had just been appointed Smith Professor of Modern Languages at Harvard and was at the beginning of a long and distinguished career of his own. He wrote for a weighty and influential journal whose editors, contributors, and subscribers constituted New England's cultural elite in the 1830s, 40s, and 50s. When Longfellow announced in the pages of the *North American* that Hawthorne was a "man of genius" and that a "new star" had arisen in the heavens, a new set of circumstances was called into being within which Hawthorne's fiction would, from then on, be read.[11] He began to receive more, and more favorable, critical attention; and his works began to assume a shape and to occupy a place in the literary scene that made him eligible, in time, for the role of American literary hero.

It is not my intention here to describe how that process took place step-by-step, but rather to show, in a series of instances, how the "circumstances" surrounding the emergence of Hawthorne's texts onto the literary scene defined those texts and positioned them, so that they became central and, so to speak, inescapable features of the cultural landscape.

II

Once Hawthorne's tales had been called to their attention, nineteenth-century critics singled out not what we now consider his great short stories—"The Minister's Black Veil," "Young Goodman Brown," "The Maypole of Merrymount"—but sketches now considered peripheral and thin. Their favorites, with virtually no exceptions, were "A Rill from the Town Pump," "Sunday at Home," "Sights from a Steeple," and "Little Annie's Ramble." Not only did these critics devote their attention almost exclusively to sketches that moralize on domestic topics and fail to appreciate what we now consider classic examples of the American short story, they "overlooked" completely those qualities in Hawthorne's writing that twentieth-century critics have consistently admired: his symbolic complexity, psychological depth, moral subtlety, and density of composition. Instead what almost every critic who wrote on Hawthorne's tales in the 1830s found particularly impressive were his combination of "sunshine" and "shadow," the transparency of his style, and his ability to invest the common elements of life with spiritual significance.[12]

It is these qualities that made Hawthorne a critical success among literary men in the 1830s and 40s, and it is on this foundation that his reputation as a classic author was built. Even the laudatory reviews by Poe and Melville, which critics take as proof of their "discernment" because in certain passages they seem to anticipate modern views, arise out of tastes and sympathies that are in many respects foreign to present day critical concerns. In a headnote to Poe's second review of *Twice-told Tales*, Richard Wilbur, for example, comments, "Poe proves his discernment by recognizing the merits of his contemporary."[13] But while Poe's reviews seem to confirm modern assessments of Hawthorne by pointing to his "invention, creation, imagination, originality," the chief merit Poe recognizes in Hawthorne's tales is one that few modern commentators have seen: their repose. "A painter," Poe writes, "would at once note their leading or predominant feature, and style it *repose. . . .* We are soothed as we read."[14] Hawthorne's current status as a major writer rests on exactly the opposite claim, namely that his vision is dark and troubled, the very reverse of that "hearty, genial, but still Indian-summer sunshine of his Wakefields and Little Annie's Rambles" which Poe admires so much and contrasts favorably to the "mysticism" of "Young Goodman Brown" which he wishes Hawthorne would rid himself of. "He has done *well* as a mystic. But . . . let him mend his pen, get a bottle of visible ink, come out from the Old Manse, cut Mr. Alcott, hang (if possible) the editor of the *Dial*, and throw out of the window to the pigs all his odd numbers of the 'North American Review.' "[15]

Melville's wonderful encomium of Hawthorne in the *Literary World*, which sees Hawthorne's works as "deeper than the plummet of the mere critic," characterized above all by their "blackness," and possessed of a vision of truth as "terrific" and as "madness to utter," comes much closer to modern criticism of Hawthorne (which quotes from it tirelessly) than Poe's reviews do.[16] But Melville's response to Hawthorne's "blackness" is not proof that he saw Hawthorne's tales as they really are, but rather proof of Melville's own preoccupation with the problem of innate depravity and original sin. What modern critics take as evidence of Melville's critical penetration—e.g., his admiration of Hawthorne's "blackness"—testifies rather to their own propensity for projecting onto what is actually a latter-day Calvinist vocabulary, their mid-twentieth-century conviction that a "tragic vision," elaborated chiefly in psychological terms, constitutes literary maturity. While Melville's reading of Hawthorne resembles modern interpretations in some respects, many of his critical observations—his pronouncements on "genius," his constant comparison of Hawthorne to natural phenomena (e.g., "the smell of young beeches and hemlocks is upon him; your own broad prairies are in his soul"), his emphasis on the "repose" of Hawthorne's intellect, on his "Indian summer . . . softness," on the "spell" of "this wizard"—testify to Melville's participation in the same romantic theories of art that dominate the mainstream reviews.[17]

It becomes clear upon examining these contemporary evaluations of Hawthorne's work that the texts on which his claim to classic status rested were not the same texts we read today in two senses. In the first and relatively trivial sense, they were not the same because the stories that made Hawthorne great in the eyes of his contemporaries were literally not the ones we read today—i.e., nineteenth-century critics preferred "Little Annie's Ramble" to "Young Goodman Brown." In the second and more important sense, they were not the same because even texts bearing the same title became intelligible within a different framework of assumptions. It is not that critics in the 1830s admired different *aspects* of Hawthorne's work from the ones we admire now, but that the work itself was different. Whatever claims one may or may not wish to make for the ontological sameness of these texts, all of the historical evidence suggests that what Hawthorne's contemporaries saw when they read his work is not what we see now. What I mean can be illustrated further by juxtaposing a piece of Hawthorne criticism written in 1837 with one written a hundred and twenty years later.

In praising Hawthorne's brilliance as a stylist, Andrew Peabody makes the following comment on a phrase from "The Gentle Boy":

> These Tales abound with beautiful imagery, sparkling metaphors, novel and brilliant comparisons. . . . Thus, for instance, an adopted child is spoken of as "a domesticated sunbeam" in the family. . . . How full of meaning is that simple phrase! How much does it imply, and conjure up of beauty, sweetness, gentleness, and love! How comprehensive, yet how definite! Who, after reading it, can help recurring to it, whenever he sees the sunny, happy little face of a father's pride or a mother's joy?[18]

No wonder, then, Hawthorne's contemporaries missed the point of his great short stories: they could not possibly have understood him, given the attitudes that must inform effusions such as these. But before dismissing Peabody completely, it is worthwhile asking if there isn't a point of view from which his commentary made good critical sense.

For Peabody, whose critical assumptions privilege the spiritualization of the ordinary and especially of domestic life, the phrase "a domesticated sunbeam" leaps immediately into view. "The Gentle Boy" becomes visible for him from within a structure of norms that nineteenth-century social historians refer to as "the cult of domesticity" and fulfills a definition of poeticity that values fanciful descriptions of commonplace things (Peabody admires Hawthorne's tales because they are "flower-garlands of poetic feeling wreathed around some everyday scene or object").[19] These critical precepts intersect with widely-held cultural beliefs about the special properties of childhood and the sanctity of the home. The child, in the nineteenth-century American imagination, is a spiritual force that binds the family together so that it becomes the type and cornerstone of national unity, and an earthly semblance of the communion of the saints.[20] Thus the "sunbeam"—associated with nature and with Heaven—"domesticated"—given a familiar human form—really is, in Peabody's terms, "comprehensive" yet "definite." The forms of apprehension that concretize the tale for him flag the phrase as a brilliant embodiment of his critical principles and moral presuppositions.

In the same way, one can readily see how a changed set of cultural beliefs and critical presuppositions has given rise to a modern commentary on the story. For example, Richard Adams writes in *The New England Quarterly* (1957) that Ilbrahim, the title character to whom the phrase "domesticated sunbeam" applies, "does not succeed" because he "is too young and weak."[21] He fails to "surmount the crisis of adolescence" and so illustrates the "common theme" of all the *Provincial Tales* which is "not basically a question of good versus evil but rather of boyish dependence and carelessness versus manly freedom and responsibility. . . . It is very much a question of the protagonist's passing from the one state to the other or of failing to do so—a question of time, change, and development."[22]

The modern critic typically does not pause to exclaim over the beauties of a single phrase, but sees the tale as a whole as the illustration of a "theme." He understands the character of Ilbrahim in the light of a psychological paradigm of human development in which childhood represents a stage that must be overcome. The ideal of human life implicit in Adams' descriptions of the story privileges individual self-realization, intellectual control, and a take-charge attitude toward experience. His beliefs about the nature of good fiction and the ideal shape of human life interpret "The Gentle Boy" for him as a story about "the protagonist's passing from the one state to the other or . . . failing to do so. . . ." He does not *impose* this interpretation on the story; that is to say, he does not apply his convictions to "The Gentle Boy" in order to make its details conform to some predetermined outline, rather, his convictions are what make the story intelligible to him in the first place.[23] And this way of rendering stories intelligible means, among other things, that Adams will not notice the phrase "a domesticated sunbeam" at all, because there is nothing in his interpretive assumptions that would make it noticeable. If someone were to call it to his attention, he would have to read the phrase ironically—as Hawthorne's sneering comment on nineteenth-century prettifications of childhood—or as an unfortunate lapse, on Hawthorne's part, into the sentimental idiom of his age. In any case, the phrase is not the same phrase for him as it is for Peabody, except in a purely orthographic sense, because it becomes visible— if it is noticed at all—from within a completely different framework of assumptions from those which produce Peabody's reading of the tale.

In both cases the text of the story represents and elaborates an amalgamation of beliefs, institutions, and practices that defines the space within which the text appears. The practice of psychiatry in the twentieth century organizes the space the text can occupy much as the existence of the Unitarian Church does in the nineteenth.

The critical vocabulary, moreover, which each critic uses to formulate his comments, extends and elaborates that space even as the text itself does. When Adams says that the protagonist's success or failure is a "question of time, change, and development," his vocabulary implicitly affirms the value of controlling experience through abstract categorization, an assumption not merely appropriate to but required by the institutional and professional situation within which he writes. In the same way, Peabody's rhetoric, full of exclamations and given to naming the tender emotions ("How full of meaning is that simple phrase! How much does it imply, and conjure up of beauty, sweetness, gentleness, and love!"), embodies just the kind of excited representation of emotional experience that his critical stance privileges, and affirms the value of precisely those feelings which—to his mind—Hawthorne so splendidly evokes. The critic's rhetoric is not a secondary or detachable attribute of his enterprise, but simultaneously its enabling assumption and final justification. When Peabody rhapsodizes over the domesticated sunbeam, when Longfellow exclaims "live ever, sweet, sweet book," when Charles Fenno Hoffman describes Hawthorne as "a rose bathed and baptized in dew," their rhetorical performance embodies the same critical strategies that make Hawthorne's tales intelligible to them, and all three—rhetoric, critical strategies, and the tales themselves—are inseparable from a whole way of looking at life.[24] The reading of fiction and the writing of criticism in the 1830s are activities rooted in beliefs about the sanctity of the home, the spirituality of children, the purifying effects of nature, the moral influence of art, and the relation of material to spiritual essences that determined what shape the *Twice-told Tales* would have for its readers at the level of the individual phrase, and at the level of the volume as a whole. Longfellow and his peers do not admire "A Rill from the Town Pump" out of bad taste; their judgment is an affirmation of their ideals no less than Adams' belief that Hawthorne chronicles "the crisis of adolescence" is an affirmation of his. We may think that the beliefs of Peabody and Longfellow are silly or outmoded, but we cannot accuse them of having *overlooked* in Hawthorne's work what they couldn't possibly have seen. One might just as well criticize F. O. Matthiessen, who holds that Hawthorne's greatness lies in his "wholeness of imaginative composition," for failing to notice that Hawthorne's prose is "as clear as running waters are" and that his words are like "stepping-stones."[25] In short, it is useless to insist that critics of the 1830s couldn't see the true nature of Hawthorne's work because of their naive literary and cultural assumptions, but that that true nature was there all along, waiting to be discovered by more discerning eyes. Rather the "true nature" of a literary work is a function of the critical perspective that is brought to bear upon it. What remains to be explained is why—if it is true that literary texts become visible only from within a particular framework of beliefs—it is always *Hawthorne's* texts that are the subject of these discussions rather than the texts of other writers. If there were nothing "in" the *Twice-told Tales* that commanded critical attention, why has Hawthorne's collection of stories and sketches come down to us rather than Harriet Beecher Stowe's *The Mayflower*? Wasn't there, right from the beginning, something unique about Hawthorne's prose that marked it as different from and better than the prose of other writers?

One can answer these questions by turning to the contemporary reviews. What the reviews show is that the novels of sentimental writers like Susan Warner and Harriet Beecher Stowe were praised as extravagantly as Hawthorne's and in exactly the same terms. Critics who admired Hawthorne's fondness for "lowly . . . scenes and characters," which they took as a sign of his "sympathy with everything human," also admired Warner's "simple transcript of country life" and "homely circumstances," which portrayed "the ordinary joys and sorrows of our common humanity."[26] They found that Hawthorne's "tales . . . are national while they are universal," and that Warner's novels "paint human nature in its American type" and "appeal to universal human sympathy."[27] Warner is commended for her remarkable grasp of religious truth, and Hawthorne for his depiction of "spiritual laws" and the "eternal facts of morality."[28] Both writers display an extraordinary understanding of the "heart."[29]

Thus it is not the case that Hawthorne's work from the very first set itself apart from the fiction of his contemporaries; on the contrary, his fiction did not distinguish itself at all clearly from that of the sentimental novelists—whose work we now see as occupying an entirely separate category. This is not because nineteenth-century critics couldn't tell the difference between serious and sentimental fiction, but because their principles of sameness and difference had a different shape. In the 1850s the aesthetic and the didactic, the serious and the sentimental were not opposed but overlapping designations. Thus, the terms "sentimental author" and "genius" were not mutually exclusive, but wholly compatible ways of describing literary excellence. Differences in the way literature is defined necessarily produce differences in the way literary works are classified and evaluated. Thus, if in 1841 Evert Duyckinck, who was arguably the most powerful literary man in New York, regarded "Little Annie's Ramble" as the high-water mark of Hawthorne's achievement, it is no wonder that other critics should subsequently have admired Warner's novel about the tribulations of an orphan girl, and seen both works—moralized pictures of innocent girlhood in a characteristically New England setting—as exemplifying the same virtues.[30] Nor is it strange that when Phoebe Pynchon appeared to brighten the old family mansion in Salem, critics praised *The House of the Seven Gables* because it was full of "tenderness and delicacy of sentiment" with a "moral constantly in view."[31] *The House of the Seven Gables* succeeded in 1851 because it was a sentimental novel; that is, it succeeded not because it escaped or transcended the standards of judgment that made critics admire Warner's work, but because it fulfilled them. To critics who took for granted the moral purity of children, the holiness of the heart's affections, the divinity of nature, and the sanctity of the home, and who conceived of the poet as a prophet who could elevate the soul by "revealing the hidden harmonies of common things," sketches like "Sunday at Home," "Sights from a Steeple," "A Rill from the Town Pump," and novels like *The House of the Seven Gables* and *The Wide, Wide World* formed a perfect continuum; it is not that these critics couldn't *see* the difference between Warner's work and Hawthorne's, but that, given their way of seeing, there *was* no difference.

This does not mean that antebellum critics made no distinction between various kinds of work, but that their principles of classification produced different groupings from the ones we are used to. *The House of the Seven Gables* and *The Wide, Wide World*, for example, were published in the same year as *Moby-Dick*, but whereas today Hawthorne and Melville are constantly seen in terms of one another, contemporary reviews of Hawthorne never even mention Melville's name. While in the 1850s there was no monolithic view of either Hawthorne or Melville, one can easily construct characterizations of their works, based on comments from contemporary reviews, that would place them at opposite ends of the critical spectrum. According to contemporary critics, Hawthorne, like the sentimental novelists, writes a clear, intelligible prose accessible to everyone (a style suitable for artists in a self-consciously democratic nation); he tells stories about recognizable people in humble settings and thus, like the writers of domestic fiction, illuminates the spiritual dimensions of ordinary life; his works, like theirs, firmly rooted in Christian precept, serve as reliable guides to the truths of the human heart.[32] Melville, on the other hand, whose work is described as being full of stylistic ex-

travagances, bizarre neologisms, and recondite allusions, emerges
as a mad obscurantist; his characters inhabit exotic locales and rant
incomprehensibly about esoteric philosophical issues; and their
ravings verge dangerously and irresponsibly on blasphemy.[33] Although many critics admired Melville's daring and considered his
work powerful and brilliant, they nevertheless did not describe it
in the terms they used to characterize Hawthorne. In their own
day, Hawthorne and Melville were admired, when they were admired, for opposite reasons: Hawthorne for his insight into the
domestic situation, Melville for his love of the wild and the re-
mote.[34]

It is easy enough to see that Hawthorne's relation to Melville
in the nineteenth century wasn't the same as it is now; and it is
easy enough to see that it wasn't the same because the criteria
according to which their works were described and evaluated were
different and that therefore the works themselves took on a different shape. But what the comparison shows is that the entire
situation within which the literary works appeared and within which
judgments were made upon them was so different in either case
that no element that appeared within these two situations could
be the same. Not only is Hawthorne in the 1850s not easily distinguishable from the sentimental novelists, and in most respects
quite distinguishable from Melville; not only did antebellum critics
have different notions about the nature and function of good literature, prize the domestic affections, and think children were
spiritually endowed; more fundamentally, once one has accepted
the notion that a literary text exists only within a framework of
assumptions which are historically produced, it then becomes clear
that the "complex" Hawthorne we study today, the Melville we
know as Hawthorne's co-conspirator against the pieties of the age,
the sentimental novelists we regard as having pandered to a debased popular taste, are not the novelists nineteenth-century readers read and that nineteenth-century critics wrote about. Even
when nineteenth- and twentieth-century critics use the same or
similar words to describe some element in Hawthorne's work, one
can see that what they mean by what they say is not the same
thing.

When a Unitarian clergyman writes that "the character of Chillingworth" illustrates "the danger of cherishing a merely intellectual interest in the human soul," he seems to be describing the same phenomenon that Donald Ringe describes when he writes that Chillingworth is "a cold, speculative, intellectual man who commits a sin of isolation which must ultimately destroy him."[35] Both writers clearly agree that Hawthorne, through the character of Chillingworth, is suggesting that the intellect alone is a dangerous guide. But what the modern critic means by Chillingworth's sin is isolation from the community, the separation of the head from the heart, and something he calls "dehumanization"; for him, Chillingworth sins by cutting himself off from "human sympathy and love."[36] The minister writing for the *Universalist Quarterly*, on the other hand, admires Hawthorne's treatment of character because it demonstrates "spiritual laws" and is "sternly true to eternal facts of morality."[37] Those facts are not the same for him as they are for Ringe. Chillingworth is damned in the minister's eyes because he is cut off not from human sympathy and love, but from "God . . . the all-good and the all-beautiful."[38] These critics may use the same words to describe Hawthorne's character, but the Chillingworth of *PMLA* transgresses the social and psychological norms of a secular humanism, while the Chillingworth of Hawthorne's era dramatizes liberal Protestant convictions about the soul's relation to God. These accounts of what Hawthorne meant to convey are not interchangeable and do not testify to the existence of some central truth in Hawthorne's text which both critics have grasped. What they show is that the critic, the context within which the critic reads, and the text that is interpreted are simultaneous features of a single historical moment. As the concept of sin changes from theological fact to metaphor for a psychological state, as the critic changes from Unitarian clergyman to professor of English, as the *Universalist Quarterly* gives way to *PMLA*, the text of *The Scarlet Letter* changes accordingly.

Because modern commentators have tended to ignore the context within which nineteenth-century authors and critics worked, their view of the criticism that was written on *The Scarlet Letter* in the nineteenth century has failed to take account of the cultural circumstances that shaped Hawthorne's novel for his contemporaries. They evaluate this criticism as if it had been written about the same text that they read, and so produce accounts of that criticism that are unrelated to the issues with which it was actually engaged. For example, three modern scholars of Hawthorne criticism all find George Loring's reply in 1850 to an attack on *The Scarlet Letter* that had appeared in the *North American Review* one of the ablest contemporary discussions of the novel.[39] It is not hard to see why these critics think so highly of Loring's defense. His essay is written in answer to a religious attack on the novel which argues that *The Scarlet Letter* is unchristian because it presents its adulterous heroine in a sympathetic light, sees "devils and angels [as] alike beautiful," deals with a "revolting" subject whose "ugliness" is unredeemed by Hawthorne's "wizard power over language," and is manifestly untrue to the realities of "God's moral world."[40] Because Loring's essay sets itself up in opposition to what seems to the modern critics a narrowly based doctrinal attack, they find the defense admirable. When Loring says, for example, that without sorrow and sin "virtue cannot rise above innocency," it looks as if he has acknowledged the complex nature of moral problems as the twentieth century views them.[41] When he says that those who think "vice stands at one pale and virtue at another" betray a "want of sympathy" which "the experience of our own temptation should remove," Loring seems to be acknowledging the existence of "the dark underside of the psyche" with which so much modern criticism has been preoccupied.[42] When he writes that "in casting [Hester] out, the world had torn from her all the support of its dogmatic teachings, . . . and had compelled her to rely upon that great religious truth which flows instinctively around a life of agony, with its daring freedom," the modern critic discerns a celebration of human individuality and an affirmation of the heroic struggle for personal freedom at all costs.[43]

But Loring's review of *The Scarlet Letter* does not escape the confines of religious controversy; on the contrary, his argument with the reviewer for the *North American* is mounted on specifically doctrinal grounds. He is just as committed as Hawthorne's harshest critics were to a view of authors as "moral and accountable beings" and to a serious consideration of "the moral and religious effects of their works."[44] His argument with Hawthorne's adversaries is not literary, but theological, and he defends Hester on the highly technical grounds that she represents a proper conception of the soul's relation to God and to sin:

> Between the individual and his God, there remains a spot, larger or smaller, as the soul has been kept unclouded, where no sin can enter, where no mediation can come, where all the discords of . . . life are resolved into the most delicious harmonies, and his whole existence becomes illuminated by a divine intelligence. Sorrow and sin reveal this spot to all men—as, through death, we are born to an immortal life.[45]

This disquistion on the "spot" belongs to a religious controversy over the sources of spiritual authority that had been going on in New England since the seventeenth century, and whose most recent manifestation was the quarrel between the Unitarians and the Transcendentalists over the authority of "forms and doctrines" as opposed to the voice of God speaking in the individual heart.[46] Loring's views in this article, published in the *Massachusetts Quarterly Review*, are an extension of those put forward by Theodore Parker, the *Quarterly*'s editor, in his famous "Discourse of the Transient and Permanent in Christianity," where he argued that "Christianity is not a system of doctrines but rather a method of attaining oneness with God"; "it does not demand all men to *think* alike, but to think uprightly, . . . [nor demand] all men to *live* alike, but to live holy."[47] Loring, who had graduated from Harvard the year Emerson gave his Divinity School Address, sees Hester as a Transcendental heroine and *The Scarlet Letter* as a manifesto of Transcendental beliefs.[48] His impassioned defense of Hawthorne is part of a political and ideological struggle then taking place between liberal and conservative branches of Protestant Christianity. The *North American*, which printed the attack, represented the Unitarian establishment at Harvard where its editor, Francis Bowen, was McClean Professor of History. Anti-low-tariff, anti-Transcendental, and anti-abolitionist (though opposed to slavery in principle), it was regarded by the bright young men of the day as a "slowcoach," whose "passengers had been taking a social nap."[49] The *Massachusetts Quarterly*, on the other hand, the direct descendant of *The Dial*, was strongly pro-abolition, reformist, and thoroughgoingly Transcendental.[50]

Loring's interpretation of *The Scarlet Letter* arises from the theological controversy (which was also a power struggle) then raging within the New England churches.[51] The very shape of his disagreement with the reviewer for the *North American* shows that the text these critics argued over had been structured by a set of interests and beliefs that we can reconstruct but no longer hold. It is just as impossible for a twentieth-century critic to argue, as Loring does, that the story of Hester's sin demonstrates the existence of a certain "spot" in the human soul as it would have been for a Transcendentalist to read it, along with Charles Feidelson, as demonstrating the "anti-conventional impulse . . . inherent in symbolism."[52] This is not simply because each critic looks at the text from a different point of view or with different purposes in mind, but because *looking* is not an activity that is performed outside of political struggles and institutional structures, but arises *from* them.

III

One such structure is the machinery of publishing and reviewing by means of which an author is brought to the attention of his audience. The social and economic processes that govern the dissemination of a literary work are no more accidental to its reputation, and indeed to its very nature, as that will be perceived by an audience, than are the cultural conceptions (of the nature of poetry, of morality, of the human soul) within which the work is read. The conditions of dissemination interpret the work for its readers in exactly the same way as definitions of poetry in that they flow from and support widely-held—if unspoken—assumptions about the methods of distribution proper to a serious (or non-serious) work. The fact that an author makes his or her appearance in the context of a particular publishing practice rather than some other is a fact about the kind of claim he or she is

making on an audience's attention and is *crucial* to the success of
the claim. Hawthorne's debut as a novelist illustrates this proposition rather strikingly.

In 1970, C. E. Frazer Clark, Jr., published an article that revealed some little-known facts surrounding the publication of *The
Scarlet Letter.*[53] Clark observed that despite Hawthorne's habit of
referring to himself as "the most unpopular author in America,"
he was much better known than he himself was aware. His satires
and sketches had been pirated liberally by newspapers up and down
the Eastern seaboard; notices, advertisements, and reviews of his
work had regularly appeared in the periodical press. And so, when
Hawthorne lost his job as surveyor of customs at Salem, it caused
a furor in the local papers.[54] The press took up the case of political
axing not because such events were so extraordinary—nothing could
have been more common with a change of administrations—but
because Hawthorne was already newsworthy. This publicity attracted the attention of James T. Fields, shortly to become New
England's most influential publisher, who until then had not printed
a word of Hawthorne's, but whose business instincts now prompted
him to visit Salem on the off-chance that Hawthorne might have
something ready for the press. Hawthorne, as it happened, did
have something on hand which, very reluctantly, he gave to Fields.
It was a story which Fields encouraged him to turn into a novel—
novels being more marketable than short fiction. Hawthorne took
this suggestion and prefaced the story with an introductory essay
on his stint in the customs house to help achieve the desired length.
As Fields suspected, Hawthorne's first book to appear after the
customs house fiasco sold remarkably well: the advance publicity
had guaranteed that *The Scarlet Letter* would be a success.

Encouraged by the attention paid to his novel, and prodded by
the ever-vigilant Fields, who saw an opportunity to capitalize on
the reputation so recently enlarged, Hawthorne, who until then
had not been a prolific writer, turned out two more novels in rapid
succession. These received a great deal of favorable attention from
well-placed reviewers, with the result that, two years after the
publication of *The Scarlet Letter*, Hawthorne was being referred
to as a classic American writer—and has been so identified ever

since. But the success of *The Scarlet Letter* and of the subsequent novels becomes fully explicable only within a larger frame of reference than the one Clark's essay supplies.

By the 1840s Irving's reputation had sagged and Cooper had alienated large portions of the reading public and the critical establishment with his attacks on American manners and his unpopular political stands. America needed a living novelist whom it could regard as this country's answer to Dickens and Thackeray, a novelist who represented both what was essentially American and what was "best" by some universal criteria of literary value. Hawthorne seemed well-suited for the role, since, as almost every critic emphasized, his work made use of characteristically American materials. Hawthorne's feel for the humbler aspects of the American scene made him attractive both as an interpreter of "spiritual laws" that know no nationality and as a spokesman for the democratic way of life. These qualities, however, as I have suggested, were shared equally by novelists like Warner and Stowe who, if anything, outdid him in this respect. What finally distinguished Hawthorne from his popular rivals was his relation to the social and institutional structures that shaped literary opinion; these associations ultimately determined the longevity of his reputation. The parallel but finally divergent careers of Hawthorne and Warner illustrate dramatically how important belonging to the right network was as a precondition for long-standing critical success.

The circle of well-educated, well-connected men and women who controlled New England's cultural life at mid-century thought of themselves as spiritually and culturally suited to raise the level of popular taste and to civilize and refine the impulses of the multitude. Any writer whom they chose as a model of moral and aesthetic excellence, therefore, had to be someone whose work had not already been embraced by the nation at large, but had been initially admired only by the discerning few. Longfellow formulates the prevailing view of Hawthorne as a writer for a cultivated minority in his review of the second edition of *Twice-told Tales*:

> Mr. Hawthorne's . . . writings have now become so well known, and are so justly appreciated, by all discerning minds, that they do not

need our commendation. He is not an author to create a sensation, or have a tumultuous popularity. His works are not stimulating or impassioned, and they minister nothing to a feverish love of excitement. Their tranquil beauty and softened tints, which do not win the notice of the restless many, only endear them the more to the thoughtful few.[55]

The "thoughtful few" to whom Longfellow refers are the people who controlled New England's cultural life before the Civil War. Once Hawthorne's work had been published by Ticknor and Fields, New England's most prominent publisher; once it had been reviewed by E. P. Whipple, a member of Fields' coterie and one of the most influential contemporary reviewers; and had become the subject of long discussions in the *Christian Examiner* and the *North American Review*, periodicals whose editors, in Sydney Ahlstrom's words, "alone constitute . . . a hall of fame of the New England flowering;" Hawthorne had gained a place in a socio-cultural network that assured his prominence because its own prominence was already an established and self-perpetuating fact.[56]

Lewis Simpson has characterized this group of literary and intellectual men who took the nation's spiritual welfare as their special charge as the "New England clerisy."[57] Simpson traces its beginnings in the passage from a theological to a literary clergy in the early years of the nineteenth century, using the career of Joseph Stevens Buckminster, a precocious young theology professor at Harvard, to exemplify the broadening of ecclesiastical authority to include general cultural matters, and especially literature. Buckminster and his associates, who founded the *Monthly Anthology*, America's most serious literary journal at the time, spoke of literature as a "commonwealth" with its own "government," that along with church and state fought for civilization against barbarism.[58] As a result of their activity, Simpson writes, "the image in the New England mind of the old theocratic polity begins to become the image of a literary polity. . . . The *Respublica Christiana* . . . becomes the *Respublica Litterarum*."[59] The metaphor of the state as a means of conceptualizing literary activity is important because it suggests the need for centralized leadership and control in cultural affairs: the choice of proper reading matter was not something that could be left to the "restless many," but rightly belonged to the "thoughtful few" whose training and authority qualified them as arbiters of public taste. The formation of a literary canon in the nineteenth century was not a haphazard affair, but depended on the judgment of a small group of prominent men, the members of the Anthology Society—clergymen, professors, businessmen, judges, and statesmen—who conceived of their task as a civic and moral duty. The power they had to determine who would be read and who would not is dramatically illustrated by the career of Richard Henry Dana, Sr., whose ardent admiration for the English Romantic poets drew scathing criticism from the Boston literati. He failed to be elected to the editorship of the *North American* (the direct descendant of the *Monthly Anthology*), and thereafter refused to contribute to it. When his essays and tales, his long poem, and the collected edition of his poems and prose elicited only a cool response from reviewers, he simply withdrew from the world, devastated by its failure to recognize his genius.[60]

This fate did not befall Nathaniel Hawthorne because he had been taken up by the second generation of the New England clerisy, whose power to shape literary opinion had been inherited from the first through an interlocking network of social, familial, political, and professional connections. William Tudor, an active member of the Anthology Society, the *Monthly Anthology*'s editorial board, became the founding editor of the *North American Review*. John Kirkland, another of the Society's original members, became president of Harvard. Alexander Everett, another member, later a minister to Spain, also went on to edit the *North American*, as did Edward Everett, who had studied German at Gottingen with George Ticknor, both of them original members of the Anthology Society. Ticknor, who preceded Longfellow as Professor of Modern Languages at Harvard, was the cousin of William Ticknor, of Ticknor and Fields, who became one of Hawthorne's lifelong friends. William Emerson, pastor of the First Church of Boston, who edited the *Monthly Anthology* for two years before the Society took over, was Ralph Waldo Emerson's father.[61]

Joseph Buckminster's father had strenuously opposed the liberal theological tendencies of his son, just as the Unitarians of Buckminster's era and beyond would oppose the radical theorizing of Emerson and his circle; but the authority to speak on spiritual and cultural issues passed smoothly down from father to son undiminished by doctrinal differences. The men who thus assumed the role of cultural spokesmen at mid-century—Longfellow, Holmes, Lowell, Whittier, and Emerson—were particularly powerful since by then Boston had become the literary center of the nation.[62] These were the men whom Caroline Ticknor records as gathering to socialize at the Old Corner Bookstore, as Ticknor and Fields was familiarly known.[63] These were the men who in 1857 "all agreed to write for the *Atlantic*, and . . . made it immediately . . . the most important magazine in America."[64] These were the men who, as Sophia Hawthorne left the cemetery after her husband's funeral, stood with bared heads as the carriage passed.[65]

It is hard to overestimate the importance of Hawthorne's connections with these men who outlived him by a score of years and who launched the periodical that would dominate literary activity in the United States for the rest of the nineteenth century. When William Dean Howells returned to Boston in 1866, he became assistant editor of the *Atlantic Monthly* under James T. Fields (Hawthorne's publisher), who had taken over the editorship from Lowell (Hawthorne's good friend). Howells, whom Hawthorne had helped get his start by introducing him to Emerson, took over the editorship from Fields in 1871, and George Parsons Lathrop, Hawthorne's son-in-law, became an assistant editor.[66] Lathrop would publish the first full-length study of Hawthorne, which Howells' close friend, Henry James, would challenge three years later in *his* full-length study. This touched off a critical controversy—notably in an essay by Howells—over whether Hawthorne was an idealist or a realist, so that it was Hawthorne whose texts critics used to argue the merits of literary realism in the 80s and 90s.[67] Meanwhile, several friends published poems commemorating Hawthorne's death; relatives, friends, and associates printed their reminiscences; Sophia published excerpts from Hawthorne's journals; and other admirers wrote pieces with titles such as "The Homes and Haunts of Hawthorne."

But most important in assuring Hawthorne's continuing presence in the cultural foreground was James T. Fields. Fields, wanting to make good on his investment, followed his former practice of putting out anything he thought would pique the public's interest in his author and managed to produce eleven posthumous editions of Hawthorne's work between 1864 and 1883. This meant, twenty years after he was dead, that Hawthorne was still being reviewed as a live author. Osgood, the successor to Fields, pushed this strategy further by adding Hawthorne to his "Little Classics" series, and in 1884, Houghton Mifflin, the successor to Osgood, capped it off by publishing *The Complete Works of Nathaniel Hawthorne* in twelve volumes edited by his son-in-law. Finally, Houghton Mifflin reinforced the image by including Hawthorne in two more series: "Modern Classics" and "American Classics for the Schools." In 1883, the academic establishment put its imprimatur on what the publishers had done. In that year, Yale allowed English literature students for the first time to write their junior essays on "Hawthorne's Imagination"—the only topic on the list that concerned an American author. Consequently, Hawthorne's texts were "there" to be drawn upon for ammunition in the debates over the question of realism that raged during the 1880s. By the end of the century, as Edwin Cady observes in his survey of Hawthorne criticism, "a minor critic might well have doubted his respectability if he failed to cite Hawthorne whether in praise of or attack against any writing in question."[68]

The prominence of Hawthorne's texts in the post–Civil War era is a natural consequence of his relation to the mechanisms that produced literary and cultural opinion. Hawthorne's initial connections with the Boston literati—his acquaintance with Longfellow at college, his residence next door to Alcott and a half mile from Emerson (his son and Emerson's nephew roomed together at Harvard), his marrying a Peabody, becoming fast friends with Ticknor and Lowell, being published by the indefatigable Fields, socializing with Duyckinck and Whipple—these circumstances po-

sitioned Hawthorne's literary production so that it became the
property of a dynastic cultural elite which came to identify itself
with him.[69] The members of this elite could not fail to keep Hawthorne's reputation alive since it stood for everything they themselves stood for. America's literary establishment, no less than
James T. Fields (who was part of it), had an investment in Hawthorne. In short, the friends and associates who outlived Hawthorne kept his fiction up-to-date by writing about it, and then
their friends took over. Consequently, when the next generation
of critics—Howells, James, and their contemporaries—came of
age, they redefined his work according to the critical tastes of the
new era. And so when the century turned, it seemed appropriate
that a volume of Hawthorne criticism should appear in 1904 celebrating the hundredth anniversary of his birth. And "by then,"
writes Edwin Cady, "figures like George Woodberry, William Pe-
terfield Trent, and Paul Elmer More had come to maturity," who,
with their "Arnoldian . . . neo-humanism" would "project Hawthorne toward the present century's Age of Criticism."[70]

During the same period, Warner's critical reputation dwindled
to nothing. Whereas critics writing before the Civil War had discussed her work alongside that of Hawthorne, Brockden Brown,
Cooper, Irving, Longfellow, and Stowe, by the 70s they had ceased
to take her novels seriously as literature and finally stopped reviewing them altogether. Under the pressure of new conditions,
Warner's work, like Hawthorne's, came to be redefined. The circumstances that created each author's literary reputation were of
the same *kind* in either case—that is, they consisted of the writer's
relation to centers of cultural domination, social and professional
connections, blood relations, friendships, publishing history, and
so on—but in Warner's case the circumstances were negative rather
than positive.

Warner's connections—such as they were—sprang from New
York rather than Boston, which at this particular period put her
at a geographical disadvantage. Unlike Hawthorne, Warner had
not lived in Concord, did not know Emerson and his circle, was
not published by Fields, had not known Longfellow at college, had
not roomed with a former President of the United States whose

campaign biography she would write and who would get her a
consulship when she needed money. Rather, she had been forced
by her father's financial failure in the 1830s to retire to an island
in the Hudson River where the family owned property, and where,
along with her maiden sister, she wrote novels to earn a living.
The Warners' poverty and their resulting social isolation affected
both what they wrote and the way their work was perceived by
contemporary audiences. As a consequence of their social isolation, the Warners threw themselves into church-centered activities
and became extremely devout followers of the Reverend Thomas
Skinner—a New Light Presbyterian who preached the importance
of faith over doctrine in religious conversion. They considered the
novels and stories they wrote their best means of doing the Lord's
work and—since they had to—of supporting themselves. These
conditions (at one point their house was in receivership and creditors took their furniture away) determined not only what they
wrote, but how much, how fast, for what kind of audience, and
for which publishers.[71] Though they had started out with G. P.
Putnam, a large commercial publisher in New York whose founder
had been a friend of their father, in the 1860s they gave most of
what they wrote to Robert Carter, a highly respected religious
publisher who could guarantee a certain number of sales. The
audience for religious books was large, stable, and provided an
outlet for the Warners that answered their need both to win souls
and to have bread on the table. Thus, at a time when changes in
the economic and social environment created the context within
which literary realism flourished, the Warner sisters guaranteed
that their novels would be read as religious rather than literary
discourse, labeled with Carter's imprint and with titles—"Stories
on the Lord's Prayer," "A Story of Small Beginnings," "The
Word"—more reminiscent of tract society pamphlets than of high
art.

Given a different cultural milieu, these conditions of production
might have guaranteed the Warner sisters lasting fame. If the religious views that characterized the attacks on *The Scarlet Letter*
in the 1850s had dominated literary criticism after the war, Hawthorne would have done well to experience a religious conversion

and switch to Carter, too. But the moral impulse behind American criticism, which had been evangelical and religious in the ante-bellum years, evolved during the 70s and 80s into a concern for the material conditions of social life. Novels which had previously appeared to contain superb renditions of American character and homely scenes imbued with universal human truths, now seemed to be full of idealized characters, authorial didacticism, and an overt religiosity that marked them as morally false and artistically naive. Warner's work became identified with an outmoded piety and a discredited Romanticism that assured its swift disappearance from the critical scene. It is not that critics suddenly discovered limitations they had previously failed to notice, but that the context within which the work appeared had changed the nature of the work itself. If Warner had had the kinds of connections that kept Hawthorne's works in the public eye, had commanded the attention of influential publishers, editors, and reviewers, her early novels might have remained critically viable as they came to be recast according to the prevailing standards. And in that case *The Wide, Wide World* might have been passed down to us as one of the benchmarks of American literary realism.[72] But when she died in 1885, there were no famous men at her funeral to write poems in her memory for the *Atlantic Monthly* or for Harvard Phi Beta Kappas to hear. She had no publisher whose commercial interests lay in bringing out posthumous editions of her work, whose friends would write retrospective evaluations of her career. There were no surviving relatives whose connections would allow them to pub-lish excerpts from her journals in prestigious places, no son to write three volumes of reminiscences, no son-in-law to write a full-length critical study and then go on to edit her complete works in twelve volumes.

What these facts demonstrate is that an author's relation to the mechanisms by which his or her work is brought before the public determines the status of that work in the world's eyes. Hawthorne's canonization was the result of a network of common interests—familial, social, professional, commercial, and national—that, combined, made Hawthorne a literary and cultural artifact, a na-tional possession. The same combination of circumstances in re-

verse reconstituted Warner's best-selling novels as ephemera that
catered to the taste of a bygone age. Nor was there a conspiracy
involved in keeping Hawthorne's reputation green while Warner's
withered. By attributing the canonical status of Hawthorne's work
to factors other than its "intrinsic" merit, I do not mean to suggest
that the merits that critics and editors discerned in that work were
not real, that they promoted work they believed was worthless or
mediocre, or that they deliberately ignored work they believed was
good. On the contrary, although a mixture of motives was bound
to be present in any individual decision to publish or write about
Hawthorne's work—friendship, family feeling, commercial gain,
professional advancement—these motives are not distinguishable
from a belief in Hawthorne's genius and the conviction that his
novels were great works of art. For that conviction is itself a contextual matter; that is, it does not spring from a pure, unmediated
perception of an author's work on the part of his admirers and
supporters (a kind of perception which, as I argued earlier, is never
possible), but is determined by the situation in which they en-
counter it. The circumstances surrounding Hawthorne's texts in
the 70s and 80s—literary, cultural, social, economic, and institutional—presented that work to its readers in such a way that it
possessed the marks of greatness. Indeed, Hawthorne's work had
by that time become one of the touchstones by which literary
excellence could be defined, for canonical texts themselves become
the bearers of the particular tradition of quality of which they are
the exemplars. To put it another way, the fact that an author's
reputation depends upon the context within which his or her work
is read does not empty the work of value; it is the context—which
eventually includes the work itself—that creates the value its readers "discover" there. Their reading is an activity arising within a
particular cultural setting (of which the author's reputation is a
part) that reflects and elaborates the features of that setting simultaneously.

At this point, someone might object that while my description
of the way Hawthorne's reputation came into being may support
the foregoing account of how Hawthorne's texts were constructed,
it does not really furnish grounds for making claims about literary

works in general. What about Melville, some readers may ask; how did his work come to be appreciated in the twentieth century if there were no relatives and friends, no critical establishment, working to keep it in the public eye? Conversely, why did Longfellow, who had all of the social and institutional advantages I have ascribed to Hawthorne, lose his place in the canon while Hawthorne maintained his? The cases of Melville and Longfellow, though they differ from Hawthorne's at the particular level, are in principle exactly the same. It is not that their work, unlike Hawthorne's, has been judged on its intrinsic merits, but rather that it has been constituted by a changing series of interpretive frames. These authors' fluctuating reputations (Longfellow is now on the verge of a revival) further illustrate how changing definitions of literary value, institutionally and socially produced, continually refashion the literary canon to suit the culture's needs.

IV

The idea that great literary works are those that stand the test of time might seem at first to have a persuasive force that no amount of argument can dispel. But the moment one starts to investigate the critical history of even a single work, the notion that a classic is a book that outlasts its age becomes extremely problematic. What does it mean to say that *The Scarlet Letter* stood the test of time and *The Wide, Wide World* did not? Which test? Or rather, whose? It was the custom house essay and not Hester's story that drew the most unstinting praise from contemporary reviewers of *The Scarlet Letter*; and it was *The Marble Faun* that, on the whole, Hawthorne's contemporaries deemed his finest work.[73] The reason for this, as I have shown, is that the criteria by which those critics judged Hawthorne were different from ours. Whose criteria then shall constitute the test? Certainly not Longfellow's: his standards belong to the "prose-like-running-waters" school. Henry James' admiration of Hawthorne was highly qualified: he believed *The Scarlet Letter* inferior to John Lockhart's *Adam Blair*.[74] The Transcendental defense of Hawthorne is not, as I have indicated, one that twentieth-century crities could make. But if we use

only modern critical criteria—assuming they could be agreed upon—
then *The Scarlet Letter* would have passed *a* test, but not the "test
of time," since that presumably would have to include the critical
judgments of more than one generation. The trouble with the
notion that a classic work transcends the limitations of its age and
appeals to critics and readers across the centuries is that one discovers, upon investigation, that the grounds of critical approval
are always shifting. *The Scarlet Letter* is a great novel in 1850, in
1876, in 1904, in 1942, and in 1966, but each time it is great for
different reasons. In the light of this evidence, it begins to appear
that what we have been accustomed to think of as the most enduring work of American literature is not a stable object possessing
features of enduring value, but an object that—because of its place
within institutional and cultural history—has come to embody successive concepts of literary excellence. This is not to say that *The
Scarlet Letter* is simply an "empty space" or that there is "nothing
there"; to put it another way, it is not to assert that no matter
what Hawthorne had written, his work would have succeeded because he had the right connections. The novel Hawthorne produced in 1850 had a specificity and a force within its own context
that a different work would not have had. But as the context
changed, so did the work embedded in it.

Yet that very description of *The Scarlet Letter* as a text that
invited constant redefinition might be put forward, finally, as the
one true basis on which to found its claim to immortality. For the
hallmark of the classic work is precisely that it rewards the scrutiny
of successive generations of readers, speaking with equal power
to people of various persuasions. It is on just this basis, in fact,
that one of Hawthorne's critics has explained his critical prominence in recent years. Reviewing Hawthorne criticism for *American Literary Scholarship* in 1970, Roy Male comments "on the
way Hawthorne's work has responded to shifting expectations during the last two decades."

   In the fifties it rewarded the explicatory and mythic analyses of the
   New Critics; in the mid-sixties it survived, at the cost of some dim-
   inution, the rigorous inquest of the new historicists and the neo-

Freudians; and now his fiction seems more vital than ever for readers
aware of new developments in psychology and related fields.[75]

In a sense, what Roy Male describes here is a capsule version of
what I have been describing throughout this essay: namely, the
various ways in which Hawthorne's texts have been reinterpreted
by critics of various persuasions. What is at issue is how to account
for this phenomenon. In Male's view, these successive reinterpre-
tations show that Hawthorne's work is "more vital than ever"
because they testify to its capacity to reward a variety of critical
approaches, each of which produces only a partial reading of it;
the text itself must be deeper and broader than any of its individual
concretizations, for there is no other way to explain how the same
text could give rise to them all. The notion that the classic text
escapes or outlasts history *must* hold that various attempts to cap-
ture it from within history (i.e., from within a particular perspective) are incomplete, for if one of them did succeed completely,
not only would interpretation have to stop; it would mean that the
classic was not universal but limited, could not speak to people in
all times and places, was not, in short, a classic.

But, as I have been suggesting, there is no need to account for
the succession of interpretations by positing an ahistorical, transcendent text which calls them forth. History—the succession of
cultural formations, social networks, institutional priorities, and
critical perspectives—does that, and the readings thus produced
are not mere approximations of an ungraspable, transhistorical
entity, but a series of completions, wholly adequate to the text
which each interpretive framework makes available. In each case,
the reading can be accounted for by a series of quite specific,
documentable circumstances having to do with publishing practices, pedagogical and critical traditions, economic structures, social networks, and national needs which constitute the text within
the framework of a particular disciplinary hermeneutic. The "durability" of the text is not a function of its unique resistance to
intellectual obsolescence; for the text, in any describable, documentable sense, is not durable at all. What endures is the literary
and cultural tradition that believes in the idea of the classic, and that

perpetuates that belief from day to day and from year to year by reading and rereading, publishing and republishing, teaching and recommending for teaching, and writing books and articles about a small group of works whose "durability" is thereby assured.

The fact is that literary classics do not *withstand* change; rather, they are always registering, or promoting, or retarding alterations in historical conditions as these affect their readers and, especially, the members of the literary establishment. For classic texts, while they may or may not have originally been written by geniuses, have certainly been written and rewritten by the generations of professors and critics who make their living by them. They are the mirrors of culture as culture is interpreted by those who control the literary establishment. Rather than being the repository of eternal truths, they embody the changing interests and beliefs of those people whose place in the cultural hierarchy empowers them to decide which works deserve the name of classic and which do not. For the idea of "the classic" itself is no more universal or interest-free than the situation of those whose business it is to interpret literary works for the general public. It underwrites their claim to be the servants—and not the arbiters—of truth, and disguises the historically conditioned, contingent, and partisan nature of the texts that their modes of construction make visible. The recognition that literary texts are man-made, historically produced objects, whose value has been created and recreated by men and women out of their particular needs, suggests a need to study the interests, institutional practices, and social arrangements that sustain the canon of classic works. It also opens the way for a retrieval of the values and interests embodied in other, non-canonical texts, which the literary establishment responsible for the canon in its present form has—for a variety of reasons—suppressed.

*   *   *

The following chapters begin the retrieval process conservatively, starting with works already in the canon that have been criticized for failing to meet the requirements of literary art. The

strategy employed in revaluing these novels is not to show that
they do in fact meet such requirements, but to change the nature
of the questions criticism puts to them and thus to change the
standards by which they are being judged. Rather than asking,
"what does this text mean?" or, "how does it work?," I ask, "what
kind of work is this novel trying to do?" My assumption in each
instance has been that the text is engaged in solving a problem or
a set of problems specific to the time in which it was written, and
that therefore the way to identify its purposes is not to compare
it to other examples of the genre, but to relate it to the historical
circumstances and the contemporary cultural discourse to which
it seems most closely linked. Within this framework, the question
of literary value undergoes a metamorphosis. Instead of asking
whether a work is unified or discontinuous, subtle, complex, or
profound, one wants to know, first, whether it was successful in
achieving its aims; and second, whether those aims were good or
bad. For the most part, I have not tried to answer these questions
head on, but have tried to describe the kind of enterprise the novel
was engaged in, in order to determine, before passing judgment
on it, what its purposes really were.

Each chapter, then, offers a reading of the novel in question
that shows what kind of work the text is doing within its particular
milieu. The shape of the argument in each case depends on the
nature of the objections the text has typically given rise to, and
on the amount of context-building necessary to make the text's
intentions understandable. As a rule the more sweeping the critical
objections are, the greater the work of contextualization required,
for the more flagrantly a text violates our notions of what good
literature is, the more its assumptions are likely to differ from ours
across a whole range of issues—issues that concern not only the
definition of literature but the purpose of human life, the nature
of power, and reality itself. The kinds of arguments necessary to
answer a charge of careless plot construction, for example (as in
the case of *Wieland* and *Arthur Mervyn*), involve a less thorough-
going account of the text's historical situation than those required
to meet the wholesale dismissal of works as non-literary and out

of touch with reality (as in the case of *Uncle Tom's Cabin* and *The Wide, Wide World*). In the chapter on *Wieland*, I have been able to argue for the novel's structural coherence by having recourse to the political context that makes sense of seeming irrelevancies in the plot. But in the chapter on Susan Warner, in order to argue for the value and significance of *The Wide, Wide World*, I have had to reconstruct the very sense of reality from which the novel sprang—its theology, its definition of power, its thematics, its language, its psychology, its conception of everyday life.

What Happens in *Wieland*

This is what happens in *Wieland*.

Four young adults—Theodore and Clara Wieland, and Catherine and Henry Pleyel—are leading the most rational and harmonious existence imaginable on a country estate on the banks of the Schuylkill River. One night, after the arrival in their midst of a mysterious person named Francis Carwin, one of them hears a strange voice and after that, it is no exaggeration to say, things go rapidly downhill. Theodore Wieland, who heard the voice, becomes introspective and morbid. Clara begins to hear voices too—men in her bedroom closet threatening to rape and kill her, other men warning her to keep off her own cottage grounds. Pleyel overhears someone say that his fiancée in Germany is dead (she is alive), and later he hears someone say that Clara, whom he loves, has betrayed him with another man (she has not). The climax comes when Wieland is visited by an apparition (he thinks it is God) commanding him, as proof of religious devotion, to kill his wife—which he does—and then demanding that he kill his children—which he also does (he has four of them). Upon learning of this, Clara falls desperately ill, but recovers in time for Wieland to break out of jail in order to kill her, too. She is saved, however, by the interposition of Carwin, whose confession that he is a ventriloquist causes Wieland to doubt whether it was indeed God's voice that commanded him to murder his family. He kills himself. Clara's house burns down. Somehow, the misunderstanding between her and Pleyel is cleared up and they go off to Europe. End of story.

This summary of *Wieland*'s main narrative exaggerates its craziness only slightly. Even Brown admits that the events he narrates are "extraordinary and rare" and that "some readers may find the conduct of . . . Wieland impossible.[1] Nevertheless, it is impossible, at the same time, not to take the story seriously. The acts Wieland commits are terrible in themselves and in the effects they have on the mind of their distraught narrator, whose desperate struggle to understand them constitutes so much of the novel's action. It is clear that Brown took these events with the utmost seriousness, too. He offers *Wieland* to us, in his foreword, as an "illustration of some important branches of the moral constitution of man," and hopes that it will "be ranked with the few productions whose usefulness secures to them a lasting reputation" (3).

What is significant about this remark is that Brown identified the value of *Wieland* with its usefulness, and therefore must have assumed that its *meaning* would be clear to his readers, since the usefulness of his book would naturally depend upon its being understood. Modern critics of *Wieland*, however, do not agree at all on what *Wieland* means and hardly any have thought of the novel as intended to have a practical use (circumstances that are not unrelated). I think the discrepancy between Brown's expectations for *Wieland*—that its practical consequences were what was important, its meaning being taken for granted—and our current account of *Wieland* as a fascinating, polysemous text that is deeply flawed from a formal point of view, can be explained by our loss of the context within which the novel was written. Modern critical expectations about the nature of literary production have replaced those that motivated the writing of *Wieland*, and the result is a variety of interpretations that reflect the concerns of twentieth century critics more closely than they do the concerns that animated Brown's novel.

Thus, critics who write from a formalist or neo-formalist perspective read the novel, naturally enough, as an expression of their preoccupation with art and artifice, or as pointing to the slipperiness of language itself.[2] A second group, representing various kinds of archetypal criticism, sees *Wieland* as dealing in universal symbols, or, more loosely, as probing "the dark side of human consciousness."[3] A third group, more interested in the history of ideas than in literary forms or psychological constants, focuses on the philosophical speculation Brown's protagonists love to engage

in, and sees *Wieland* as arguing the merits and demerits of Calvinist
pessimism as against those of Enlightenment rationalism.[4] This
group, I think, comes closest to reconstructing Brown's own intentions. But whatever their specific orientation, almost all the
critics assume that Brown was trying to write what in the twentieth
century we have come to think of as a good novel—that is to say,
a carefully crafted, intellectually dense, stylistically polished ex-
ploration of some enduring moral, psychological, or philosophical
problem. Virtually all scold Brown for his repetitiveness, incon-
sistency, digressiveness, and general carelessness, citing the novel's
hasty composition and the fact that Brown was an inexperienced
craftsman as the source of *Wieland*'s artistic defects.[5]

The problem that underlies these criticisms appears in its starkest
form in an essay by Nina Baym somewhat misleadingly titled "A
Minority Reading of *Wieland*." The essay argues that *Wieland* is
a failed tragedy that could have succeeded if only it had been
handled properly. Baym reasons that since *Wieland* concerns the
fate of a single individual, therefore the story ought logically to
show the development of that individual in some detail. "The
success of the story, so singleminded as it is, will depend on the
handling of Wieland himself; how the mania will develop in him.
The audience must be made to hang on every step of the progression, suspended in that profound alembic of pity and fear with
which a tragic fall is experienced."[6] Because he does not concen-
trate on Wieland's "slow decline into madness," but concentrates
instead on Clara's mystification at the bizarre events and on her
obsession with Carwin, Brown, according to Baym, driven by the
desire to produce "immediate effects," "sacrifices the story line,"
sacrifices character development, and sacrifices the long-term coherence of his novel, which deteriorates into "Gothicism" and
"sensation."[7] While Baym's critique of *Wieland* is severer than
some (hence the label "minority" reading), the principles that
animate it underlie most of the strictures that critics have voiced
over Brown's handling of the novel form. *Wieland* is evaluated
and described in terms of aesthetic and psychological norms that
assume that the primary focus must be on an individual character,
that action must reveal character, and that character must reveal

internal psychic processes rather than public and social ones. Given these criteria, Brown's novel necessarily seems defective, since it offers no coherent account of why Wieland committed the murders, never focuses on Wieland's character per se, presents no step-by-step description of his transformation, and includes much material that seems psychologically irrelevant to it. If one assumes that *Wieland* was conceived as a tightly constructed "study in dementia," there is no alternative but to conclude that it is seriously flawed.

While I do not wish to deny the relevance of some modern discussions of the novel, especially those that emphasize its relation to the intellectual trends of its day, I think that there is a better way to explain what happens in *Wieland*, one that seeks to understand the text, as Brown did, in the light of its use. Brown staked the reputation of his novel not on its claims to artistic merit, but on its efficacy. This means that the key to *Wieland*'s meaning lies in the historical situation that the novel itself attempted to shape. And while this contextual reading of the novel will be no less a product of modern critical assumptions than those I have described above, it provides the bizarre and painful events of *Wieland* with a more satisfactory explanation than has yet been available, because it is able to account for portions of the text that have hitherto been seen as irrelevant, inadvertent, or simply "bad."

That explanation begins with a single fact. The first thing that Brown did when he finished writing *Wieland* was to send a copy to Thomas Jefferson, who was then Vice President of the United States. Since Brown was an unknown writer who had no personal connection with Jefferson, this gesture suggests that he believed his novel's "usefulness" lay in the area of national politics, that perhaps he saw his book not so much as a work of art in our modern sense of the term, but as an attempt to influence public policy. But since *Wieland*, to our eyes at least, has no obvious political content, the question then becomes, what bearing could it possibly have on affairs of state?

The very fact that this question arises is an index of the distance that separates modern ways of thinking about literature from those that prevailed when Brown was alive. The question assumes, for example, that literary and political discourse normally occupy separate realms and fulfill separate functions, and that a novel that does not refer explicitly to political matters therefore has nothing to do with them. But as Joseph Ellis points out in his study of the post-Revolutionary era, "our presumption that it is possible to think and talk about the arts as distinct from society—or, for that matter, the isolated individual as independent of society—is a legacy of the 19th century." Eighteenth-century Americans, says Ellis, "lacked our modern understanding of the word 'culture' as a transcendent realm of sensibility divorced from the ordinary events of the mundane world"; to them "the artistic, political, and economic life of any society . . . was a single thing."[8]

In what follows I will argue that Charles Brockden Brown was a product of the society Ellis describes in a way and to a degree that modern criticism has not fully recognized. That *Wieland* was not designed as a well-made novel, but as a political tract. That Brown sent *Wieland* to the Vice President because he wanted to bring about a change in government policy. That his novel is directed toward solving the problems of post-Revolutionary society. And that *Wieland* is worth attending to not because it manages to *escape* the limiting features of its particular historical situation, but because it presents a shocking and uncharacteristically negative view of what it meant to survive the War of Independence. If Thomas Paine and Thomas Jefferson wanted to convince the populace of the glories of independence, Brown wanted no less to warn people of its horrifying consequences—a motive he shared, if not in its specific content, then certainly in its general nature, with all literary men of his era.[9]

In the 1790s, when Brown wrote, literary discourse was regularly used, especially on this side of the Atlantic, as a vehicle for political statements in exactly the same way that the Augustans, on whom American men of letters modeled themselves, had used satire as a weapon to attack political adversaries. National politics, in the Revolutionary and post-Revolutionary decades, was the dominant theme of American writing; whether they wrote in a critical or celebratory vein, American authors devoted themselves almost exclusively to subjects that concerned the future of the republic.[10]

The first American epic poem, Timothy Dwight's *Conquest of Canaan*, is an allegory of the Revolution told as the story of the Book of Joshua. Joel Barlow's *Vision of Columbus* (a poem Kenneth Silverman calls "the most serious American poem of the eighteenth century") was written specifically in answer to the question "Was America a Mistake?" (a question *Wieland* seems to answer in the affirmative).[11] The Connecticut Wits, frightened by the civil violence of Shays' Rebellion, composed a miscellany in twelve installments entitled *The Anarchiad*, attacking "the Anti-Federalists & Advocates for Mobs and Conventions."[12] In 1787 *The Columbian Magazine*, to which Brown contributed, serialized a novella-length piece called *The Forester, an American Tale*, a satirical allegory of America's relations with Britain from the time of Elizabeth through the Revolution. Another anonymous writer for the same periodical used the conventions of the novel of seduction to glorify American revolutionary morals in *Amelia, or the Faithless Briton*. And just as American authors and editors felt it their patriotic responsibility to address themselves to issues of national importance, political leaders felt it incumbent on them to support literary enterprise. George Washington told Matthew Carey, who founded *The Columbian* and the *American Museum*, the country's best periodical, that magazines strengthened the nation by creating an informed citizenry: "I consider such easy vehicles of knowledge," he said, "more happily calculated than any other to preserve the liberty, stimulate the industry and meliorate the morals of an enlightened and free people."[13] American writers of Brown's generation saw themselves as shapers of public morality; and not only that, they saw themselves as helping to guide the ship of state as well. Joel Barlow sums up their attitude succinctly in his introduction to *Advice to the Privileged Orders*: "To induce the men who now govern the world," he wrote, "to adopt these ideas, is the duty of those who now possess them."[14] To have political ideas, to express them in literary form, and to attempt thereby to influence "the men who now govern the world" was not only standard practice in Brown's day, it was the raison d'être of an American author. Thus, for a young novelist steeped in the atmosphere of post-Revolutionary Philadelphia to send his first work of fiction to the Vice President was hardly an extraordinary gesture—on the contrary, it was a natural extension of the motives that impelled him to write in the first place.

Brown, in fact, had meditated at some length on how "genius and virtue" might best "labour for the public good."[15] In the letter he sent Jefferson accompanying *Wieland*, he defends his book against the traditional charge that novels are frivolous time-wasters and corruptors of the youth, arguing that "fictitious narratives through an artful display of incidents, . . . the powerful delineation of characters and the train of eloquent and judicious reasoning" deserve as much respect as "social and intellectual theories, and the history of facts in the processes of nature and the operations of government."[16] In an early essay, "Walstein's School of History," he had reached the conclusion that not only were "abstract systems and intellectual reasonings" inferior, as moral instruments, to "the detail of actions" in an "eloquent narration," but that "the medium of books"—and specifically of fiction—was a *better* means of effecting "public good" than the "legal or ministerial authority" that men such as Jefferson possessed.[17] For, he reasons, the fates of great statesmen like Cicero and Pombal "evince the insufficiency of the instrument chosen by them, and teach us, that a change of national opinion is the necessary prerequisite of revolutions."[18] Brown had no wish to foment revolution but he had developed some rather precise notions of how writing fiction might change national opinion. And specifically he believed that in order to exert the maximum effect on readers a novelist should "select, as the scene . . . of his narrative, that in which those who should read it, should exist," thus "forcibly suggesting[ing] . . . the parallel between [their] state and that described."[19] In *Wieland*, following the example of Godwin's *Caleb Williams*, Brown intended to offer his readers a picture of "things as they are" in America of the 1790s.[20] And given the context in which Brown wrote, that could only mean that he intended to address the great political issues that occupied the minds of most men alive in his day. For most people writing in the late eighteenth century, to investigate "things passing in the moral world" was not to discuss matters that were separate from the great questions of revolution and reform, but to meet them head on. For, as I will suggest later, whether one was for or against the Constitution, for or against the French Revolution, for or against Jeffersonian democracy, turned largely on whether one believed that men were by nature fit to govern themselves or needed the restraining force of an entrenched ruling order. Thus when Brown announces in the advertisement to his novel that his purpose is not "selfish" or "temporary," but "aims at the illustration of some important branches of the moral constitution of man," he is signaling his intention to enter a dialogue that had engaged civic-minded men and women since the age of Locke and Rousseau over the nature of man, the proper forms of civic representation, and the right of citizens to overthrow their government. These debates, which had given rise to two opposing pictures of the consequences of revolution, form a background against which Brown's grotesque narrative, subtitled "an American Tale," begins to make sense.

The first of these pictures is one which it is difficult for us who read this novel at the safe distance of almost two centuries to be fully cognizant of. I refer to the extreme instability of political and social life in the years immediately following the Revolution. It was not clear in the 1790s whether there would be a United States next year or the year after, much less in the 1980s. Thus, the events Brown had recently lived through gave considerable support to the awful picture that Loyalists before the Revolution had drawn of what would happen if there were a civil insurrection.

"Suppose," wrote Charles Inglis in *The True Interest of America Impartially Considered* (1776), "suppose we were to revolt from Great Britain, declare ourselves Independent, and set up a Republic of our own. . . . All our property throughout the continent would be unhinged; the greatest confusion, and most violent convulsions would take place. . . . The common bond that tied us together, and by which our property was secured, would be snapt asunder. . . . A Declaration for Independency would infallibly disunite and divide the colonists."[21] In the minds of the Loyalist minority, not only would independence lead to anarchy and chaos, but these conditions would inevitably give birth to demagoguery and thence to tyranny so that, as James Chalmers argued in a reply to Paine's *Common Sense*, "Independence and Slavery are synonymous terms."[22]

Views like these were not simply the paranoid fantasies of a conservative elite, but were widely shared and drew substantive support from the history of the colonists' relation to authority. "I have learnt from experience," writes Lord Dunmore, governor of Virginia, "that the established Authority of any government in America, and the policy of Government at home, are both insufficient to restrain the Americans."[23] Riots, mob actions, and the raising of semi-private militias were recurrent features of American civil life before the Revolution; and in the decades that preceded the writing of *Wieland*, the country was threatened by civil insurrection in the doctors' riot in New York, Shays' Rebellion in western Massachusetts, and the Whiskey Rebellion in Pennsylvania.[24] Mob violence was endemic; there were fist fights in state and federal legislatures; ordinary people took to the streets, destroying property and beating men; dueling became widespread; "everything," writes Gordon Wood, "seemed to be coming apart, and murder, suicide and drunkeness were prevalent."[25]

But, in opposition to the actuality of political chaos and social and economic disarray, Jeffersonians were painting a picture of the consequences of revolution in America that described this country as a haven of security and freedom, a place where men and women, contrary to the dire predictions of Federalist alarmists, curbed their passions and their selfishness in the interests of the public good. Ideologically committed to the belief that men were able to govern themselves when educated in right principles of virtue, and allied politically and economically with the small farmers who needed a liberal monetary policy in order to survive, Jeffersonians emphasized the dangers of government interference in private affairs. Moreover, the need to forge a national identity for a miscellaneous collection of people who were united in practically nothing but their living on the same side of the Atlantic, and the need to attract labor and capital to American shores, gave rise, in the writings of Jefferson, Crèvecoeur, and others, to a crude exaltation of America as the Promised Land that completely ignored the tumultuous, uncertain tenor of American life.[26] Europeans, in these characterizations of the Old and New Worlds, are said to be "suffering under physical and moral oppression," while Americans, conversely, love simplicity and domesticity, cultivate the rural virtues of independence, self-reliance, and frugality, enjoy "the tranquil permanent felicity with which domestic society in America blesses most of it's (sic) inhabitants, . . . [and] follow steadily those pursuits which health and reason approve. . . ."[27] Crèvecoeur, speaking in the character of the sturdy yeoman, tells the European traveler that "if he travels through our rural districts," what he will find is not

> the hostile castle and the haughty mansion, contrasted with the clay-built hut and miserable cabin, where cattle and men help to keep each other warm, and dwell in meanness, smoke, and indigence. A pleasing uniformity of decent competence appears throughout our habitations. The meanest of our log-houses is a dry and comfortable habitation. Lawyer or merchant are the fairest titles our towns afford; that of a farmer is the only appellation of the rural inhabitants of our country. . . . There, on a Sunday, he sees a congregation of respectable farmers and their wives, all clad in neat homespun, well mounted, or riding in their own humble wagons. There is not among them an esquire, saving the unlettered magistrate. There he sees a parson as simple as his flock, a farmer who does not riot on the labor of others. We have no princes, for whom we toil, starve, and bleed; we are the most perfect society now existing in the world.[28]

In writing *Wieland* Brown shows that Crèvecoeur's picture of sturdy yeomen living in rural decency is not the Republican idyll it pretends to be. *Wieland*'s landscape, like Crèvecoeur's, contains no hostile castles or haughty mansions, no squires, lawyers, or magistrates, no princes who oppress the poor; people do not toil, starve, and bleed; they prosper, and in their spare time read Cicero and play chamber music. But instead of being a depiction of "the most perfect society now existing in the world," *Wieland*'s rural decencies are the seedbed of a holocaust. Dramatizing the precariousness of Crèvecoeur's "perfect" society, the novel's plot offers a direct refutation of the Republican faith in men's capacity to govern themselves without the supports and constraints of an established social order.

The two protagonists of *Wieland*, Clara and her brother, Theodore, are ideal products of that faith, having been raised according to the most enlightened Republican notions of proper education. The maiden aunt who cares for them is the perfect combination of indulgence and resolution. The young Wielands are instructed in "most branches of useful knowledge" but are "saved from the corruption and tyranny of colleges and boarding schools" (III, 20). For their religious education they are "left to the guidance of [their] own understanding"; their religion, Clara explains, "was the product of lively feelings, excited by reflection on our own happiness, and by the grandeur of external nature" (III, 22). While Theodore's character resembles his father's in its tendency to melancholy and in his fondness for dwelling on serious moral issues, his mind, unlike his father's, "was enriched by science, and embellished with literature" (III, 23). Moreover, Wieland's studiousness, and his Calvinistic bent are happily offset by the liberal views of his best friend, Henry Pleyel, who has spent some years in Europe and is of a gay and ardent disposition. "Their creeds," writes Clara, "were in many respects opposite. . . . Pleyel was the champion of intellectual liberty, and rejected all guidance but that of his reason." "My brother," she says, "was captivated with his friend," and as a result of his influence had "laid aside some part of his ancient gravity" (III, 25). The third generation of Wielands embody America's passage from Puritan narrowness to large-minded enlightenment views not only in their character and education, but in the setting and activities Brown assigns to them.

The temple their father had built to his vindictive God on the banks of the Schuylkill has been converted by the children into a summerhouse where they carry on their cultural pastimes. It now contains a bust of Cicero and a harpsichord; "here we sung, and talked, and read, and occasionally banqueted, . . . here the performances of our musical and poetical ancestor were rehearsed, . . . here a thousand conversations, pregnant with delight and improvement, took place"(III, 24). The Wielands live in a rationalist's paradise. They are uncorrupted by ancient prejudice and oppressive institutions; their lives are not worn with labor (their fortune exempts them from the need to work); they are free from the effects of political turmoil ("The sound of war had been heard, but it was at such a distance as to enhance our enjoyment . . . Revolutions and battles, however calamitous to those who occupied the scene, contributed in some sort to our happiness" [IV, 26].); Theodore marries Pleyel's rich, beautiful, vivacious, and "remarkably congenial" sister, who is also Clara's best friend; they have four beautiful children, and in this privileged setting pass "six years of uninterrupted happiness" (IV, 26). "We gradually withdrew ourselves from the society of others, and found every moment irksome that was not devoted to each other" (III, 21). No mode of existence, it seems, could be more self-sufficient or better calculated to support human life on the most favorable terms. But it is these ideal conditions that spawn the horrors that are about to occur. The question the novel poses, then, is: given the material prosperity of the Wielands, given the ideal nature of their intellectual, moral, and religious education, their location in an innocent rural environment, their freedom from social or political pressures of any kind, given all this, how can one account for the series of catastrophes that ensue? If the Wielands represent, in Crèvecoeur's language, "the most perfect society now existing in the world," how can one explain the transformation?

But "explain" is, in some sense, precisely the wrong word. The story of *Wieland*'s transformation is told by Clara, Wieland's sister, whose overwhelming desire is to find an explanation for the confusions that surround her—the voices she hears in her bedroom, Pleyel's hostility towards her, and, above all, her brother's terrible acts—but no satisfactory explanation is ever found. Clara, most of whose actions and speculations take place at night, is literally and metaphorically in the dark. She strives continually to find some concrete, rational basis for understanding the events she relates, but continually fails. Her uncertainty is only exacerbated when, at a climactic moment, it appears that there may after all be a rational explanation for Wieland's behavior. For no sooner does the explanation arrive than it is withdrawn.

When Francis Carwin, the stranger whose appearance in the Wielands' circle coincides with the mysterious "voices" they hear, finally confesses to having played on them a series of ventriloquist's tricks, it seems at first that the mystery of Wieland's transformation has been solved. But the explanation that Carwin's ventriloquism seems to represent fails at the crucial point. Although he confesses to having been the cause of all the other confusions, Carwin categorically denies having been the voice that commanded Wieland to murder his wife and children. And although there is no way to be sure he isn't lying, there is no way to prove that he is. This "explanation" merely transposes the mystery from Wieland's behavior to Carwin's. Far from being a solution to the problem of what happens in *Wieland*, Carwin is the embodiment of it.

Carwin, who first appears in the guise of a plowman, and then turns out to have studied with the Jesuits, is the quintessential child of revolution, a self-made man who changes his religion, his nationality, his occupation, his social position at will (he has been both Catholic and Protestant, American and European, rustic and cosmopolitan). Carwin's successive identities, like his assumption of the voices of others, are the logical outcome of the social situation the Wielands inhabit, one in which the insignia of social stratification have been stripped away in the name of equality, and all sources of authority are potentially suspect.

Carwin, whose whimsical tricks precipitate the Wielands' downfall, replicates on the level of individual identity the social and epistemic voids the Wielands confront. He is the living embodiment of a society in which there are no markers that define and fix the self. In political terms, he is one of the "new men" the Federalists feared, who suddenly appeared out of nowhere, "specious, interested, designing men," "respectable neither for their property, their virtue, nor their abilities," who now took the lead in public life.[29] Rather than being the cause of the calamities that surround the Wielands, Carwin is merely a symptom of the emptiness that makes them possible. When something happens that troubles their relations with one another, the Wielands have no authorities of any kind on hand to tell them what to do: no kings or princes; no officials of the court; no priests of the church; no professors from the university; no judges; no representatives of "society," or of commerce; not even a neighbor to give some friendly advice. Because the social spaces of *Wieland* are empty, the space of authority is vacant in a double sense. For since they lack any external means of checking their own perceptions, when even the littlest thing disturbs their pastimes—a few words whispered by a prankster on the night air—neither reason, nor an acquaintance with "most branches of useful knowledge," nor freedom from the corrupting effects of institutions, nor their love for one another can help the Wielands to distinguish truth from falsehood or right from wrong.

Brown's picture of the disintegration of the Wielands' miniature society is a more or less direct reflection of Federalist skepticism about the efficacy of religion and education in preparing citizens to govern themselves.[30] The Federalists wanted to create a new kind of government which did not require a virtuous people in order to maintain it; they wanted a system that would by its very nature "protect the worthy against the licentious."[31] What makes *Wieland* striking in this regard is its suggestion that when institutional supports are absent, it is not so much a question of protecting the worthy against the licentious as of protecting citizens, worthy or otherwise, against themselves. It is not Carwin who murders his wife and children, but Wieland, the devout, well-educated farmer, the very epitome of the man on whom Jeffersonians staked their vision of Republican order. Because he lives in a world where authority is not vested in particular institutions of a visible and external sort, Wieland has no satisfactory way of classifying and interpreting his experiences. The "wilderness" in which he lives, as Alan Axelrod observes, "offers nothing to check a misguided leap of faith," for in a world already devoid of the "tempering influence of city civilization," democratic revolution removes not only the social controls that might have prevented Wieland's crime, but stable structures of perception and judgment as well.[32]

Though Clara's continual searching after explanations for the mysterious events that befall her makes her seem the opposite of her brother, who *knows* that God has spoken to him, their differing behavior arises from the same cause. Whereas Wieland, whose "days have been spent in searching for the revelation of [God's] will" (XIX, 165), fills the vacuum of authority by inventing a source of authority outside himself whose "commands" he feels bound

to obey, Clara is unable to decide among alternative versions of
the truth. Speaking of her efforts to explain her brother's terrible
act, she says:

> My opinions were the sport of eternal change. Some times I con-
> ceived the apparition to be more than human. I had no grounds on
> which to build a disbelief. (XX, 180).

The absence of "grounds" on which to build either belief or
disbelief is the problem that confronts the central characters in this
novel. The vacuum of authority permits the random violence that
kills the Wieland children at the same time that it removes the
possibility of ever understanding it. Poised between unsatisfactory
and irreconcilable explanations of Wieland's madness, Clara vac-
illates between the Calvinism of Wieland and the rationalism of
Pleyel, but instead of finding a third explanation, she simply gives
up. "I care not," she writes, "from what source these disasters
have flowed; it suffices that they have swallowed up our hopes and
our existence" (XXVI, 233). Clara never finds out whether it was
Carwin who imitated the voice of God, or whether it was God
himself who spoke to Wieland, or whether the voices were, in
Pleyel's words, "a deception of the senses" (IV, 34) because, Brown
is saying, she never can. When the whole order of society has been
shaken from top to bottom by the convulsions of civil rebellion,
there is no way of knowing what is or is not the case since the
world that would be the object of this knowledge is not defined
by the stable set of social practices which determine what knowledge is.[33]

Indeed the answer to the question "what happens in *Wieland*?"
has already been supplied before the main events of the story have
even begun to unfold, and it has been supplied by Clara herself.
The Wielands' catastrophe does not stem from anything they have
done or neglected to do, but from their history, which is to say
from their position as orphans of civilization in the New World.
In a series of apparently gratuitous episodes, recounted at the very
beginning of the narrative, Brown sets up the conditions that not
only explain, but require the disaster that finally occurs.

The first of these episodes concerns the protagonist's grandfather, a young Saxon nobleman, who, while on vacation in Hamburg, falls in love with a merchant's daughter, whom he marries, against the vehement protests of his parents, and as a result is disinherited by his family. "All intercourse ceased, and he received from [his family] merely that treatment to which an absolute stranger, or detested enemy, would be entitled" (I, 6). After a brief career as a playwright, the young man dies "in the bloom of his life" and is "quickly followed to the grave by his wife" (I, 7). This sketchy recital of events seems to serve, at best, as a formulaic piece of background information, and at worst as evidence of Brown's penchant for irrelevancy. And it is succeeded by a longer, more eventful narrative of the fortunes of this Wieland's son whose pertinence is equally unclear.

Apprenticed by his merchant grandfather to a London trader, he passes "seven years of mercantile servitude," performing "laborious," "mechanical," and "unintermitted labour" (I, 7). His unfurnished mind is filled with unnameable longings, but having no education, he does not even know what he lacks. One day he discovers a Camisard text lying in a corner of his garret, and this accident determines the shape of his entire life. Because the Camisards' is the God of a dissenting sect, whose commands are not interpreted by a church hierarchy or by the traditions of a community, his authority is much more oppressive than that of the traditional religions he replaces. Since his will can be divined only by the individual worshiper, and therefore has no prescribed limits, Wieland's attempts to obey this inscrutable deity turn his life into an excruciating ritual of obedience.

Hence arose a thousand scruples to which he had hitherto been a stranger. . . . He imagined himself beset by the snares of a spiritual foe, and that his security lay in ceaseless watchfulness and prayer. . . . The empire of religious duty extended itself to his looks, gestures, and phrases. . . . He laboured to keep alive a sentiment of fear, and belief of the awe-creating presence of the Deity. Ideas foreign to this were sedulously excluded. To suffer their intrusion was a crime against the Divine Majesty inexpiable but by days and weeks of the keenest agonies. (I, 9)

This second Wieland, after emigrating to America in a doomed attempt to convert the Indians, marries, has children, and becomes the successful proprietor of a farm. There he builds on the banks of the Schuylkill River a temple, devoid of ornament or symbol, where he worships his deity alone every noon and midnight. There, after a period of protracted spiritual anguish, in which he fails to carry out an unnamed command from God, he "explodes" one night, during his act of solitary worship, and shortly thereafter dies from festering wounds whose source no one can explain.

These stories of the prehistory of the Wieland family, though they seem only tenuously related to the main business of the novel, are not only relevant to it, but essential, and typical of the way Brown's plots operate. For in *Wieland*, a book about the consequences of revolution, the little tale of a man who married, long ago, against his parents' wishes, sets up a pattern of revolt and retribution that is the basis for the entire work. The paramount question in America in the 1790s was, can people get away with revolution? Is it safe to break the bonds that have held a society together? Is it possible to rebel against one's father and still survive? Brown's answer to these questions is no, no, and no, an answer which the episodic plot of *Wieland* drives home again and again.

The story of the first Wieland lays down the proposition that it is impossible to rebel against legitimate authority and not be destroyed. At the same time it recapitulates one phase of the developments that led to the founding of the American republic.[34] The story of Wieland's grandfather represents, in telescopic form, Europe's passage from an aristocratic, agrarian, feudal order (represented by Wieland's noble Saxon origins), to a middle-class commercial society (represented by the Hamburg merchant's daughter); and his marrying outside his kinship group records the weakening of the social codes that held that aristocracy together and protected its power. Declassed and disinherited, the elder Wieland becomes an economic and social orphan, someone who makes a living through entrepreneurial activity (he becomes the founder of the German theatre) and has no traditions to pass down to his heirs. His story is succeeded by its logical sequel in which the elder Wieland's son, a child of social miscegenation, lives out the consequences of his father's transgression in a more prolonged and painful form.

Whereas his father had rebelled against the strictures of an aristocratic social order, the second Wieland *has* no authority to rebel against and, therefore, nothing to live by. His father had been able to make a living by turning his aristocratic education in the arts to use; but the son, who lacks this cultural advantage, is mentally as well as economically unequipped. For this second Wieland, James Chalmers' prediction has come true: for him, independence and slavery *are* synonymous terms. With no family and no social structure to guide him, he submits himself to the harshest regimen his mind can devise, the will of a tyrannical deity. Thus, when Wieland, like the first Puritan settlers, comes to America in search of religious "freedom," the freedom he finds to worship as he chooses does not save him from a life of mental servitude. Like the Puritans, he makes an unsuccessful attempt to convert the Indians, and, as he grows more prosperous materially, like them falls prey to spasms of religious anxiety. In the story of the second Wieland, which represents a second stage in the coming of civilization to the New World, Brown seems to suggest that transporting into a wilderness people whose outlook has been shaped by a set of grim beliefs is not only not to liberate them in any significant sense, but to give free reign to their instinct to enslave themselves. In what seems almost a parody of antinomian behavior, Brown's suggestion that the second Wieland has died of guilt—the victim of a God of his own devising—extends the critique of Calvinist theology which many critics agree the novel offers. But that critique is part of a broader attack on the naively optimistic views of human nature which would do away with the external controls that might have forestalled this pathetic suicide. In what Joseph Ridgely has called "the empty world of *Wieland*," where men are characteristically left to their own devices, the cruelty they visit on themselves and on each other outstrips anything that the authorities they have deposed could have imagined.[35] Whenever, in this novel, an existing authority is deposed, a worse one rushes in to fill the vacuum.

And this was no mere fantasy on Brown's part. When, only a few years before *Wieland*'s publication, the Revolution in France had turned into a Reign of Terror, people in the United States began to be afraid that the same thing would happen here. America, after all, had served as a model for the French Revolution, and the precariousness of civil life in the Federalist era suggested to many citizens that events in this country might follow the French example.[36] There was talk of a "second Cromwell"; the "turbulence" and "mobbishness" that were already in evidence convinced Jefferson's opponents that more democracy was not the answer. "If the people will not erect any barriers against their own intemperance and giddiness," explained one editorial writer, "or will not respect and sustain them after they are erected, their power will soon be snatched out of their hands, and their own heads broken with it—as in *France*."[37] To curb the violent tendencies that could produce another Robespierre was considered an "act of patriotism."[38] And in this sense, *Wieland* is a patriotic novel: its main action, in an attempt to alert people to the dangers of mob rule, realizes the Federalist nightmare. The third Wieland, raised in the vacuum of authority his forefathers had created, goes insane; and his "Transformation" from sturdy yeoman to homicidal maniac is intended, as Brown's subtitles tell us, as a prototypically "American Tale."

The inescapability of Wieland's homicidal behavior, despite the "ideal" conditions in which he was raised, is pointed to yet again before his disintegration begins in an episode that has always seemed to *Wieland*'s critics Brown's most egregious sin against formal economy. In addition to their own children, Theodore and Catherine Wieland had adopted a fifth child, an orphan girl of fourteen named Louisa Conway, the daughter of a woman also named Louisa Conway, who comes from a wealthy London family, and of a Major Stuart, whose military duties had called him to Germany after three years of marriage. The major is absent for some time, longer than he had expected, and on his return finds that his father-in-law's house is in mourning. Louisa and her infant daughter have disappeared and are never heard from again until, years later, while on a trip to America, the husband finds his daughter living with the Wielands, the mother having long since died, the victim of "incurable griefs" (IV, 28). The introduction of the Louisa Conway story at the beginning and again at the end of the novel seems to make no sense, and critics have never been able to account for it except as an instance of Brown's uncontrolled impulse to proliferate subplots. It is, according to Fred Pattee, "the most serious structural defect" in the novel, a direct result of Brown's "headlong rapidity of composition" and inevitable "slovenliness": there is, says Pattee, "no reason for Louisa Conway's presence in Wieland's family."[39]

But in fact Louisa Conway's story is essential precisely because it seems so gratuitous, which it is in any number of ways: Wieland and Catherine already have four children, making a fifth seem quite unnecessary; Louisa Conway makes her appearance only to disappear immediately and completely; we never hear another word about her except to learn that she has been massacred along with the Wieland children; moreover, Louisa Conway is not even related to the Wielands, and therefore it seems especially unjust that she should share their fate. But it is because Louisa Conway has nothing to do with the Wielands that her story is significant. Her story is not part of theirs but parallel to it. Louisa Conway's mother, we learn at the end of the book, like the Wielands' ancestor, had transgressed the norms of her society. While her husband was away, the young wife had fallen in love with a seducer and, helpless to change her feelings, she had fled England disguised as a boy in order to hide her shame.[40] The mother dies for her transgression as the Wielands' grandfather had, in the bloom of youth, leaving her daughter behind to the consequences that (we now know) must inevitably befall the children of people who have dispossessed themselves. Louisa Conway's story has "nothing to do" with the Wielands' because her daughter would have died whether or not the Wielands had adopted her. The child has been sentenced to death not by Theodore Wieland's madness but by her own mother's trespass. Her fate is sealed no matter what she does, just as the Wielands' catastrophe is certain before the first false voice is heard.

When the Wielands' grandfather took the first fatal misstep and

married below his station, when Louisa Conway's mother left her
father's house ashamed and in disguise, they set in motion a train
of circumstances that would not be played out until both families
are decimated. In effect, then, the correct answer to the question
"what happens in *Wieland*?" is "nothing." The novel's principal
scenario, in which revolt against patriarchal authority brings suffering and death, has already been played out several times before
the story proper ever gets underway. The murders that occupy its
narrative center are only a bloodier, more shocking, and inevitable
repetition of what has already occurred. In an early debate over
Cicero's oration for Cluentius, Wieland and Pleyel argue over
whether Cicero had intended to "make the picture of a single
family a model from which to sketch the condition of a nation"
(IV, 30). This, of course, is exactly what Brown intended in writing
Wieland, whose story replicates the history of civilization in the
New World. The Wielands are done in not by any moral weakness,
intellectual oversight, or defect in their education; they are casualties of history viewed from the perspective of men who had
watched in fear the bloodbath that followed the French Revolution.

With these observations in mind I would like to return to the
criticisms of *Wieland* outlined at the beginning which, in addition
to citing Brown's digressiveness, focused on his failure to show
the inner development of his central character, to create suspense,
or to develop the main line of action step-by-step.[41] The cultural
discourse of the Federalist era suggests that the sort of "progression" which interested Brown and his contemporaries was not that
of an individual's "slow decline into madness," but of a nation's
decline into violence and anarchy.[42] *Wieland*'s immediate context
suggests that Brown's frame of reference is not a concern for the
psychodynamics of a deranged personality, nor yet Aristotelian
canons of unity, or of probability and necessity, as Baym suggests,
but the disintegration of social life that Jefferson's opponents believed was endangering the life of the republic.[43] Given these background assumptions, it is appropriate that the plot does not focus
on the evolution of individual character and has, indeed, no interest
whatever in character—conceived as the fate of a single person.

Character, in *Wieland*, is the function of socio-political situations which define, or fail to define, human possibilities and limits. *Wieland*'s plot, rather than presenting a character's "slow decline into madness," presents a series of transformations of a paradigmatic event in which characters who are successive reincarnations of one another enact the same catastrophe over and over again. Events in this novel do not "develop" or form a "progression"; they do not involve "suspense." Events in *Wieland* are related to one another not, as in Aristotle, as cause and effect, but as variations of a single ideological proposition, which states and restates itself with increasing intensity as the narrative lengthens. What they say in the case of Wieland's grandfather, his father, and Wieland himself, and in the case of Louisa Conway, is always the same thing: that death is the price of revolution. *but at the command or in the name of God.*

What this analysis suggests, finally, is that one can make more sense of *Wieland*'s bizarre features—its sensationalism, its repetitions, its apparent digressiveness—if one reads the novel not as an object to be analyzed in modern psychological or aesthetic terms, but politically, as a plea for the restoration of civic authority in a post-Revolutionary age. Brown wanted to convince people that it was time to stop the progressive liberalization of the structures of authority which was leading the country into civil chaos. And therefore his message to the Vice President is, not coincidentally, the same as Carwin's favorite warning to his victims—to "Hold!"

Two years later, with the publication of *Arthur Mervyn*, Brown seems to have rescinded the order. This time, in an apparent reversal of his position in *Wieland*, he uses the resources of fiction not to restrain action or to forecast disaster, but to furnish citizens of the republic with a strategy for plunging ahead.

III

The Importance of
Merely Circulating

I. MARAVEGLI

Toward the middle of part I of *Arthur Mervyn*, Mervyn, who has
been working for a kindly Quaker farmer named Mr. Hadwin,
decides that he has to make a trip to Philadelphia to find a young
man named Wallace whose life may be in danger. Although Mervyn does not know Wallace personally, he knows that he is engaged
to marry Mr. Hadwin's elder daughter, that he is "without kindred
and probably without friends, in the city," and that he is of a
"frank and generous spirit." "Incessantly pursued by the image of
this youth, perishing alone, and in obscurity," Mervyn decides that
he must find him, "friendless and succourless" as he is and "supply
to him the place of protector and nurse."[1]

Arthur goes to the city and after a series of inquiries ends up in
the house of a wealthy merchant named Thetford (with whom he
has had an oblique acquaintance), but the house is deserted by all
except a man who is dying of the plague in one of the upper
bedrooms. This man, Mervyn learns through further inquiry, is
"the only descendent of an illustrious house of Venice, . . . devoted
from his childhood to the acquisition of knowledge and the practice
of virtue," (I:XVI, 153) who, while pursuing his studies in America, had befriended a widow and her seven daughters and had become engaged to one of the girls. He had been on the verge of
embarking for Europe when the plague struck Philadelphia and
he had "hastened to the rescue of the Walpoles from the perils
which encompassed them" (I:XVI, 154). But he arrived only to
find that they had all died of the fever, which he is about to die
of himself when Mervyn discovers him. On his features "the traces

of intelligence and beauty were undefaced," and Mervyn muses that though the life of Wallace (the man he had set out to rescue) was of value to "a feeble individual [Susan Hadwin], . . . surely the being that was stretched before [him] and who was hastening to his last breath was precious to thousands" (I:XVI, 147). This youth is fittingly named Maravegli (an ancient form of the Italian word for "marvels"). And Mervyn declares that he was "one in whose place I would willingly have died" (I:XVI, 147).

What are we to make of this? Arthur Mervyn sets out to rescue someone else's fiancé and finds another man, who has tried to rescue *his* fiancée, dying of the plague. Here is the image Mervyn had dreamed of—a man dying "friendless and succourless"—but the victim is not the man he had been looking for. Instead, he is another stranger, a person of even more extraordinary abilities and accomplishments than Wallace, for whom Mervyn declares himself willing to die. Nevertheless, it is Maravegli who dies and is soon left behind in the helter-skelter forward movement of the story. Yet, who is he, and why has he been introduced? Why does Mervyn meet, not the person he seeks, but another man who resembles both that person *and* Mervyn himself in that he risks his life for others and is himself the object of rescue (for, in the opening scene of the novel, Arthur Mervyn had been rescued selflessly from the plague by a kind and generous person to whom *he* was a complete stranger, the same person to whom he is now telling this story)? Moreover, the person whom Arthur seeks, this Wallace, is, unbeknownst to him, someone he has already met, the very same person who rescued him, in a manner of speaking, when he first came to the city.

What are we to make of these coincidences and repetitions? The episode I have described, with its uncanny connections and mirroring of other incidents, is not anomalous, but typical of the events in this novel. It reproduces both the labyrinthine movement of Brown's narrative and the sense of what it is like to be caught in the repetitive convolutions of its plot. We are always rushing off with this hero on half-formed quests that lead down unfamiliar streets, only to find that we've been there before, faced the same faces, been surprised by the same events.

The role of coincidence in Brown's fiction, as Norman Grabo has demonstrated, is so pervasive that it requires an explanation beyond what any of the traditional generic categories can supply.[2] *Arthur Mervyn* has been identified as a *bildungsroman*, as a Gothic tale of terror, as a study in moral ambiguity, and as a romance; but these designations do not succeed in accounting for the sense of déjà vu, of being trapped in the same predicament, the doubling, tripling, and quadrupling of weirdly interconnected persons and events that the reader constantly encounters in this novel.[3] The effort to assimilate *Arthur Mervyn* to the norms of modern criticism has led critics to conclude that, like *Wieland*, it is a flawed attempt to imitate more perfect models.[4] "In a touchstone test of merit, [Brown] would fail almost completely" says Warner Berthoff in the introduction to the Rinehart edition of *Arthur Mervyn*. "There is often a glaring contrast between the rich promise of his conceptions and the haphazardness of their execution."[5] By "haphazardness," Berthoff refers to the seemingly gratuitous repetitions of Brown's plots, and to the introduction of apparently superfluous characters such as Maravegli who are suddenly discovered and "marvelled" at, only to be immediately forgotten.

But Brown's description of *Arthur Mervyn* in "Walstein's School of History" provides some insight into how one might approach the problem of repetition and apparent irrelevance here, as it did in the case of *Wieland*. He says that *Arthur Mervyn* (which he refers to under the title "Olivo Ronsica") represents a "model of right conduct" in which the reader is intended to see the parallel between his own situation and that of the hero and so be excited to emulate the hero's behavior.[6] To compose such a narrative, says Brown, is "the highest province of benevolence" (151). It is a story, he insists, from which "it is not possible for any one to rise without some degree of moral benefit" (156), for it "shews us how temptation may be baffled, in spite of ignorance, and benefits be conferred in spite of poverty" (154–155). Whatever modern criticism may have made of Brown's novel, there can be no question how he himself conceived it: he wrote in order to benefit the mass of men, who like his hero are poor, friendless, and ignorant, and he saw himself as a servant of "benevolence" rather than of the Muse. The problem, then, for anyone who wishes to understand the original intent of *Arthur Mervyn* as a whole, is to explain how its apparently mindless reiterations and stark implausibilities can be seen as an extension of the author's benevolent aims. With this purpose in mind, it will be helpful to return to the incident in which Mervyn, setting out to rescue Wallace, discovers instead the illustrious Maravegli, for the way in which that incident amplifies and reproduces itself illustrates the way the whole novel is organized.

The Maravegli incident, typically, reenacts a situation that has already occurred several times. The first instance in which one character rescues another is Dr. Stevens' rescue of Mervyn. In return for Stevens' kindness, Mervyn, who has no money or worldly goods of any kind, repays him by telling the story of his life—a narrative which occupies the entire first half of the novel and which Stevens, who is the narrator of most of the story, is telling to us. The second incident of rescue, which occurs early in Mervyn's narrative, is his rescue of a young man named Clavering who looks uncannily like him. Clavering too has been driven from home by his father and like Arthur Mervyn is skilled with the pen. The "amiable and unfortunate" Clavering bequeaths to Mervyn, in payment for his care, a portrait of himself—a pictorial double of the story Mervyn is telling Stevens. Clavering, like Maravegli, does not survive, but he turns up later in the story, posthumously, so to speak, when Arthur Mervyn is mistaken for him by his employer's landlady (an instance of mistaken identity that will be repeated more than once).

The third instance of rescue is the one in which Wallace, on the pretext of offering Arthur shelter for the night, tricks him into entering the house of a wealthy merchant (it is Thetford, the same man in whose house Mervyn discovers the dying Maravegli), where Mervyn is locked in a dark bedroom which he discovers is already occupied.

The fourth rescue, even more dubious than the third, takes place when Mervyn, wandering the streets, hungry and penniless, begs alms from a wealthy passerby who takes him in, dresses him in fine clothes, and gives him the position of personal secretary. This man is Welbeck, the villain, who shares the premises with a young woman named Clemenza Lodi, whom he introduces as his daughter but who is in fact his mistress. Clemenza Lodi, we soon learn, is the sister of the man whom *Welbeck* had found dying of the plague, had pitied and cared for (the fifth rescue), and from whom Welbeck received, in exchange for his care, a small fortune and a life story. Thus, Vincenzo Lodi, who also, coincidentally, looks just like Arthur Mervyn, tells his story to Welbeck, as Welbeck tells his to Mervyn, as Mervyn tells his to Stevens, who is telling the whole thing to us.

I have now reached the point, which arrives sooner or later in most serious discussions of Brown's novels, where the critic begins to sound like the child who, when asked what the movie she has just seen was about, proceeds to tell you the entire story from beginning to end. This is not because Brown is a naive writer whom the critics unwittingly fall to imitating, but because the story, as these compulsive recapitulations attest, delivers its messages by enacting over and over again the same few scenes. The scene of rescue, which I have been tracing through the first quarter of the novel, reaches new intensities of repetition as part I draws to a close. For Mervyn, fleeing to the country in old clothes and hungry again, starts the cycle up by letting himself be rescued by the kindly Mr. Hadwin, the rural counterpart of Dr. Stevens. And once again, the tables turn. It is from Hadwin's house that Mervyn sets out to rescue Wallace (who previously had rescued Mervyn although he doesn't know it and whom he eventually does rescue, after finding Maravegli—another would-be rescuer and rescuee). In the course of rescuing Wallace, Mervyn is given shelter by yet another kind gentleman—a man named Medlicote—and is helped by still another, named Estwick. Finally, Mervyn, who has come down with the fever himself in his attempt to save Wallace, and has taken refuge in Welbeck's empty house, hears in one of the upper rooms the voice of a man named Colvill, a studious and solitary youth (like Mervyn) who was also the seducer of Mervyn's sister (whom Mervyn greatly resembles). But, as it turns out—and by now, no coincidence is too great—it is not the voice of Colvill that Mervyn hears, it is the voice of *Welbeck*, who is *imitating* Colvill; Welbeck, whom Mervyn had helped to escape from Philadelphia after he had murdered a man named Watson, and whom Mervyn believes to be dead; Welbeck, who had previously rescued Mervyn, and whom *Colvill* had rescued and nursed back to health when he (Welbeck) was wandering in the "forests of New-Jersey" (I:XXI, 194)!

As soon as one begins to bear down on these repetitions, what emerges most clearly—besides their stark implausibility—is the abstract nature of the message they convey. Like *Wieland, Arthur Mervyn* is a novel that must be read structurally—that is, as a series of abstract propositions whose permutations and combinations spell out a message to the reader, a message whose intent is to change the social reality which the narrative purports to represent. But whereas *Wieland*'s episodes present the reader with a paradigm of hopelessness, *Arthur Mervyn*'s scenarios describe the conditions under which it is possible to survive in the new nation, inciting the audience to modes of behavior that will lead to happiness and prosperity. I am not arguing that *Arthur Mervyn* be seen as a kind of young man's guide to success—although it can be taken that way. Rather, I think that the main character, insofar as he can be distinguished from other characters, sets forth the ground rules which everyone in the society must obey if the social order is to survive. Plot—in the sense of a developing action, which offers an initial problem, complications, a climax, and denouement—has no place in this narrative. There is no "main action" in any recognizable sense because all of the episodes are transformations of a few paradigmatic situations for which they spell out alternate scenarios.[7] These scenarios, as Brown suggests in "Walstein's School," are invested with a transitive force, for in encouraging readers to see the parallel between the hero's situation and theirs, they are calculated to confer moral benefit. But it is not only Mervyn whose behavior is intended as exemplary.

If plot in the accepted definition has no place in *Arthur Mervyn*, so character, in the sense of individual identity, is nonexistent. In this novel the self is dispersed among several possible representatives simultaneously, each of whom becomes for the reader that "model of . . . conduct"—Stevens, Mervyn, Clavering, Wallace,

Welbeck, Hadwin, Maravegli, Estwick, Medlicote, Colvill—which s/he must learn to emulate or shun.[8] Indeed, the character of Mervyn himself is not even conceived in exclusively human terms, for by the end of the narrative his outlines have become so blurred—in the sense that he is identified with so many other characters, and he has himself played so many roles, and performed so often that of the go-between or intermediary—that he becomes both less and more than a character—an impulse of energy, rippling through society itself.

If Arthur Mervyn is not to be regarded as a character in the normal sense, but as the occasion for the enactment of certain paradigmatic situations, then it is the situation that should command our attention. What the Maravegli episode and all of its forbears and descendants suggest is that the model of right conduct that Brown wishes his readers to make their own is benevolence, figured as the rescue of one man by another. Toward the end of part I, which concludes this round of rescues, Arthur Mervyn follows his own example; he decides that he will henceforth dedicate himself to the rescue of the unfortunate by offering to become "governor" of the city's hospital, a place of filth and misery, where the attendants laugh at the tortures of the dying and get drunk on cordials intended for the relief of their patients. At the beginning of part II, this admirable impulse takes on a more realistic form with Mervyn's decision to apprentice himself to Stevens and become a doctor. But there is more to Brown's notion of benevolence than would seem to be implied by this endlessly repeated parable of the good Samaritan.

The aim of benevolent action is something that Brown repeatedly refers to as "the welfare of mankind." What this seems to mean is that individual human behavior is benevolent only insofar as it promotes the good of the community, a good conceived here not simply as the saving of individual lives, but as the support of those activities necessary for the functioning of society as a whole. To do good in Mervyn's world means not simply to perform acts of corporal mercy (even Welbeck and Colvill do that), but also to act according to the rules that govern the way society communicates with itself and sustains itself. What this means will presently become clear.

But first it is important to note that in offering benevolence, understood as acting for the good of the community, as a model of right conduct, Brown is cleaving to that ideal of republican virtue which based the prosperity of the state on the character of its individual citizens. An idea that had been central to political theorizing since the Renaissance, republican virtue was, in the words of J. G. A. Pocock, "a civic and patriot ideal in which the personality was founded in property, perfected in citizenship," and characterized above all by its active participation in the life of the *polis*.[9] That participation in *Arthur Mervyn* does not mean taking part in government per se—in this novel, as in *Wieland*, no one seems to be in charge—but taking responsibility in a private way for the welfare of those one meets in the course of going about one's business. Thus, one of Mervyn's most engaging and irritating features is his chronic incapacity to keep his nose out of other people's affairs, "business" and "affairs" being the key to the special brand of republican virtue that is at play here.

Whereas an agricultural mode of life had formed the basis of Jefferson's ideal of virtue—honesty, industry, and frugality flourishing uncorrupted on the farm—Brown's ideal reflects the Federalist concern with trade, manufacture, sound currency, credit, and generally, with a concept of America as a nation for which commerce within and without its borders is the lifeblood.[10] For Brown, exchange is the process by which both nations and individuals assume an identity, attain their majority, become viable; obeying the rules of exchange is the process by which Arthur Mervyn exemplifies benevolence in its most inclusive form.

Early in the novel, when Mervyn begins to tell his story to Dr. Stevens, it is clear that he is doing so as a way of repaying the doctor for his kindness. Mervyn's story has exchange value within the situation—it satisfies the curiosity of Stevens and his wife and affords them a long evening's entertainment—but as his narrative unfolds it acquires a value that is greater than at first appears. Wortley, a friend of Stevens, knows of Mervyn's association with

Welbeck and suspects him of being an arch-dissimulator, too; thus, Mervyn's story, by clearing him of suspicion, reestablishes the value of his character as well. Moreover, in the course of revealing the multitudinous treacheries of Welbeck, so as to exculpate himself, Mervyn brings to light a series of forgeries, thefts, and seductions and thereby leads to the restitution of stolen property, the rescue of a woman, and the clearing up of various misunderstandings. So the passing on of information in this episode works in several ways at once: as repayment for a favor, as a means of satisfying curiosity, as a means of reestablishing the value of character, and as a way of putting into circulation information, previously withheld, that will allow certain sums of money as well as certain individuals to regain their proper place in the circulatory system. (The parallels between people and money intensify as the novel progresses). And because Mervyn tells his story to Stevens, Stevens subsequently teaches him to save lives, a skill that will be thereby put back into circulation, and so on.

The value of information as currency whose value multiplies when it enters the social system plays a role throughout the novel. Offering an account of oneself as a form of payment for rescue, giving a "life" for a life, persists in the episode where Clavering gives his portrait to Mervyn in exchange for his care; Welbeck, similarly, tells the story of his life to Mervyn in order to earn his help in escaping from Philadelphia after he has murdered Watson; and Vincenzo Lodi, in the incident where Welbeck rescues him, tells a life story that purchases attendance on his death and a promise to look after his estate. In each of these instances, the information imparted allows characters to act for the benefit of others. (Whether or not they do so is another story). Mervyn can let Clavering's relatives know what has become of him; Welbeck can take care of Clemenza; Mervyn, who comes into possession of Welbeck's ill-gotten gains, can return various sums of money to their rightful owners, and so on. The exchange of information is bound up with other transactions, monetary and sexual, that are important to the well-being of large numbers of people. The telling of stories puts back into circulation pieces of information and sums of money, and, in the case of Clemenza, a woman who would otherwise have been lost, and so allows the larger society to work more effectively. To tell the truth and tell it whole is as important an injunction in the world of *Arthur Mervyn* as benevolence itself. In fact, it is inseparable from it. Information must be given freely and it must be given whole, because either to withhold or falsify the truth always produces bad consequences (Brown had written an entire story on the dangers of secrecy in domestic relations called "A Lesson on Concealment"). On innumerable occasions, Mervyn suffers by keeping secrets (chiefly his own and Welbeck's); and he constantly warns of the perils of holding information back: "Secrecy may seldom be a crime," he pontificates to himself, "a virtuous intention may produce it; but surely it is always erroneous and pernicious" (I:XVII, 162). And on another occasion he declares: "My understanding had been taught, by recent occurrences, to question the justice, and deny the usefulness of secrecy in any case" (I:XXII, 199).

But the telling of stories does not happen spontaneously. Stories are told in response to gratuitous acts of benevolence which are not generated by the system of exchange but set it in motion. Benevolence has a ripple effect: acts of mercy engender acts of restitution (the telling of stories) that engender other acts of restitution (giving back money, passing along information) in a continuing series. In short, benevolence begets itself; it is contagious.

II. WELBECK

It may be no accident then that the disease from which most of the rescued characters die or are saved in the novel is contagious also—the yellow fever plague, a malign infestation that sweeps through the city and kills indiscriminately (the noble Maravegli is struck down while the unreliable Wallace survives; Hadwin succumbs but Welbeck is untouched). The plague, which robs people of their individual lives, is a generalized threat to the life of the city—a kind of "social ill"—whose source is not located in any particular person or event, but is "epidemic," systemic. Those who are kind to others, like Estwick and Medlicote, and Mervyn himself, and those who can actually cure the sick, like Stevens, not only relieve the suffering of individuals, but are restorers of health to the community as a whole, for they set going a chain reaction that benefits not only the person they save, but other people too, and so start a kind of backfire of benevolence, or anti-plague plague, to combat the forces that threaten "the welfare of mankind."

Stories contribute to the anti-plague forces by putting into circulation other modes of currency that the society needs, principally information about money and property that permits stolen goods to be returned to their rightful owners. Stolen goods are usually acquired in the novel through a process of "disinformation" or fraud that operates in exactly the same way as the yellow fever: it is an infection which, once introduced into the system, spreads out of control. "Disinformation" can take the form of ignorance or deceit, but in both cases it is harmful. When Arthur sets out on his journey to Philadelphia as a "barn-door simpleton," (II: XXIV, 434) he is easily defrauded by two innkeepers, who take advantage of his ignorance and overcharge him scandalously for the scant fare they provide. As a result, he cannot pay the toll when he crosses the Schuylkill and has to depend on the charity of others for shelter and food. These events trace in miniature the pattern of disinformation as a spreading disease that dominates the opening of part II, where the absence of true knowledge assumes its more virulent form—that of fraud. "If men were guided by justice in the acquisition and disbursement [of property]," Brown writes in "Walstein's School," "the brood of private and public evils would be extinguished" (152). For fraud, like benevolence, sets off a chain reaction. In part II, Welbeck, the Thetfords, Wortley, Mrs. Wentworth, the Watsons, and the Maurices, not to mention Arthur Mervyn, are caught in a net of sharp dealing, forgery, usury, and theft which it takes all of Arthur Mervyn's prodigious energies to untangle. It is quite clear that in Brown's eyes what is bad for commerce is bad for the country as a whole, and vice versa. The restoration of stolen property replaces the rescue of the sick, in this portion of the novel, as the principal means of doing good.

The prominence given to financial transactions in *Arthur Mervyn* is no mere idiosyncrasy of Brown's, but a reflection of a general belief in the late eighteenth century that a nation's welfare depended in large part on prosperous trade. Historians conceived of commerce not just as a source of economic benefits, but as a civilizing force that had important social and political ramifications.[11]

> Commerce [writes the great Scottish historian William Robertson] tends to wear off those prejudices which maintain distinction and animosity between nations. It softens and polishes the manners of men. It unites them by one of the strongest of all ties, the desire of supplying their mutual wants. It disposes them to peace by establishing in every state an order of citizens bound by their interests to be the guardians of public tranquillity. As soon as the commercial spirit acquires new vigor, and begins to gain an ascendant in any society, we discover a new genius in its policy. . . . In proportion as commerce made its way into the different countries of Europe, they successfully turned their attention to those objects, and adopted those manners, which occupy and distinguish polished nations.[12]

The leaders of the Federalist party in the United States pursued policies calculated to foster the growth of commerce and thus to garner that tranquillity and order, that distinction and polish, which Americans so avidly desired in the years following the Revolution. In the 1790s Alexander Hamilton's fiscal program attempted to implement these goals through the establishment of a sound monetary system, which he believed was the sine qua non of a viable economy.[13] Thus, Mervyn's role in setting to rights all sorts of twisted financial dealings had a significance in the 1790s that is lost on us today because the ways in which currency is misappropriated, misrepresented, and misused in this novel have specific reference not only to financial conditions that prevailed when Brown was writing, but to a conception of commerce that gave those conditions their particular shape. The most telling episode, in this regard, involves the disposition of Vincenzo Lodi's fortune; it occurs at the end of part I, and comes as close to being a major climax as is possible in a narrative of this sort.

Arthur Mervyn has accidentally come into possession of a portion of Lodi's fortune, which was secreted in a book that he had taken from Welbeck's house. He has the money on him during his effort to save Wallace from the plague, and Welbeck, returning to his house to look for this book, finds Mervyn, who has taken refuge there.

When he first discovers Arthur Mervyn lying sick in his house, Welbeck is (understandably) beside himself with frustration:

> "What is this? Are you here? In defiance of pestilence, are you actuated by some demon to haunt me, like the ghost of my offences, and cover me with shame? What have I to do with that dauntless, yet guileless front? With that foolishly, confiding, and obsequious, yet erect and unconquerable spirit? Is there no means of evading your pursuit?" (I:XXI, 191–192)

The answer to the last question is no, since Arthur will hound Welbeck to death with his good intentions—though Mervyn would be equally justified in feeling himself haunted by Welbeck, whom he believes to be dead (these characters haunt one another in a way that suggests their interdependence). But Welbeck, his outburst over, suddenly decides to give up searching for what he came for, to abandon hope of his own survival, and to devote himself to Arthur Mervyn in a Mervyn-like gesture of selfless benevolence:

> "Yes. Mervyn! I will stay with you. I will hold your head. I will put water to your lips. I will watch night and day by your side. When you die, I will carry you by night to the neighbouring field; will bury you, and water your grave with those tears that are due to your incomparable worth and untimely destiny. Then I will lay myself in your bed and wait for the same oblivion." (I:XXI, 193)

But naturally nothing of the kind occurs. Welbeck tells Mervyn the story of his failed suicide (he tried to drown himself), of his rescue by Colvill in the forests of New Jersey, and of his desire to recover the book Vincenzo Lodi had given him, which he suspects contains some money. Mervyn, true to form, foolishly confides that he has the money and intends to give it to Clemenza. Welbeck starts, "as if he had trodden on a mine of gold," and proceeds to reason, threaten, and cajole Arthur into giving him the money. But Mervyn refuses to give in. "I will not repeat," he says, "the contest that succeeded between my forbearance and his passions," but he goes on to describe himself and Welbeck as if they were lovers engaged in an erotic combat: "sometimes his emotions would mount into fury, and he would approach me in a menacing attitude, and lift his hand as if he would exterminate me at a blow. My languid eyes, my cheeks glowing, and my temples throbbing with fever, and my total passiveness, attracted his attention and arrested his stroke" (I:XXII, 205). Finally, Welbeck, apparently torn by terrible inner conflict, starts muttering to himself incoherently, and, looking around to make sure no one else is in the room, makes a last confession. The notes, he says, are forged. He only wants them back in order to destroy them so that innocent people will not suffer for his crime. At this moment, they hear footsteps approaching, and in the time it takes Welbeck to go to the door, Mervyn jumps out of bed, seizes a candle, and burns the money. When Welbeck realizes what Mervyn has done, he goes berserk: "Maniac! Miscreant!" he cries. "To be fooled by so gross an artifice! The notes were genuine. *The tale of their forgery was false"* (I:XXIII, 210, my italics).

This scene dramatizes the villainies of Welbeck in a way that organizes all at once the novel's haphazardness and makes the meaning of benevolence clear. Welbeck is the arch-subverter of the social currency: he is a seducer—both of women and of men (he almost succeeds in seducing Arthur in this scene and, as we have learned from an earlier confession, has in fact seduced several women); he is a counterfeiter (he has earlier confessed to Mervyn that he chose this profession upon arriving in America, and has in fact forged other documents); and he is a liar, whose very confessions of forgery cannot be trusted. Welbeck attacks the social system at its base by subverting the means by which it reproduces itself, sustains itself, and communicates with itself. As seducer, counterfeiter, and liar, Welbeck destroys the value of women, money, and information, the currency that social life depends on. He is the negative of which benevolence is the positive, undermining the system that benevolence sets in motion. Thus he is the "ghost" of Arthur Mervyn in more senses than one, for everything that Welbeck does must be exorcised by his benevolent counterpart. As the "enormity of his transgressions and the complexity of his frauds" come fully to light in part II, Arthur Mervyn devotes himself to undoing the tangle of lies, forgeries, and seductions in which he and Welbeck's other victims are entrapped.

It may be difficult for readers to take Arthur Mervyn's benevolent efforts seriously, much less my efforts to wrest social significance from them, given the bizarre hilarity of the scene I have just described. Yet the issues at stake in the struggle over Vincenzo Lodi's fortune *are* serious, and would have seemed so to Brown's audience. The difficulty of maintaining "sound currency" was a major problem in the years following the Revolution. The value of continental currency had dropped to practically nothing (the government redeemed it at one cent on the dollar, whence the expression, "not worth a continental"). There was a shortage of currency of any kind, since the British blockade had stopped the flow of goods to and from the colonies. In cities the British had occupied, even local commerce had fallen off as artisans left to find jobs in the country. The consequent shortage of manufactured goods after the war affected the balance of trade severely, so that when Brown was writing *Arthur Mervyn* there was still a shortage not only of sound currency but of specie of any kind with which to carry on business.[14]

But if the absence of money created a downward economic spiral, its presence had the opposite effect. James Henretta's account of how the economy got back on its feet aptly characterizes the way in which money put into circulation tended, like benevolence, to beget itself.[15] The cycle began in cities like Philadelphia, which, because they were closer to the rich West Indian market and could build ships more cheaply, eventually took the thriving West Indian trade away from Britain and France. This created capital that could be invested in other business ventures and raised the salaries of workers already engaged in the West Indian traffic. This, in turn, created a demand for additional goods and services which began to be met by merchants who now had enough capital to start new manufacturing enterprises. "Injected into the life of the port cities, the money created by commerce had a 'multiplier' effect on the level of business activity; it was 'used' two, three, or four times as it passed from hand to hand and from business to business."[16]

It is not hard to see then why the burning of Vincenzo Lodi's fortune was a disaster not just for the desperate Welbeck but for the economy as a whole. Nor is it hard to see why, in part II, the body of Watson is exhumed in order to recover the money he had carried in a belt beneath his clothing. Putting money into circulation had an exponentially benevolent effect—but only if the money was good. If to keep money out of circulation was to rob the nation of its lifeblood, to forge currency was to poison the whole system. Though the economy grew again because of the European wars of the 1790s, Hamilton's protective tariff legislation, federal assumption of the state debts, the issuance of public securities, and the establishment of a national bank—problems of unsound currency remained until the second half of the nineteenth century. Despite Hamilton's efforts, America had no single standard currency after the Revolution. State bank notes were still the primary form of exchange and the worth of these notes varied with the banks' printing and lending policies. Since so many different currencies were in circulation, not only was the value of currency uncertain, but counterfeiting was a major problem as well.[17] Thus, while Welbeck's stratagems may look fanciful to us, they were not at all uncommon when Brown was writing. Arthur Mervyn's attempts to mend the damage done by Welbeck's frauds and forgeries are tied to two of the major issues of the era—the establishment of a sound monetary system and the stimulation of flagging commerce. To keep money, already in short supply, out of circulation and to weaken the already shaky economic system through counterfeiting and stealing were sins against the "welfare of mankind" not in any displaced, analogical sense, but in fact.

III. CARLTON

Against this background, some of the irrelevancies of the second half of *Arthur Mervyn* make a good deal more sense than they otherwise might. Part II begins by introducing a character who, like the unfortunate Maravegli of part I, at first appears to have nothing to do with the rest of the story. Stevens learns that a young acquaintance of his named Carlton is in prison for nonpayment of debts. Carlton, who had inherited these debts from his father, had worked assiduously as a copyist (Mervyn's only skill besides the plow, you will remember) to pay them back. But because of a small remaining sum which he was unable to meet, he had been thrown in jail by a vengeful creditor. When Stevens receives an unsigned message imploring him to come to the debtors' prison, he goes there in the expectation of finding his friend. But whom does he meet when he enters the bowels of this miserable institution—a counterpart of the grisly hospital in part I—but Arthur Mervyn! Stevens' surprise redoubles when Mervyn leads him to a room in which, lying on a bed, he discovers the emaciated form of (who else?) Welbeck, who has been thrown into jail for nonpayment of debts by *his* creditors. And that is not all. For we learn that Arthur Mervyn's father, defrauded of his money by the infamous seductress Betty Lawrence, and in a state of pitiful drunkenness and penury, has ended his life in debtors' prison. The introduction of Carlton epitomizes the way Brown's narrative works on two levels. First, Carlton, like the string of minor characters we meet in part I, is important because he is *like* other characters; his situation resembles theirs. What happens to him has meaning as a possible solution to the problem that his situation poses. In contrast to Welbeck and Sawny Mervyn, debtors who made no attempt to pay back what they owed, Carlton furnishes a "model of right conduct." A poor young copyist, orphaned, with a single sister, and a protégé of Stevens, he is also another of Arthur Mervyn's doubles.

But Carlton is integral to the novel on another level because his situation is isomorphic with that of thousands of people in the country at the time. One of the most hotly debated issues of the

Federalist era was the question of how debts should be paid. Farmers who had borrowed money before the war when prices were high found themselves having to pay their debts with money earned from commodities whose value had declined. The shortage of currency with which to pay these debts and the resultant tight lending policies made it difficult to obtain credit for the purchase of seed and equipment needed to generate more income. Debtors and small farmers, therefore, wanted the state governments to issue paper currency so that they could pay back their loans, borrow money, and raise the price of their goods, while large landowners and merchants opposed this because they were suspicious of the value of state-issued paper currency. "The courts," say the authors of *An Economic History of the United States*, "were flooded with cases involving . . . debtors who could not meet their obligations."[18]

Brown's readers would have seen Carlton in the context of the struggle between debtors and creditors that was then taking place in the courts and state legislatures. Given this context, his having been imprisoned, and imprisoned unjustly, for debt, means that he already belongs to a "plot" that exists in the minds of Brown's contemporaries. Carlton is integral to the narrative of *Arthur Mervyn* because the unity of a novel does not exist independently of the circumstances in which it is being read; what is relevant or irrelevant depends upon its readers' framework of assumptions. Though Carlton seems to us just another of an irritating array of intrusive minor characters who are found languishing along the path of the "central" character, he is no less central than Mervyn himself. Indeed, he *is* Mervyn in another form. Carlton's plight dramatizes the operations of justice and injustice in "the acquisition and disbursement [of property]" which was an unavoidable issue in 1800.

IV. ACHSA FIELDING

The other unavoidable issue for a novelist attempting to show his readers, by example, how to live, is marriage. "Next to property," Brown writes in "Walstein's School," "the most extensive source of our relations is sex" (152). Having demonstrated the proper modes of exchanging information and goods, Brown sets himself to exemplify an ideal exchange of affections. Determined that he will not be guilty of the "sentimental softness" that characterizes most "fictitious history" dealing with the subject, Brown solemnly declares that when knowledge and skill are brought to bear in depicting marriage, the result will "enable men to evade the evils and secure the benefits of this state"(153). In order to illustrate the proper principles of wife-selection, Brown has Arthur Mervyn choose between two candidates—a rich, older woman named Achsa Fielding, who is intelligent, well-educated, worldly, prudent, sexually experienced, and rather peculiar looking, and a pretty young girl from the country with whom he has fallen in love. This girl, Eliza Hadwin, is innocent, uneducated, poor, a virgin, alone in the world and, it would seem, an obvious choice for Arthur, who comes from a rural background himself. But he promptly decides against her.

Mervyn reasons that having come so lately from his cottage into the world, his education is still "defective," his views still "limited." Since coming to the "busy haunts of men" he has learned more than in all his years on the farm; and from this he deduces the "immaturity" of his own understanding and the progress he is still capable of making. "Books and inanimate nature were cold and lifeless instructors. Men, and the works of men, were the objects of rational study. . . . The influence of manners, professions and social institutions, could be thoroughly known only by direct inspection" and "the joys of a settled existence" appreciated only "by those who have tried all scenes; who have mixed with all classes and ranks; who have partaken of all conditions; and who have visited different hemispheres and climates and nations" (II:VIII, 293). In short, Mervyn decides that he is too young to get married, doesn't know enough yet, and may change a great deal as a result of experiences he hasn't yet had. "Might not my modes of judging undergo essential variations? Might I not gain the knowledge of beings whose virtue was the gift of experience and the growth of knowledge? Who joined to the modesty and charms of woman, the benefits of education, the maturity and steadfastness of age . . .?" (II:IX, 292).

But the real reason that Mervyn decides against Eliza is not so much that *he* isn't ready as that she is even less so. Eliza Hadwin is exactly like Arthur as he was before he left home. Despite her beauty, her sweetness, and her devotion to him, Eliza's "extreme youth, rustic simplicity and mental imperfections" (I:IX, 292) put her out of the running. Brown violates the norms of sentimental fiction on this point just as he had said he would: his hero chooses age over beauty, experience over innocence, wealth over poverty, the city over the country, and worldly sophistication over innocence and purity. Not only does he choose a woman who is "sedate" and "prudent," (II:XXI, 397) short, dark, has "the eye of a gypsy" (II:XXIV, 432), is not a virgin and is much older than he, he chooses a woman who is not even a native American; in fact, Achsa Fielding was not only born in England, where she married and had a child—she is also a Portuguese Jew.

Racial and ethnic purity are no more to be valued in this novel than sexual purity is. Just as "those who have tried all scenes, . . . mixed with all classes, . . . partaken of all conditions" are in a better position to judge the value of what they have at home than those who have always stayed there, the healthy society, like the well-furnished mind, is crossbred. The reason Arthur Mervyn can't marry Eliza Hadwin, as he himself is dimly aware, is that she is like an unminted coin: a person who has not yet gone into circulation and therefore lacks definition, experience, knowledge: the qualities one acquires from moving around in the world. The fact that she is not "used"—still a virgin in every conceivable way— which makes her attractive by conventional standards, is just what depreciates her in Mervyn's eyes. Mervyn, who started out just like Eliza, has now become a more valuable commodity than she because of his adventures in the city. Tempered and polished by his experiences, Mervyn's value has appreciated. He must choose a wife higher on this cosmopolitan scale of value than he, one who will polish and shape him until his value is equal to hers. People, no less than money and information, must be circulated in order for a society to prosper. And it is just as important, in Brown's view, for a woman to be sophisticated as it is for a man.

In fact, it is more important, because women are the chief facilitators of the more intimate forms of social exchange—those sexual and emotional transactions that are the goal which all the other forms of exchange exist to foster and preserve. Arthur believes that he "was formed on purpose" for this type of gratification: "to love and to be loved; to exchange hearts, and mingle sentiments with all the virtuous and amiable, whom my good fortune had placed within the circuit of my knowledge, I always esteemed my highest enjoyment and my chief duty" (II:XXI, 396). But he cannot enter into the exchange of hearts until he has proved himself worthy in the other forms, where he learns the principles of reciprocity and openness that keep exchange alive. In love, as in commerce, to eschew secrecy, to offer freely what one has and not hold back, to keep everything in circulation is paramount. "I felt no scruple," says Arthur, "on any occasion, to disclose every feeling and every event. Any one who could listen, found me willing to talk. Every talker found me willing to listen" (II:XXI, 397). Especially Achsa Fielding. When Arthur Mervyn first talks to her, he opens himself up to her immediately.

> The first moment I engaged her attention, I . . . related the little story of my family, spread out before her all my reasonings and determinations, my notions of right and wrong, my fears and wishes. All this was done with sincerity and fervor, with gestures, actions and looks, in which I felt as if my whole soul was visible. Her superior age, sedateness and prudence, gave my deportment a filial freedom and affection, and I was fond of calling her *'mamma.'* (II:XXII, 397)

This is not a sign of regression to the Oedipal stage in the protagonist, but a mark of the value of Achsa Fielding. The authority Mervyn feels emanating from her allows him to express himself volubly, unrestrainedly. "My eyes glistened as I spoke. In truth, I am in that respect, a mere woman" (II:XXII, 398).

To be "a mere woman" in this respect is to become more like what the novel holds out as the ideal of human conduct: to be open and forthcoming in all the modes of human exchange. Arthur Mervyn is going to become like Achsa Fielding (who is even more emotional than he), just as Eliza is going to become more like

Arthur Mervyn. The good society that commerce brings about tends towards homogenization, and the mingling of sentiments between lovers is only a more intimate form of the mingling that takes places across the whole spectrum of public life. Indeed, Mervyn's relation to Achsa Fielding might stand as an embodiment of the term *doux commerce* which the French used to express the civilizing and refining effects of trade. "The origin of the epithet '*doux*,' " Albert Hirschmann suggests, "is probably to be found in the 'non-commercial' meaning of *commerce*: besides trade, the word long denoted animated and repeated conversation and other forms of polite social intercourse and dealings among persons (frequently between two persons of the opposite sex)."[19] It is in this expanded sense of the word *commerce*, rather than in our own more restricted sense, that the principle of commerce, or exchange, can be said to rule the world of *Arthur Mervyn*. The kinds of exchange which I have argued the novel concentrates on—exchange of information, of money, of sentiments—are all implied in the single term *commerce* as it was then understood. If individuals, like nations, are softened and polished by commerce, then it is not so surprising that Brown's protagonists should come to resemble coins, that precious specie, which, when passed from hand to hand, has a 'multiplier' effect. Like the talents in the Biblical parable, human beings like Eliza Hadwin who are buried in the country are less valuable to society than those who circulate.

Thus Brown's model of social relations is just as anti-Jeffersonian as his concept of individual virtue, for its posits a cosmopolitan mixing of nationalities, ethnic groups, and social classes that "commerce" alone can effect. Arthur Mervyn, the barn-door simpleton, is redeemed by his choice of the city over the country. Warned by the examples of Wallace, Welbeck, and the Thetfords, rescued and educated by Stevens, awed by Maravegli, cared for by Estwick and Medlicote, a rube like Arthur can aspire to become a doctor and win the hand of a cosmopolitan lady who is rich and his social superior. He can move in the same circles as that woman of property and standing, Mrs. Wentworth, a friend of Achsa Fielding, and owner of the palatial dwelling formerly lived in by Welbeck.

V. COLVILL

But Welbeck stands as a reminder that the delights of circulating are obtainable only when people follow the rules that govern social exchange. People whose circulation has been under-the-counter, so to speak, can never "mingle sentiments" as Arthur Mervyn and Achsa Fielding do, because once discovered, their illicit activity damages their value on the marriage market. Like forgery, illicit sex poisons the system of exchange by damaging the value of the currency involved in making transactions. In fact, seduction is a form of social counterfeiting because people who engage in sexual relations that are not publicly sanctioned must hide what they are doing from other people and, often, from themselves. (Betty Lawrence hides her seduction of Sawny Mervyn from Arthur, and Arthur's father hides from him the fact that he is going to marry her. The woman who first seduces Welbeck "had no trouble" in deceiving him. Welbeck's seduction of Watson's sister involves his deceiving her—he pretends he shares all her views—at the same time that she deceives herself. When Welbeck lives with Clemenza Lodi, he pretends to Arthur that she is his daughter. And when Colvill, the seducer of Arthur's sister, first appears on the scene, he seems to be a studious, sensitive, morally correct young man.) In all cases illicit sex prevents the actors from engaging in that legitimate "exchange of hearts" that marriage represents. Whether the seducer or the seducee is male or female, seduction is uneconomical, a waste—it spoils the value of the merchandise. A woman who has been seduced is damaged goods, no longer negotiable in the marriage market. The child of a seduction has no place in society. And the male seducer, once discovered, must leave town; and so he, too, is out of commission in a social sense—withdrawn from circulation.

But despite Arthur Mervyn's exemplary behavior in the matter of choosing a wife, he also bears a striking resemblance to one of the novel's most flagrant seducers: the mild-mannered Colvill— a character who, like Carlton and Maravegli, has no relation to the plot in a linear sense, but whose situation, like theirs, is one with which the novel is centrally concerned. Colvill's behavior serves as a touchstone for how not to act in relation to women; and so, like Welbeck, he is an inversion of the hero.

Colvill appeared in Arthur Mervyn's neighborhood one day to take up the post of schoolmaster. A man of "learning and genius," "gentle and modest" of demeanor, "his habits," says Mervyn, were "abstemious and regular." "Meditation in the forest, or reading in his closet, seemed to constitute . . . his sole amusement and employment" (I:XX, 187). At the end of a year, however, a young woman appeared to have fallen prey to the arts of a seducer, and the villain turns out to be Colvill, who is discovered to have practised the "same artifices . . . with the same success upon many others" (I:XX, 188). The victim, in this case, is none other than Arthur Mervyn's sister, who, to escape shame, has killed herself. "She was innocent and lovely," says Mervyn. "My soul was linked with her's by a thousand resemblances and sympathies. . . . She was my . . . preceptress and friend" (I:XX, 188).

If the incident suggests an identification between Mervyn and his sister—they are "linked . . . by a thousand resemblances"—it also suggests a likeness between Mervyn and Colvill. For Mervyn had been a gentle and blameless young man of studious habits who preferred meditation in the forest and reading in his closet to social activity. Arthur Mervyn is the double of Colvill and of his sister simultaneously, both seducer and seducee. But the resemblances are more complicated still. For the voice that Mervyn identified as Colvill's when he was sick with the plague in Welbeck's house, belonged to Welbeck, and Welbeck's relation to Colvill is that of a double also (he, too, is an accomplished seducer). So Colvill functions here as a link between Mervyn and Welbeck, a kind of bridge character in the way that Wallace was. But the resemblances do not stop here, for Colvill had rescued Welbeck, just as Mervyn will later attempt to rescue him when he is dying in jail, and as Welbeck, conversely, has already rescued Mervyn. Thus Mervyn, again, is both agent and patient, victim and victimizer. In the scene that follows the story of Colvill, Welbeck will try to seduce Arthur Mervyn, verbally, and the process will be described, as we have seen, in erotic terms. The question that these complicated mirrorings raise is: why, in a novel whose purpose is to guide its audience into the paths of virtuous action, is there so much confusion between the villain and the hero? Are the resemblances inadvertent, or do they have a purpose? And if they have a purpose, what can it be?

Welbeck starts out in circumstances much like Arthur Mervyn's. His father is "insolvent" and he has to make his way in the world without patrimony. His inability to do so through honest (if bumbling) endeavor, as Mervyn does, stems not from his ignorance of correct principles, but from his irresistible impulse toward "reputation . . . and opulence" (I:XI, 100). What makes Welbeck particularly pathetic is that, although he knows how he ought to act, he is incapable of following his own precepts. "What it was that made me thus, I know not," he confesses to Arthur.

> "I can talk and can feel as virtue and justice prescribe; yet the tenor of my actions has been uniform. One tissue of iniquity and folly has been my life; while my thoughts have been familiar with enlightened and disinterested principles. Scorn and detestation I have heaped upon myself. Yesterday is remembered with remorse. To-morrow is contemplated with anguish and fear; yet every day is productive of the same crimes and of the same follies." (I:IX, 85)

Welbeck confesses all this in hopes that his story will "inspire" Mervyn with "fortitude" and "arm" him with "caution" (I:IX, 85). In the light of Welbeck's "hope," Arthur Mervyn's similarity to Welbeck begins to make sense.

Welbeck's susceptibility to guilt and remorse, his knowledge of the principles of virtue and justice, as well as the countless structural parallels that connect him with Mervyn, make him another version of Mervyn himself. Arthur Mervyn *could* have turned out like Welbeck if he had given in to those impulses that his constant association with and mirroring of Welbeck suggest that he possesses, in common with the rest of mankind. The way the narrative message works for Brown's audience is this: If you—who resemble Arthur Mervyn—imitate his example, you will end up as he does— happy and provided for. If, on the other hand, you—who also resemble Welbeck—give in to the impulses in yourself that Welbeck gave in to, your fate will be like his. Ultimately, Welbeck and Arthur Mervyn are the same person—the reader—for whose life Brown's novel sketches alternate scenarios. We are intended to gain, as Mervyn does, from the "contemplation" of Welbeck's "misery," "new motives to sincerity and rectitude" (II:XIII, 334), the assumption being that somehow *we*, who read this book, are still malleable like Mervyn and can learn to be better than we now are. That our impulses toward reputation and opulence are not, like Welbeck's, irresistible. And that in our case, unlike his, knowledge of the right principles will make a difference, because when these principles are enacted in a fiction, rather than being enunciated abstractly, they have the power to excite emulation.

But if that is the case, if, that is, the distinction between Mervyn and Welbeck must sometimes seem to break down in order for the reader to see his resemblance simultaneously to both characters, so that he can be instructed by both—if this is so, then one wants to know why the novel occasionally risks sacrificing its moral efficacy in another strangely similar fashion. There are moments in *Arthur Mervyn* when everything is in danger of being turned upside down. When Welbeck on his deathbed accuses Arthur Mervyn of being the cause of all his woes, his eloquence is such that we almost believe him. It seems for a moment as though Arthur Mervyn's disclosure of Welbeck's past has been a dastardly act, disloyal, opportunistic, and self-seeking. Again, when we hear the story that Mervyn's former neighbor tells about his "criminal intimacy" (II:II, 230) with Betty Lawrence, about his infamous laziness and other peculiarities (that he used to knit stockings, for instance), we almost begin to believe that Mervyn has been pulling the wool over our eyes, that Wortley's accusations are true, and that we don't know the half of it. This volatility in our view of Mervyn is related to the farcical tone that intrudes in scenes like the one where Mervyn burns the money that had belonged to Vincenzo Lodi, or the one where he declares his love for Achsa Fielding in a manner so clownish and juvenile that it is impossible to imagine what she sees in him. Moments like these, in which despite all his good intentions, or perhaps because of them, Mervyn seems utterly ridiculous, produce feelings of giddiness as one teeters between opposite interpretations of what is going on, and contribute to the roller-coaster effect of the novel's headlong motion. There is nothing to do at such times except plunge ahead, hoping that the uncertainty will be cleared up soon. And indeed, this is what we do most of the time anyway as readers of *Arthur Mervyn*, for the reader never gets an overview of things in this novel, which, as a developing action or pattern of cause and effect, hardly exists "as a whole." Just as the hero is frequently trapped in small, enclosed spaces—a closet, a bedroom, a basement, an attic—the reader is also trapped in the bewilderingly rapid succession of episodes and can never see beyond the confines of the situation at hand. Which is exactly Arthur Mervyn's dilemma. "Ushered into . . . a world of revolutions and perils," Mervyn is aware that he lacks "forethought" and "the wisdom of experience," that his behavior is often "ambiguous and hazardous, and perhaps wanting in discretion." But, he reasons, "we must not be unactive because we are ignorant. Our good purposes must hurry to performance, whether our knowledge be greater or less" (II:XI, 322, 323).

The plot of *Arthur Mervyn* rushes forward with the same "headlong expedition" as its hero, unable, at times, to control its own impetuous career. Like its hero, the novel has the energy of youth and the ability to take chances—the chance, for instance, of momentarily losing the reader's faith in its protagonist. Its trajectory, like Mervyn's, is "hazardous," and perhaps "wanting in discretion." "Without reflecting on what was due to decorum and punctilio," (II:XXV, 440) Brown, like Arthur, charges ahead, intent on carrying out his benevolent aims. As Mervyn says to Mrs. Wentworth, "Why fluctuate, why linger, when so much good may be done?" (II:XVI, 361).

VI. MARAVEGLI

But the headlong forward movement of the narrative is always a backward movement as well. As Arthur takes the bit in his mouth and hurtles down the track of his good intentions, he is always running into people he has met before, or whose histories are intertwined with his own, whose fortunes have affected his without his knowing it, or are about to do so. There is no way ahead in this novel that does not lead into the past, revealing new connections among the characters, and multiplying resemblances among them. When Arthur set out to rescue Susan Hadwin's fiancé, he had no way of knowing that the man he sought had already sought him out and made him the butt of a joke, or that he would be mistaken for this same man by someone who had done him a good turn. These coincidences suggest that the person he finds instead of Wallace—the brilliant but unfortunate Maravegli—may not be the total stranger he seems. Given the rebarbative tendencies of the characters in this novel, it is mere accident that no further mention is made of Maravegli, that no package arrives from Leghorn, on a ship owned by the Thetfords, containing a fortune intended for his dead fiancée but which finds its way into Welbeck's hands, or perhaps Wallace's. These coincidental connections, which are after all not coincidental, point to a deeper connection still, which is the implication of every character in every other character's fortunes. When Arthur Mervyn looks upon the wasted but still noble features of the dying Maravegli, it is himself he sees. There are no separate characters in *Arthur Mervyn* because no man is ever distinct from the collectivity that contains him; the hero and his many avatars are not to be understood as individuals, nor even as aspects of a single character, but as representing certain possibilities within a social system. The "radical discontinuities" that Berthoff and others have discovered in Brown's plot are a logical impossibility, given the assumptions that underlie his depiction of the social world.[20]

Everything that Arthur Mervyn does is discontinuous in the sense of being ad hoc, or, in Berthoff's phrase, "loosely tied" to what he has just been doing. The incidents, like the characters, hang together by virtue of being parts of the same social whole. And that whole does not consist merely of the world depicted in Brown's text, but of the world in which it was written and read. In this respect Maravegli is no more and no less "integral" to the story than Mervyn himself. And the same is true for Carlton, Estwick, Medlicote, Clavering, and an honest businessman named Williams (an antidote to the Thetfords) who turns up near the end in connection with Arthur's restoration of money to a family of women named Maurice. These characters, like Mervyn himself, are important only because their situations resemble those of other characters and those situations are important only because they resemble the experience of contemporary readers. In Maravegli's case, the parallel is not far to seek. For just as hundreds of people had gone to debtors' prison after the Revolution, or been stung by defaulters, or found themselves with worthless currency, or counterfeit notes, or no money at all, so thousands had died of the yellow fever plague.

Maravegli is as much a part of the "plot" that already structured the consciousness of Brown's readers as Carlton is, but this is not simply because Brown's readers had seen people dying of yellow fever. As I shall argue later in discussing the context of sentimental fiction in the 1850s, what a person sees when watching someone die depends upon the framework of assumptions that structure his or her observation. Brown's rendering of the plague, and his readers' experience of it, have a common origin in contemporary notions about disease, contagion, the care of the sick, and people's obligations to their neighbors, to strangers, and to the "welfare of mankind." The intelligibility of *Arthur Mervyn* is a function of the modes of perception and classification, the hierarchies of value that structured day-to-day reality in the 1790s. Thus Matthew Carey's contemporary history of the epidemic, *A Short Account of the Malignant Fever which Prevailed in Philadelphia, in the Year 1793*, conveys the same sense of "what happened" as *Arthur Mervyn*, for Carey and Brown share a common frame of reference. Both men, for example, write about the plague for the same reason. They offer their accounts (Brown subtitles his novel *A Memoir of the Year 1793*) as, simultaneously, historical record and civic propaganda. In the process of describing how people behaved towards one another in this emergency, both writers actively seek to inspire in their readers the attitudes they believe *should* govern human behavior at such times. Carey's catalogue of instances in which Philadelphians selflessly risked their lives to save others replicates the many rescues of *Arthur Mervyn*, and his portrait of Joseph

Inskeep serves as a model for emulation in exactly the way that Brown's benevolent rescuers do:

> Amidst the general abandonment of the sick that prevailed, there were to be found many illustrious instances of men and women, some in the middle, others in the lower spheres of life, who, in the exercise of the duties of humanity, exposed themselves to dangers, which terrified men, who had often faced death without fear, in the field of battle. . . . Foremost in this noble groupe stands Joseph Inskeep, a most excellent man in all the social relations of citizen, brother, husband, and friend.—To the sick and the forsaken has he devoted his hours, to relieve and comfort them in their tribulation, and his kind assistance was dealt out with almost equal freedom to an utter stranger as to his bosom friend.[21]

Inskeep, like Stevens, is the epitome of good citizenship; "a most excellent man in all the social relations," he devotes himself fearlessly to the sick and the forsaken. Carey clearly intends his description of Joseph Inskeep to serve as a model of right conduct in exactly the way Brown's characters function. His account of this man's benevolence becomes, for Carey, a way of participating in the work of benevolence himself.

> Could I suppose that in any future equally-dangerous emergency, the opportunity I have seized of bearing my feeble testimony, in favour of those worthy persons, would be a means of exciting others to emulate their heroic virtue, it would afford me the highest consolation I have ever experienced.[22]

That consolation is the reward Brown hoped for in offering Arthur Mervyn's adventures as a model for the citizens of a new nation.

VII. BROWN

The foregoing account of *Arthur Mervyn* may seem to contradict my interpretation of *Wieland*, in that the attitudes these novels express toward the possibility of life in the New World seem diametrically opposed: in *Wieland*, a prediction of disaster; in *Ar-*

thur Mervyn, a projection of success. But while the novels are antithetical psychologically, they are perfectly continuous in an ideological sense. The continuity lies in their common refusal of a Jeffersonian ideology of virtue. Whereas in *Wieland* Brown attacked the Republican ideal by exposing its dangers, in *Arthur Mervyn*, still meditating how justice and virtue might best labor for the common good, he elaborates the Federalist alternative. In the debate between commercial and agrarian interests, coastal versus inland points of view, Brown, like Hamilton, faced toward Europe rather than toward the frontier. No less than the rural atrocities of *Wieland* Arthur Mervyn's delighted disquisitions on the benefits of travel and experience run directly counter to the Republican philosophy of those Revolutionary officers who founded the Order of the Cincinnati after the war. Modeling themselves on the Roman hero who returned gratefully to the plough after having served as consul, they exalted husbandry over military or government service as an ideal form of patriotism.[23]

In offering a physician rather than a farmer as ideal citizen and pillar of the state, *Arthur Mervyn* challenges the Republican philosophy of *Notes on the State of Virginia*, just as *Wieland* had challenged the *Declaration*. In Query XIX, Jefferson writes:

> Those who labor in the earth are the chosen people of God. . . . Corruption of morals . . . is the mark set on those who . . . depend for [their subsistence] on the casualties and caprice of customers. Dependence begets subservience and venality, suffocates the germ of virtue, and prepares fit tools for the designs of ambition. This [is] the natural progress and consequence of the arts. . . . The proportion which the aggregate of other classes of citizens bears in any state to that of its husbandmen is the proportion of its unsound to its healthy parts. . . . The mobs of great cities add just so much to the support of pure government, as sores do to the strength of a human body.[24]

In pursuing one of those despised "arts"—medicine—Brown's model citizen prepares himself to *heal* the sores of the body politic, not to become one. The art of medicine, in this narrative, is more powerful for social good than anything "those who labor in the earth" are capable of. Thomas Hadwin, an honest husbandman in

the Jeffersonian sense, can feed the penniless Mervyn in time of
need, but his rural occupation does not protect him from ills that
affect the whole society and leaves him helpless to combat the
plague that finally sweeps him and his family away—all but one.[25]
Dr. Stevens, on the other hand, can save lives and propagate his
virtue by teaching others how to heal; in *Arthur Mervyn*, true virtue
resides in the city, where people learn to practice those arts of
"commerce" in the broadest sense, that enable them effectively
to multiply the public good.

IV

No Apologies for the Iroquois: A New Way to Read the Leatherstocking Novels

I have argued that the novels of Charles Brockden Brown ought to be read as attempts to diagnose and prescribe for the American body politic in its post-Revolutionary phase. Whereas *Wieland* imagines a scene of carnage as the consequence of too much revolution, *Arthur Mervyn* suggests that circulation, or whatever encourages a society to communicate with itself through commerce, marriage, and the exchange of information, may offset the damage revolution does by knitting together the parts of the social whole. When Arthur Mervyn marries a wealthy, sophisticated widow, born in England of Portuguese-Jewish parentage, it is clear that social intermixture, for Brown, is a key to stability and progress.

Arthur Mervyn's marriage to Achsa Fielding is exactly the kind of union that never takes place in *The Last of the Mohicans*. The crossing of ethnic, national, and class boundaries in this novel does not produce a healthy cosmopolitanism, but has the same effect that revolution does in *Wieland*: bloodshed. Both Cooper and Brockden Brown were afraid of anarchy, and both were afraid of what happens when clear lines of authority, explicit social insignia, and the codes that govern them disappear; but whereas Brown, in his more optimistic moments, believed that a code of conduct founded on benevolence, could provide a model for republican social harmony, Cooper, by the time he wrote *The Last of the Mohicans*, had no such expectation. By the 1820s, a sense of the conflict of interests within American society had increased to such an extent that the most popular novel of the decade depicts the confusion that results when people whose beliefs and customs bear no relation to one another, who share no common fund of values, come into collision on territory to which they all have a legitimate claim.

It is hard to see Cooper's novel as performing the kind of civic function that I have ascribed to *Wieland* and *Arthur Mervyn* because, to a modern audience at least, its mode of representation seems even less appropriate than theirs as a vehicle for considering political and social issues. Peopled by storybook savages and cardboard heroes, and dotted with scalpings and hairsbreadth escapes, *The Last of the Mohicans* seems to cater to a popular taste for melodrama rather than to serious-minded speculation on the national good. Indeed, even the most sympathetic of Cooper's critics in this century have been hard put to it to explain why they should continue to be fascinated by a novel which, by their own accounts, is replete with sensationalism and cliché. But it is precisely those features of the Leatherstocking tales that have made them a target either of critical disdain or of critical apology which enable these narratives to treat cultural problems in a manner both comprehensive and broadly intelligible.

In order to understand the difficulty Cooper's sensationalism presents for modern interpreters, it will be useful to examine a scene in which the most objectionable elements of Cooper's melodramatic mode are on display. In Chapter XXXII of *The Last of the Mohicans*, for example, Cora, who has been carried off by Magua for the last time, stops unexpectedly on a ledge of rocks and cries out, "Kill me if thou wilt, detestable Huron, I will go no farther!":

> The supporters of the maiden raised their ready tomahawks with the impious joy that fiends are thought to take in mischief, but Magua suddenly stayed the uplifted arms. The Huron chief, after casting the weapons he had wrested from his companions over the rock, drew his knife and turned to his captive with a look in which conflicting passions fiercely contended.
> "Woman," he said, "choose; the wigwam or the knife of le Subtil!"[1]

This moment, which epitomizes the problem that has plagued

Cooper criticism ever since Mark Twain ridiculed *The Deerslayer* in the late nineteenth century, has all the color and suspense that made the Leatherstocking novels so enormously popular in their own day, and the melodramatic features that have caused them to be relegated to the category of children's literature in our own.[2] Robert Spiller, who was Cooper's greatest champion in this century, refers to Cooper's plots as "the usual soufflé of escapes, rescues, and pursuits," full of "stock artifices" and "threadbare formulas."[3] And although these words were written in 1947, they reflect a view of Cooper that remains essentially unchanged. It has been echoed recently by Eric Sundquist in *Home as Found: Authority and Genealogy in Nineteenth-Century American Literature*, which begins by describing Cooper's frontier as "an area of impossibility populated by stick figures mouthing stylized handbook creeds."[4]

These labels seem richly deserved by the passage just quoted. Cora and Magua *are* stick figures: she is a virtuous Christian maiden whose life and virginity are in peril; he is a dark Byronic hero torn by violent emotions. She speaks in archaisms and he in the childlike idiom that Cooper thought appropriate for primitive people. The phrase Cooper uses to describe Magua's expression—"in which conflicting passions fiercely contended"—is itself a cliché. The characters pause on a ledge of rocks reminiscent of Mrs. Radcliffe's beetling crags to enact a scene so stilted and improbable that it is no wonder modern critics are embarrassed.

We associate scenes like this with forms of mindless mass entertainment that flatten the complexities of experience, rob human situations of their psychological depth and moral significance, and present a travesty of life that excites the instincts while playing on the worst prejudices of a credulous audience. One's tendency to reject this kind of writing, with its stereotyped characters and sensational events, is virtually automatic; so much so, that contemporary critics who write about Cooper not only assume that their readers will condemn this aspect of his work, but rush to do so themselves. "Such images," writes Richard Slotkin, "were developed as [a] means of reducing the complexities and ambiguities of the American situation to a simple, satisfying formula."[5] Before addressing themselves to what they believe are the valuable qualities in Cooper's fiction, his critics, almost to a man, feel obliged, as Slotkin does, to make apologies for the most obvious features of his work, and by so doing reinforce the negative attitudes they are trying to eliminate. If one looks closely at the strategies the critics employ, the nature of the problem comes into clearer focus.

Wanting to convince their readers that Cooper is worthy of attention despite his artistic flaws, scholars try to neutralize the traditional objections to his fiction in one of two ways. The first is to posit a distinction between the "surface" and the "depth" of Cooper's work, a distinction which enables them to discard as superficial what they find embarrassing (often the entire plot) and to declare significant those features that satisfy their critical expectations. Thus, R. W. B. Lewis writes of *The Deerslayer*: "the plot is little more than a medley of captures and rescues, scalpings and shootings . . . but the 'action' of the story as distinct from the plot—what is really going on in the novel—is something far more significant. . . ." A. N. Kaul, following suit, declares that whatever meanings there might be in *The Pioneers*, "they are not to be found in the intricacies of its story."[6] Cooper criticism is dotted with phrases like these: "for all the surface awkwardness and nonsense," "far more compelling than the surface force of the plot machinery," "a chaos of the surface only."[7] In an afterword to *The Prairie*, J. W. Ward, epitomizing this formulaic tradition of apology, concedes that Cooper's tableaux are melodramatic, that his details are implausible, and that his language is declamatory, only to claim that "beneath the bungled surface of his fiction . . . lies a 'yearning myth'."[8] The tactic these critics share derives ultimately from D. H. Lawrence's influential essay on Cooper which conceives the task of understanding Cooper as a mining operation. It implies that if we will only dig down far enough through the mud and slush of Cooper's stale conventions, we will find some deep underlying theme or conflict that justifes and gives value to the whole.[9]

A weaker version of this strategy substitutes for the surface–depth dichotomy a contrast between center and periphery, according to which the main plot (the apparent center) distracts attention from what is truly valuable in Cooper (the real center). Yvor Winters, who regards Cooper's plots as "comic opera material," believes that his major contribution lies in the virtuosity of his rhetorical experiments, scattered here and there throughout the canon.[10] For Henry Nash Smith, "a flimsy plot that hinges on a childish misunderstanding" in *The Pioneers* "is merely a framework to hold together a narrative focussed about an entirely different problem" which is the "emotional and literary center of the story."[11] And for Lewis, again, "instances" which are "by no means the usual focus of Cooper's tiresome, conventional plots, are the index of his real achievement. . . . The most illuminating clashes and insights occur on the margins" of his fiction.[12]

Both types of rescue operation attempt to persuade the reader that what appear to be the main features of Cooper's work are in fact nugatory and must not be allowed to blind us to its actual merits. But these efforts to save Cooper from himself only make matters worse. The center–periphery model has to declare so much of each novel inessential to the main point that Cooper becomes, as he does for Winters, a man of "fragments," whose virtues are to be found only in the interstices of his work. On the other hand, if one accepts the idea that the objectionable elements are merely surface features which obscure the underlying meaning, then one must ask how the meaning is to be arrived at, since presumably one can approach it only *through* the surface that is acknowledged to be a "chaos," "bungled," full of "awkwardness and nonsense."

The contradictoriness of this position stems from the theoretical bind that critics who admire Cooper necessarily find themselves in. Discovering that they admire novels whose most obvious features are an embarrassment, they must either explain those features away or change their standards of literary evaluation. The choice, in other words, is between declaring Cooper's characters and plots "marginal" or "superficial," and thereby throwing out nine-tenths of the work, or accepting the stereotypes and sensationalism, and thereby opening the door to a debased standard of aesthetic judgment. It is precisely this sense that Cooper's work cannot be defended on artistic grounds that gives Cooper criticism its apologetic tone. It is certainly the reason why Cooper's novels appear far less frequently on college reading lists than the novels of Hawthorne, Melville, or James, and why an admission of ignorance about Cooper, among English department members, is less a shameful confession than a subtle boast. It is a boast which, not long ago, I made myself.

Until a few years ago the only novel of Cooper I had ever read was *The Deerslayer*, at age nine, in a large uncomfortable chair, in a dark house, on a long summer vacation. I retain nothing of what I read then except the image of a man standing in the woods with a gun in his hand. Though my field of specialization is nineteenth-century American literature, I managed to earn my degrees and teach for several years without ever reading one of Cooper's novels. Trained on the close reading of texts, on stylistic analysis, and fine points of psychology and epistemology, I had no interest, I thought, in interminable stories of adventure which critics used to support their big ideas about "the American experience" and "man on the frontier." In Cooper's morally secure forests, where good and evil were clearly known, I thought I would surely starve.

Then I inherited a course and a reading list from one of my colleagues and was forced to read *The Last of the Mohicans*. It was like nothing I had ever taught before, or, for that matter, studied. It was bloody and lurid and totally unbelievable, and at the same time almost fantastically complex—though not with the kind of complexity I was used to. Cooper's style had none of the literary denseness and difficulty I had come to expect of great literary prose; his ideas were not hard to grasp. He did not worry about the nature of reality or the mind's relation to it. He had no ambiguities worth shaking a stick at, and yet I began to see him as a profound thinker, one who was obsessively preoccupied not with the subtle workings of individual consciousness, but with the way the social world is organized. His attempts to make sense of how men live in groups bore a close resemblance to Lévi-Strauss' analyses of primitive myth.[13] Armed with this discovery, I decided that Cooper was an author whom I had been prevented from reading by prejudices formed during my education. His work seemed powerful and moving in the teeth of a hundred well-known faults, but I could not explain its power or its intricacy in any literary vocabulary that was available to me.

I found myself, in short, in exactly the position of most recent admirers of Cooper—liking his work but finding that it failed to vindicate my assumptions about the nature of great literature. As R. W. B. Lewis has said, "it is hard to locate the source of Cooper's power" because "we look for it in the wrong places."[14] I do not think, however, that the right place to look is on the margins of his fiction, as Lewis has done, nor—following Lawrence—in some hypothetical underground region. I believe that the source of Cooper's power lies neither in the interstices nor in the depths of his work, but rather, like Poe's purloined letter, in plain view. What has been overlooked in the effort to protect Cooper from the charge that he relies too much on formulas and stereotypes are the formulas and stereotypes themselves. It is, I will maintain, the supposed weaknesses of Cooper's Leatherstocking novels that constitute their greatest strength. It is those elements that embarrass us the most that both account for Cooper's tremendous popularity in his own day and provide us with the best reason for studying him now.

As a way of testing this assertion, let us return to the scene on the ledge where Cora and Magua are so luridly juxtaposed. On the face of it, that scene appears to forfeit any claim to serious attention. If one looks at it from a psychological perspective, the confrontation is empty. Cora and Magua hurl their challenges at each other; and the next thing we know, they are both dead. Although this is the climactic moment of their lives, we learn nothing of how it feels to them or what it means. Cooper's utter lack of curiosity about the inner lives of his characters is not a feature of this scene alone but of every scene in the novel. He simply has no interest in the drama of the individual psyche which is the central subject matter of modern fiction. He gives us emotions—hatred and lust in Magua, terror and defiance in Cora—but they have no subtle contours, no intricacy, no nuance. The emotions are as stylized and schematic as Cora and Magua themselves. And if we look back from this final moment in their lives, we will find that these characters lack not only psychological depth, but any trace of what is normally termed character development as well. As the novel progresses we acquire new information about them both—Cora is the daughter of a crossbred West Indian woman; Magua has lived among foreign tribes, a traitor and an alien—but the characters themselves never grow or change. Like Leather-stocking, neither experiences anything resembling the education of the hero that is the staple of classical nineteenth-century fiction. We do not see them evolving from within through a series of moral choices that simultaneously create their destinies and control the narrative line. On the contrary, although Magua cries out to Cora, "Woman . . . choose," Cora never gets the opportunity; instead Uncas comes hurtling down on them from above, propelled by the purely external force of the plot machinery. Whatever it is that determines fate in this novel, it is not premeditated acts of the individual will.

If Cooper's characters lack development and lack interiority, it is not because these absences are compensated for by a richly detailed picture of the society in which they move. Cora and Magua are just as unsatisfactory when judged by the standards of the novel of manners as they are when judged in psychological terms, because the points on the social map that would allow one to chart their positions with exactitude are missing. A government, an aristocracy, a clergy, a judiciary, shared customs governing marriage, work, the education of the young—everything, in short, that goes to make up a coherent social order is missing. Cora and Magua cannot have the same kind of definition that we expect from the characters in Jane Austen because the already-constituted social world that must exist in order for people to *be* individuals in a social sense does not exist in *The Last of the Mohicans*. Not only is there hardly a topic on which Cora and Magua could have a conversation; the very possibility of conversation, which is the staple of the novel of manners, is precluded, since that is an activity that depends both for its existence and for its subject matter on a set of social conventions that Cora and Magua do not share.

If the way to understand these characters, then, is neither as in-depth psychological portraits, nor as figures in a novel of manners, one could argue, as many critics have, that the way to see them is as the dramatis personae of a myth.[15] That is, the way to save characters like Cora and Magua is to abandon the idea that Cooper was writing an English novel and to invoke Richard Chase's famous distinction between the novel and the romance.[16] In romance, characters need not resemble the people in Thackeray or George Eliot, whose lives are enmeshed in the dense fabric of a particular time and place. Since the figures of romance do not have their being within society, they are thought to represent universal categories that transcend the limitations of any specific historical moment. In this way of reading, Magua becomes the incarnation of some extra-human force—the wildness of nature, the primitive urges of man's irrational self—and Cora becomes the embodiment of civilization, or the superego, or the principle of the eternal feminine.

This approach to Cooper's characters has the advantage of being able to justify them as stereotypes because, unlike the other approaches I have outlined, it does not use the standards of literary realism as a basis for analysis but rather those of allegory. Allegory, however, is a literary mode in which the characters usually represent unalterable concepts such as justice, mercy, law, or freedom. Critics who identify Cooper as a romancer interpret the Leatherstocking tales, accordingly, as expressions of primordial truths that transcend, or lie "deeper" than, history. While this position accurately identifes Cooper's characters as allegorical, it has the effect of limiting his fables to the repetition of one or another "eternal" paradigm and makes of Cooper a forerunner of Jung, Freud, Joseph Campbell, or Mircea Eliade. This way of reading the Leatherstocking novels not only divorces them from their political and social context, which Cooper's best critics have shown is a crucial determinant of his fiction;[17] it also fails to account for the configuration of his adventure narratives at the level of detail, preferring to rest in broad generalizations about the archetypal nature of the novels, based on one or two selected incidents.[18]

But I am convinced that it is unnecessary to set aside or apologize for the surface characteristics of Cooper's fiction for any reason whatever. Cooper need not be found wanting because his characters are not psychologically profound, or because his settings lack the dense texture of society novels; his plots need not be ignored in favor of a few great archetypal images; and the status of his novels as social theory need not be maintained by conceding their technical ineptitude. A closer look at Cora and Magua on their cliffside will show that it is possible to dispense with these concessions by reading the Leatherstocking tales neither as modernist fiction manqué, nor as ahistorical romance, nor as inartistic social commentary, but as social criticism written in an allegorical mode.

Let us acknowledge at once that it is fruitless to make out a case for Cora and Magua on the grounds of psychological insight or social realism. And let us assume also that they do not represent transhistorical entities such as the id or the Great Mother. And finally, let us assume that the information we do have about them is exactly what we need to know, and then see what this information suggests about the kind of novel Cooper was writing.

Cora is the product of the marriage between the Scottish Colonel Munro, a commander of British forces in the American colonies, and the daughter of a West Indian gentleman, whose wife was the descendant of a Negro slave. "Ay, sir," says Munro as he explains Cora's lineage to Heyward, "that is a curse entailed on Scotland, by her unnatural union with a foreign and trading people" (XVI, 159). The "foreign and trading people" to whom the Scottish Munro refers are the English; and the "curse" is his involvement in the miscegenation initiated by the English whose mercantile impulse brought them into contact with alien races. Heyward is much put off by this description of Cora's background, and Munro is obviously upset by it too, although he is even more disturbed at Heyward's reaction. Already, one begins to see that Cooper's focus in constructing his character is on the mixture of nationalities and races that Cora represents and on the social problems that this mixture will pose.

Magua is the product of unnatural alliances also; his entire history is recounted in terms of radical conflict. He is born a Huron chief but, as a result of drinking whiskey given him by the French, is cast out of his tribe, becomes a wanderer, and is finally driven into the camp of the Mohawks who are his own tribe's hereditary enemies. Magua's initial exile is blamed on the "Canada fathers" who "came into the woods and taught him to drink the fire-water." "Was it the fault of le Renard that his head was not made of rock? . . . Who made him a villain? 'Twas the pale-faces . . ." (XI, 102). When he goes on the warpath against his own people, again the white intruders are indirectly blamed for Magua's betrayal: "the pale-faces have driven the red-skins from their hunting grounds, and now, when they fight, a white man leads the way" (XI, 103). While he is fighting for the English, under the leadership of Munro, Magua commits the blunder that leads him ultimately to the fatal clifftop. He gets drunk again and is whipped by Munro as a punishment. When Magua relates the incident to Cora, she claims that her father has only done justice:

> "Justice!" repeated the Indian. . . . "Is it justice to make evil, and then punish for it! Magua was not himself; it was the fire-water that spoke and acted for him! But Munro did not believe it. The Huron chief was tied up before all the pale-faced warriors and whipped like a dog."
>
> Cora remained silent, for she knew not how to palliate this imprudent severity on the part of her father, in a manner to suit the comprehension of an Indian. (XI, 103)

The gap in comprehension that Cora knows she cannot bridge represents, in microcosm, the problem that occupies the entire novel. Magua cannot comprehend the white man's justice because he sees with Indian eyes; as far as he is concerned, the firewater was responsible for his behavior, and since it is the white men who gave him the firewater, it is they who should be held to account. Munro, for his part, does his duty by his lights as a British officer and carries out justice according to the customs of military discipline. The gap in understanding and the conflict it engenders are not the result of a moral flaw on either side, nor even of limitation of vision; the conflict is the result of fundamental and irreconcilable dissimilarities of outlook which are culturally based.

It is the *fact* of these dissimilarities and what they may or may not mean for the future of American society that form the true subject of *The Last of the Mohicans*. Even within the incident from

Magua's history that I have just sketched, Cooper's interest in the phenomena of cultural difference, the bifurcations that mark men and things off from one another, surfaces several times over. The whiskey that Magua drinks, for instance, is always referred to as "fire-water," a term that denotes an unnatural conjunction of opposites. Magua identifies the firewater as a foreign substance because of its association with the "Canada fathers." Hence, when he takes it into his body he is crossing a cultural boundary: the result is disorientation and loss of identity on an awesome scale. This initial crossing of a cultural line sets in motion a series of such transgressions which lead Magua further and further away from his original position in the social world. The first time he drinks the firewater, Magua loses his identity as a Huron. The second time he loses his status as a chief: "the . . . chief was tied up before all the pale-faced warriors and whipped like a dog." And as a result of the whipping, he damages his stature as an Indian male; to hide the signs of his shame, he must go about with his body covered "like a squaw."

> "See!" continued Magua, tearing aside the slight calico that very imperfectly concealed his painted breast; "here are scars given by knives and bullets—of these a warrior may boast before his nation; but the gray-head has left marks on the back of the Huron chief that he must hide, like a squaw, under this painted cloth of the whites." (XI, 103)

The conjunctions of opposed terms that mark this description— warrior-squaw, knives-bullets, breast-back, painted breast-painted cloth, Huron-white—are not coincidental; nor are they only a feature of this passage in Magua's history—as we have seen, Cora, too, represents a conjunction of opposites of a different kind. Rather, an obsessive preoccupation with systems of classification— the insignia by which race is distinguished from race, nation from nation, tribe from tribe, human from animal, male from female— dominates every aspect of the novel. Conflicting loyalties, divergent customs, disparate codes of honor, habits of deportment, styles of dress, modes of knowledge and of skill—these occupy the narrative commentary at every turn. They are the chief topics of conversation among the characters as well as the bases for their interaction; they underlie the skirmishes, battles, and the massacre that punctuate the story line, and are the foundation of the great scenes of political debate and public ceremony at the novel's close.

If one thinks of *The Last of the Mohicans* as a meditation on *kinds*, and more specifically, as an attempt to calculate exactly how much violation or mixing of its fundamental categories a society can bear, then the characters of Cora and Magua do not appear to be crude caricatures, or defective versions of characters in other novels. Rather, they can be seen to function as starkly opposed cultural types whose confrontation on the cliff suggests the violent repulsion that exists between the social categories they represent: Indian versus white, male versus female, warrior versus virgin, pagan versus Christian. The meaning of the scene they enact consists in the irreconcilable conflict between these categories, and that is why the characters are and *must be* stereotyped. Cora and Magua are stick figures who mouth stylized handbook creeds because they must delineate in as fixed and definite a way as possible the cultural categories they embody. The presence of psychological complexity, moral development, or subtle individualization would make them worse than useless, since these features would serve only to distract attention from and blur the issues with which the novel is dealing. Not only would it be ludicrous for Cooper to pause at this moment on the cliff to trace the progress of a new perception through a character's consciousness—as James, for example, is constantly doing—but such a description would have no meaning in a narrative where thought is articulated as the interaction among kinds and classes of men.

It is necessary to ask at this point why a meditation on "kinds" should be the subject of an American novel in 1826, and why such a novel should have been written by Cooper. Cooper's preoccupation with questions of national, racial, and ethnic mixing would seem to follow naturally from the multi-ethnic composition of his native New York State. In 1805, Timothy Dwight calculated that the population of New York City could be broken down into at least thirteen different groups which he arranged "according to their supposed numbers":

1. Immigrants from New England
2. Original inhabitants, partly Dutch, partly English
3. Immigrants from other parts of this state
4. Immigrants from Ireland
5. Immigrants from New Jersey
6. Immigrants from Scotland
7. Immigrants from Germany
8. Immigrants from England
9. Immigrants from France
10. Immigrants from Holland
11. Jews

"To these," he says, "are to be added a few Swedes, Danes, Italians, Portuguese, Spaniards, and West Indians."[19] (Dwight leaves out the second largest ethnic group in the colonies—Africans— who were themselves subdivided into Ibos, Mandingos, and other tribes.) What is most surprising about this list, aside from the anomaly of classifying people from New Jersey, New England, and "other parts of this state" as immigrants in the same sense as people from Germany and France, is its documentation of the heterogeneous ethnic composition of this country from its earliest days. We normally think of the problems of immigration as belonging to a later period, but the polyglot composition of New York City in 1805 was not new either to the city (eighteen languages were spoken on its streets when New York was still called New Amsterdam) or to the other colonies, though their degrees of ethnic heterogeneity varied. Pennsylvania, because of its policy of religious tolerance, was as polyglot as New York. And while, for the opposite reason, Puritan New England had remained relatively homogeneous, "even in . . . towns like Sudbury and Hingham, Massachusetts, there had been tension between colonists from different regions of England." By 1790, according to a recent study of American nationalism, "two centuries of immigration had made the former English colonies a mosaic of peoples."[20]

Dwight's comment on the mosaic phenomenon provides some basis for understanding why Cooper might have seen ethnic difference as a problem in the 1820s. "Among so many sorts of persons," says Dwight, "you will easily believe it must be difficult, if not impossible, to find a common character; . . . the various immigrants themselves, and to some extent their children, will retain the features derived from their origin and their education. . . ."[21] Cooper treated this problem in *The Pioneers* with something of the same complacency that marks Dwight's comment on it here. The sleigh that pulls into view in chapter IV of that novel carrying a Frenchman, a German, an Englishman, and an American indicates that Cooper is concerned about how people of disparate backgrounds can coexist peacefully in the new nation. When the sleigh almost falls over a cliff but is saved in the nick of time by a man whose ancestry is "mixed" in a special way, the rescue foreshadows the comic resolution of the problem of assimilation which the novel finally arrives at. Oliver Effingham, who saved the occupants of the sleigh, is a classificatory son of the Indian tribe that originally inhabited the land now called Templeton. He is the actual son of the Tory Major to whom the land was deeded by the British crown; and when he marries Elizabeth Temple, daughter of the present (American) owner, their union resolves not only the competing claims of rival nations, families, and races, but rival religious affiliations as well—Elizabeth comes of Quaker and Oliver of Episcopalian stock.

The hope of peaceful coexistence among people of various nationalities but of like racial composition is metaphorized in *The Pioneers* by the "composite order" of the architecture of Templeton Hall, the invention of a wandering mechanic, "a perfect empiric in his profession," whose architectural philosophy represents the pragmatic American way of dealing with social problems. "The composite order, Mr. Doolittle would contend, was an order composed of many others, and was intended to be the most useful of all, for it admitted into its construction such alterations as convenience or circumstances might require."[22] The composite order, whose "facilities . . . presented themselves to effect a compromise," is Cooper's symbol for a nation "composed of many others" (French,

German, English), a society in which diverse claims such as those of the Effinghams and Temples can be accommodated because it "admits into its construction such alterations, as convenience or circumstances might require."

But the coexistence of religious and national groups within the same community, and even within the same family, is only a subset of the larger problem Cooper addresses in *The Last of the Mohicans*. The first human character to appear in *The Pioneers* is a black man who is not part of the merry group rescued by Effingham, but a slave owned by Richard Jones, a cousin and dependent of Judge Temple, because Temple, who is a Quaker, is not supposed to own slaves. Just as Africans are not included in Dwight's census, so Agamemnon, as the slave is called, is not included in the "composite order" Cooper imagined in 1824. No such "order" exists in *The Last of the Mohicans* (1826), which takes on the deeper problem of race. The marriage of Oliver and Elizabeth in *The Pioneers* is possible because Oliver is not an Indian in fact, which is to say, by blood, but only in an honorary sense. When Cora faces Magua on *their* clifftop, the situation admits of no compromise because Magua is a red man and Cora is white: there is no choice to be made between the wigwam and the knife of le Subtil because the Anglo-Saxon tradition of racial purity would not permit it.[23]

That tradition and the problems it posed for white European occupation of the American continent lie at the basis not only of *The Last of the Mohicans*, but of scores of novels dealing with white–Indian relations published during the 1820s and 30s. For it was at this time that the white European colonizers' relation both to the native Indians and to the imported African population had to be confronted. In a letter of 1826 quoted by Richard Drinnon in his monumental study of America's treatment of the Indians, James Madison wrote: "Next to the case of the black race within our bosom, that of the red on our borders is the problem most baffling to the policy of our country."[24] With independence and national status achieved, the nation's continued westward expansion and the growth of the slave-dependent plantation system required a rationale for dealing with non-white peoples. "What

American intellectuals did," says Winthrop Jordan, summing up what has now become the consensus on this issue, "was, in effect, to claim America as a white man's country."[25] Concretely, this meant that "the English, whose racially conscious culture and long history of antagonism toward neighboring Celts predisposed them to dealing harshly with less advanced people, joined other whites in eliminating Indian competitors and in forcing blacks into subordination."[26] The two key events in understanding American attitudes toward race relations during this period are the founding of the American Colonization Society in 1816 and Monroe's policy of Indian removal formulated in 1824.[27] The colonization effort, as Lawrence Friedman points out, attempted to maintain America's image of itself as a white man's nation by physically transporting blacks to another continent.[28] The Indian removal policy had much the same result; it effectively prevented the mixing of Indian and white populations by removing the Indians to lands west of the Mississippi.[29] Jordan suggests that, whatever other motives were at work, the separatist policies arose out of a need for self-identification. "In the settlement of this country," he writes, "the red and black peoples served white men as aids to navigation by which they would find their own safe positions as they ventured into America."[30] It is perhaps not too much of an exaggeration to say that the Indians who populate American novels of the 1820s and 30s served, in Jordan's terms, "the need of transplanted Englishmen to know who they were."[31]

Between the War of 1812 and the Civil War, Americans wrote seventy-three novels dealing with Indian–white relations—many of them calling attention to their subject matter by having Indian names such as *Hobomok, Ish-Noo-Ju-Lut-Sche, Tokeah, Kabaosa, Saratoga, Osceola, Eoneguski, Altowan*, and *Elkswatana*.[32] Louise Barnett observes in her study of the genre that these novels no longer focus on the problem of white survival, as the captivity narratives had, but on the inevitable white domination of the continent.[33] With few exceptions, the white hero and heroine marry at the end, the bad Indian or Indians are killed, and the good Indian either dies, or dies out because he has no heirs. Barnett shows that these novels almost universally lament the passing of the noble Indian race while at the same time affirming that civilization must supplant savagery and Christianity, paganism. "By the union of the white American couple at the conclusion," she writes, "and by the death or defeat of the foreign whites, the frontier romance conveyed a historical truth which transcended the particulars of specific battles and wars: the ongoing possession of the North American continent by whites who had overcome the native inhabitants, and who had, by also expelling foreign whites, insisted upon a new national identity."[34]

Cooper's Leatherstocking novels are no exception to this pattern. They establish the racial identity of Americans, as Jordan suggested, by positing the Indians as "not us" in a general sense, and at the same time use Indians to represent specific alternatives to American society as it was presently constituted.[35] Cooper's good Indians often embody "lost" virtues associated with the heroes of epic, romance, and the Old Testament, while the tribal life they lead incorporates values associated with pre-Revolutionary stability and cohesiveness. Their racially and ethnically homogeneous societies, hierarchical, governed by ancient customs and traditions, dignified, rooted in and respectful of the past, stand for a (quasi-feudal) way of life, imagined to be ordered and secure, that Americans believed they had lost when they overthrew the British crown. It is the use of Indians to represent qualities that white America lacked that motivates the nostalgia for Indianness pervading these fictions, even as they affirm the impossibility of union with the "dusky" race and acquiesce in its extermination.

But a dream of union, a vision of the brotherhood of man, which these novels explicitly reject, is the antithetical principle that gives these attempts to deal with the problem of "kinds" their pathos.

> *How good it is, O see,*
> *And how it pleaseth well,*
> *Together, e'en in unity,*
> *For brethren so to dwell,*

sings David Gamut at the outset of *The Last of the Mohicans* (II, 26). And the vision of unity the Psalm evokes is repeated at the end when Colonel Munro turns to the Indian maidens who have sung his daughter's funeral song and says: "Say to these kind and gentle females, that a heart-broken and failing man, returns them his thanks. Tell them, that the Being we all worship, under different names, will be mindful of their charity; and that the time shall not be distant, when we may assemble around his throne, without distinction of sex, or rank, or colour!" (XXXIII, 347). But Cooper's vision of brotherhood is only an etiolated version of the dream of a peaceable kingdom that had inspired an earlier generation. Benjamin Rush, who was a contemporary of Brown's, in his "Plan for a Peace Office of the United States," proposes that "the following inscription in letters of gold" be painted over the door:

PEACE ON EARTH—GOOD-WILL TO MAN.
AH! WHY WILL MEN FORGET THAT THEY ARE BRETHREN?

and on each of the walls of the apartment, the following pictures as large as the life:

1. A lion eating straw with an ox, and an adder playing upon the lips of a child.
2. An Indian boiling his venison in the same pot with a citizen of Kentucky.
3. Lord Cornwallis and Tippoo Saib, under the shade of a sycamore-tree in the East Indies, drinking Madeira wine together out of the same decanter.
4. A group of French and Austrian soldiers dancing arm and arm, under a bower erected in the neighborhood of Mons.
5. A Santo Domingo planter, a man of color, and native of Africa, legislating together in the same colonial assembly.[36]

The scale on which Cooper addresses the problem of unity is no less grandiose than the one Rush imagined, for it involves Americans, Englishmen, Scotsmen, Frenchmen, Delawares, Iroquois, and even the animal kingdom. But Cooper turns away finally from the possibility of union, with an elegiac gesture that mourns not so much the passing of the "wise race of the Mohicans" as the dream of human brotherhood. The impossibility of such reconciliations as Rush pictured is the issue the novel seeks to come to terms with through its obsessive juxtaposition of characters whose function is to typify the degrees and divisions of social life.

The grotesque concatenations of events that these juxtapositions produce are what stand, in the Leatherstocking tales, in lieu of a plot. Just as the human figures in Cooper's frontier fiction have the static quality of integers in a mathematical equation because they stand for fixed values in a system of value, so the plot has an air of artificiality and contrivance because it, too, answers the requirements of an abstract design. The various combinations and confrontations of characters, groupings, and regroupings test the possibilities of coexistence in a series of episodes that produce the improbabilities Cooper's critics have called "soufflés" and "comic opera material." But these combinations, no less than the stereotypes, are absolutely central to the novel's aims. There could be no harsher test of this proposition than an examination of what, from the standpoint of realistic fiction, is surely the most ridiculous sequence of events in *The Last of the Mohicans*: I mean the series of disguises that the major characters assume in the course of rescuing two of their number from the Huron camp. Prefaced by a scene in which Heyward mistakes David Gamut for a Huron, and a pond of beavers for an Indian war party, this episode tries the reader's credulity further still, as each disguise gives way to one more absurd than the last.

In order to rescue Alice from the Hurons, Heyward disguises himself as an Indian buffoon, Hawkeye disguises himself as a Huron conjurer disguised as a bear, and Alice is disguised as a sick Indian woman. After Alice has been spirited out of the enemy camp by these means, in order to rescue Uncas, Hawkeye disguises himself as David Gamut, Uncas disguises himself as a *real* bear, David Gamut disguises himself as Uncas, and Chingachgook disguises himself as a beaver!

This incredible sequence of events violates every conceivable standard of common sense, not to mention principles of formal economy or thematic relevance. For these machinations, simultaneously cumbersome and farcical, Yvor Winters' designation "comic opera material" seems almost too kind. This judgment on Cooper's plots stems from preconceptions we have about what a plot should be, preconceptions which derive chiefly from Aristotle. Aristotle held that events should follow one another "as cause and effect," that they should never deviate from the rule of probability or necessity, and that "the structural union of the parts [should be] such that, if any one of them is displaced or removed, the whole will be disjointed and disturbed. For a thing whose presence makes no visible difference, is not an organic part of the whole." It is according to this definition of plot that Cooper's series of masquerades is irredeemable. In direct contradiction to every requirement of Aristotle, Cooper's plots substitute the elaborate for the economical, the extraneous for the relevant, the gratuitous for the necessary, and the impossible for the probable.

But in a narrative whose goal is "a perfect understanding of the minute and intricate interests, which had armed friend against friend, and brought natural enemies to combat by each other's side" (XIX, 198), what seem to be absurd excrescences from an Aristotelian point of view are supremely functional formulations of a vital issue. Were Cooper attempting to explore the relationship between sin, guilt, and the individual's relation to his community, one carefully developed disguise, such as Chillingworth's in *The Scarlet Letter*, would have served him well. But in *The Last of the Mohicans*, whose subject is cultural miscegenation, seven disguises are better than one. For the series of masquerades acted out by the principal characters in escaping from the Huron camp recapitulates in rapid succession all of the major societal conflicts with which the novel has been concerned. Each of the characters crosses a boundary line into a category that represents the opposite of his or her actual place in the social structure. At the same time, the exchange of roles reinforces some trait already present in the character, suggesting the possibility of a common bond between categories that are supposedly antithetical.

Heyward, for instance, crosses the line of race and national allegiance by becoming an Indian loyal to the French, but retains his bumbling naiveté in his character as a buffoon. The fair-haired Alice of unmixed Scottish ancestry becomes her pure antithesis by taking the place of an Indian woman; but Alice's physical helplessness is emblematized by the fact that the woman is dying. David

Gamut, the man of religion, becomes an Indian warrior, crossing the barriers of race and calling simultaneously, but his loyalty and courage in protecting the weak are reflected in his impersonation of Uncas, the most noble and fearless of the Indians. Uncas and Chingachgook cross the line that divides men from other species, each in a direction that emphasizes a dominant aspect of his nature—Uncas as the ferocious bear, Chingachgook as the sagacious beaver. But the delicate calibration of these juxtapositions is most strikingly illustrated in the disguises of Hawkeye. Because from a cultural standpoint he is both white and Indian, Hawkeye crosses the racial line in two directions. In his first disguise as a Huron conjurer, he crosses the lines of racial, tribal, and national affiliation, and reinforces his character as a trickster. His second disguise as a fanatically devout psalmist moves him back across the racial and national lines in the other direction. The psalmist's unswerving faith and intense dedication to his calling reflect the highmindedness and spirituality in Natty's character, at the same time that they counterbalance the killer instinct that he also possesses, signified by his assuming the guise of a bear.

I have argued that the subject of *The Last of the Mohicans* is the question of how and whether men can dwell together in unity, and that in this context the series of disguises can be seen to recapitulate the major societal conflicts within the novel, carefully matching each character with his or her cultural opposite in a collapse of antithetical identities. The significance of these complicated mergers becomes clear as we move from the disguise episode into the final scenes of the novel where all the categories that the disguises had conflated are wrenched violently—and permanently—apart. The Delawares fight the Hurons and virtually wipe them out; the Indians mourn their dead chief, Uncas, and the whites go off together in a group. Alice will marry the grandson of her father's best friend, but Cora and Uncas are buried separately. None of the lines of race, tribe, nationality, or calling which the disguises had seemed to obliterate has been erased in fact. Men are men, and animals are animals; the Delawares hate the Hurons and always will, and there will be no marriage between any Indian chief, either Magua or Uncas, and the daughter of

Munro. If we look at the disposition of the characters at the novel's close, it appears that nothing remains of the nicely calculated mergers, based on some slight similarity, that the disguises had brought about. The barriers which it had seemed safe to cross are once again impassable. How is it, then, that at one moment in the narrative, the distinctions of kind are all suspended and in the next they are back in force? The answer lies in the special conditions under which the category shifts took place. By putting on a disguise, none of the characters risks his or her identity in the least. The costumes the protagonists wear do not penetrate below the surface; they can be removed at will; their function in fact is to shield them from their adversaries by preventing any real contact between opposing kinds from taking place. If the protagonists had shown their true identities to the Hurons, the result would have been death. The boundaries are crossed with perfect impunity because the trespass is only an illusion. For it is only in the realm of illusion, in the fiction of disguise, in songs like David Gamut's at the beginning and the song of Indian maidens at the end, in Munro's dream of a heaven without distinctions of sex, or rank, or color—that unity can ever appear.

But it is not as if the only alternative to that unity toward which the novel gestures somewhat wistfully is the chaotic and violent concussion of alien groups that is the major portion of the action. The burden of the novel's meditation on kinds, finally, is to suggest that the ideal form of human society consists neither in the obliteration of all distinctions nor in the jarring of savage races, but rather in a proper respect for the "natural" divisions that separate tribe from tribe and nation from nation. When the white man came to the North American continent, he disturbed the natural and hereditary distinctions that had obtained immemorially among the Indians. As Hawkeye explains:

> "So that the Hurons and the Oneidas, who speak the same tongue,
> or what may be called the same, take each other's scalps, and the
> Delawares are divided among themselves; a few hanging about their
> great council fire, on the their own river, and fighting on the same
> side with the Mingoes, while the greater part are in the Canadas, out

of natural enmity to the Maquas—thus throwing everything into disorder and destroying all the harmony of warfare." (XIX, 196–197)

The condition whose passing Natty laments is not one of peaceful coexistence among the members of a homogeneous group, for "harmony," insofar as it can be achieved among men, is not a question of the absence of strife or of differences. Rather, life at its best, for Cooper, as for Hawkeye, consists in a "harmony of warfare," by which Cooper means the maintenance of traditional lines of distinction between nation, race, tribe, class, age, sex, occupation, religion, and the like. There never will be a time when men live together without distinctions. Knives will always be either of French or of English formation. Men will always kill one another, and when they do, it will be according to the fashion of their kind—either with knives or with guns, and if with guns, some will use shotguns and some will use rifles, and if they use rifles, some will be short and some will be long.

What is to be avoided, in short, is not strife, which is inevitable, but the confusion of mutually exclusive systems of classification, which is what occurs when disparate cultures collide with one another. The result is the suspension of all rules: instead of warfare, massacre. That is why the central event in *The Last of the Mohicans* is the wholesale slaughter of the English by the Hurons at Fort William Henry. The violence of the massacre, which is dwelt on in horrid detail—a Huron bashes an infant's brains out against a rock and buries his hatchet in the skull of its mother—deliberately emphasizes the breakdown of all social controls.

Death was every where, and in his most terrific and disgusting aspects. . . . The flow of blood might be likened to the outbreaking of a torrent; and as the natives became heated and maddened by the sight, many among them even kneeled to the earth, and drank freely, exultingly, hellishly, of the crimson tide. (XVII, 176)

The fiendish Hurons drinking the blood of their white victims is an inverted, magnified image of Magua's drinking the white man's firewater—and its logical consequence. The first violation of boundary leads inevitably to the last.

Cooper's plots follow their own rule of necessity as rigidly as the plots of Sophocles, but the rule is different. At the end of *The Last of the Mohicans*, like cleaves to like and opposites separate; the representatives of disparate groups may cross only within certain carefully defined limits: Heyward's union with Alice crosses the line of sex but not the lines of class, nationality, or race; Hawkeye and Chingachgook pledge eternal friendship uniting Indian and white, but the sexual boundary remains uncrossed and they remain social isolates, for within a social structure even such a union as theirs cannot be tolerated. Although an aide-de-camp of Montcalm makes a token appearance at the funeral of the English commander's daughter, his presence does not signify a union between the English and the French, but is merely a diplomatic gesture made within the code that governs two European nations at war. The novel's plot is an almost algebraic demonstration of the thesis that the stability and integrity of a social order depend upon maintaining intact traditional categories of sameness and difference *within* that order, and on preserving the system as a whole from the disruptive influence of an alien culture. Hawkeye asks:

> "Did you see the fashion of their knives? were they of English or French formation? . . . Had they held their corn-feast, or can you say any thing of the totems of their tribe?" (XXII, 225, 226)

In order to be fully human in Cooper's eyes, a person must belong to one class, one totem, one tribe; for the cultural coordinates that give a person a physical, social, and spiritual identity are the source of all human dignity and worth. This is the reason for Natty Bumppo's almost fanatical assertion throughout the novel that he is "a man without a cross," by which he means that he is of unmixed blood, pure stock. Of all the characters in the novel, except Magua, Natty runs the greatest risk of losing his identity, for he wears a medley of white and Indian garments, carries both the knife and the gun, wanders restlessly over border after border, frequents the company of Indians, and has at least seven different names. Only by clinging to the notion that he has remained true to his "gifts" as a white man and a Christian, can Natty preserve that sense of cultural belonging without which he would have become another Magua—for a villain in Cooper's calculations is someone who is not true to his kind.

To say that Magua is a villain, however, is somewhat misleading. Magua is a "bad" character not because he has some characterological weakness or has made an incorrect choice; he is bad because his position in the social organization of the novel violates the boundaries that must be kept intact in order for social harmony to exist. Goodness and badness are never at issue in *The Last of the Mohicans* but are simply given from the start, because they do not depend upon acts of the individual will, but upon the position a character occupies in the branching divisions and subdivisions of social life. Instead of comparing Cooper's plots and characters, then, to those of classical nineteenth-century fiction, where individual moral choice *is* at the center of attention, we must recognize that Cooper's novels constitute a drama of an altogether different sort, a drama whose purpose is to work out the rules of coexistence that make human society possible in the first place. The Indians and maidens of his adventure stories are not cardboard figures to be laughed at or lamented over; his plots are not a series of clumsy devices strung together in haste. His characters are elements of thought, things to think with; and the convolutions of the plots, the captures, rescues, and pursuits of the narrative, are stages in a thought process, phases in a meditation on the bases of social life that is just as rigorous and complicated in its way as the meditations of Strether by the river.

*   *   *

The Last of the Mohicans, Wieland, and *Arthur Mervyn* have had for some time a secure place in the canon of American fiction. Therefore, in arguing that these works should not be judged by the standards of modern literary criticism but seen as agents of cultural formation, I have not had to justify taking them seriously in the first place. Despite the defects critics persist in finding in these novels, they are considered legitimate objects of literary study. This is not true of the texts that form the basis of the next two chapters, *Uncle Tom's Cabin* and *The Wide, Wide World*. Because these novels appealed to a mass audience, because they were enormous commercial successes, because they are based on a world view now considered to be, at best, unrealistic and outmoded, because they were designed to move their audiences to action, because they were written by, about, and for women, they have been excluded from the literary canon, and indeed have often been used by critics to exemplify everything that great literature is not: sentimental, pious, trivial, self-deluded, ephemeral, and propagandistic.

The next two chapters make the same kinds of arguments for taking sentimental fiction seriously as the previous chapters have made for the value of *Wieland, Arthur Mervyn*, and *The Last of the Mohicans*, for there are continuities between the criticisms of Brown and Cooper and those launched against Warner and Stowe. The chief of these are the charges of melodrama and artistic ineptitude, objections that spring from a lack of awareness, on the critics' part, of the cultural conditions generating these works. But partly because the sentimental novels were written in an era whose world view was specifically repudiated in the twentieth century, and partly because they were written by women, and therefore often addressed themselves to the concerns of a female audience, the assumptions that animate them are much more difficult to make credible than those that motivated the novels by earlier, male authors. Reconstructing sympathetically the discourse out of which domestic fiction springs, and for which it is also responsible, requires a considerable effort of imagination, especially in the case of a writer such as Susan Warner, whose best-selling novel does not even have a concern for slavery to make it seem important today.

Its importance was indisputable, however, in the 1850s when critics still believed that literature's main purpose was to be edifying, and the reading public had been steeped in religious and moral discourse. At a time when the national welfare was thought to depend upon the Christian virtue of individual citizens, and when bringing the whole world to Christ was conceived as a goal of national existence, stories about orphan girls whose trials of faith teach them to submit to God's will did not seem irrelevant to the collective civic enterprise. The internal dramas of sin and salvation that occupy the domestic novels of the 1850s were no less engaged in deliberating on issues of national political significance than was Cooper's narrative of the wars between the French and the English and their Indian allies a quarter of a century earlier. Indeed, the sentimental novelists could not have been so phenomenally successful unless their work had met some deeply felt national exigencies. The novel which, above all others, answered the needs of the times was Harriet Beecher Stowe's *Uncle Tom's Cabin*: a work which, for that very reason, has not been accorded a place in the literary pantheon.

V
Sentimental Power:
Uncle Tom's Cabin and the
Politics of Literary History

Once, during a difficult period of my life, I lived in the basement of a house on Forest Street in Hartford, Connecticut, which had belonged to Isabella Beecher Hooker—Harriet Beecher Stowe's half-sister. This woman at one time in her life had believed that the millennium was at hand and that she was destined to be the leader of a new matriarchy.[1] When I lived in that basement, however, I knew nothing of Stowe, or of the Beechers, or of the utopian visions of nineteenth-century American women. I made a reverential visit to the Mark Twain house a few blocks away, took photographs of his study, and completely ignored Stowe's own house—also open to the public—which stood across the lawn. Why should I go? Neither I nor anyone I knew regarded Stowe as a serious writer. At the time, I was giving my first lecture course in the American Renaissance—concentrated exclusively on Hawthorne, Melville, Poe, Emerson, Thoreau, and Whitman—and although *Uncle Tom's Cabin* was written in exactly the same period, and although it is probably the most influential book ever written by an American, I would never have dreamed of including it on my reading list. To begin with, its very popularity would have militated against it; as everybody knew, the classics of American fiction were, with a few exceptions, all succès d'estime.

In 1969, when I lived on Forest Street, the women's movement was just getting underway. It was several years before Chopin's *The Awakening* and Gilman's "The Yellow Wallpaper" would make it onto college reading lists, sandwiched in between Theodore Dreiser

and Frank Norris. These women, like some of their male counterparts, had been unpopular in their own time and owed their
reputations to the discernment of latter-day critics. Because of their
work, it is now respectable to read these writers who, unlike Nathaniel Hawthorne, had to wait several generations for their cham-
pions to appear in the literary establishment. But despite the influence of the women's movement, despite the explosion of work
in nineteenth-century American social history, and despite the new
historicism that is infiltrating literary studies, the women, like Stowe,
whose names were household words in the nineteenth century—
women such as Susan Warner, Sarah J. Hale, Augusta Evans,
Elizabeth Stuart Phelps, her daughter Mary, who took the same
name, and Frances Hodgson Burnett—these women remain excluded from the literary canon. And while it has recently become
fashionable to study their works as examples of cultural defor-
mation, even critics who have invested their professional careers
in that study and who declare themselves feminists still refer to
their novels as trash.[2]

My principal target of concern, however, is not feminists who
have written on popular women novelists of the nineteenth century, but the male-dominated scholarly tradition that controls both
the canon of American literature (from which these novelists are
excluded) and the critical perspective that interprets the canon for
society. For the tradition of Perry Miller, F. O. Matthiessen, Harry
Levin, Richard Chase, R. W. B. Lewis, Yvor Winters, and Henry
Nash Smith has prevented even committed feminists from recognizing and asserting the *value* of a powerful and specifically female
novelistic tradition. The very grounds on which sentimental fiction
has been dismissed by its detractors, grounds which have come to
seem universal standards of aesthetic judgment, were established
in a struggle to supplant the tradition of evangelical piety and moral
commitment these novelists represent. In reaction against their
world view, and perhaps even more against their success, twentieth-century critics have taught generations of students to equate
popularity with debasement, emotionality with ineffectiveness, religiosity with fakery, domesticity with triviality, and all of these,
implicitly, with womanly inferiority.

feminization of Am. culture

In this view, sentimental novels written by women in the nine-teenth century were responsible for a series of cultural evils whose effects still plague us: the degeneration of American religion from theological rigor to anti-intellectual consumerism, the rationali-zation of an unjust economic order, the propagation of the debased images of modern mass culture, and the encouragement of self-indulgence and narcissism in literature's most avid readers—women.[3] To the extent that they protested the evils of society, their protest is seen as duplicitous—the product and expression of the very values they pretended to condemn. Unwittingly or not, so the story goes, they were apologists for an oppressive social order. In con-trast to male authors such as Thoreau, Whitman, and Melville, who are celebrated as models of intellectual daring and honesty, these women are generally thought to have traded in false ster-eotypes, dishing out weak-minded pap to nourish the prejudices of an ill-educated and underemployed female readership. Self-deluded and unable to face the harsh facts of a competitive society, they are portrayed as manipulators of a gullible public who kept their readers imprisoned in a dream world of self-justifying clichés. Their fight against the evils of their society was a fixed match from the start.[4]

The thesis I will argue in this chapter is diametrically opposed to these portrayals. It holds that the popular domestic novel of the nineteenth century represents a monumental effort to reorganize culture from the woman's point of view; that this body of work is remarkable for its intellectual complexity, ambition, and resource-fulness; and that, in certain cases, it offers a critique of American society far more devastating than any delivered by better-known critics such as Hawthorne and Melville. Finally, it suggests that the enormous popularity of these novels, which has been cause for suspicion bordering on disgust, is a reason for paying close atten-tion to them. *Uncle Tom's Cabin* was, in almost any terms one can think of, the most important book of the century. It was the first American novel ever to sell over a million copies and its impact is generally thought to have been incalculable. Expressive of and responsible for the values of its time, it also belongs to a genre, the sentimental novel, whose chief characteristic is that it is written by, for, and about women. In this respect, *Uncle Tom's Cabin* is not exceptional but representative. It is the *summa theologica* of nineteenth-century America's religion of domesticity, a brilliant redaction of the culture's favorite story about itself—the story of salvation through motherly love. Out of the ideological materials at their disposal, the sentimental novelists elaborated a myth that gave women the central position of power and authority in the culture; and of these efforts *Uncle Tom's Cabin* is the most dazzling exemplar.

I have used words like "monumental" and "dazzling" to describe Stowe's novel and the tradition of which it is a part because they have for too long been the casualties of a set of critical attitudes that equate intellectual merit with a certain kind of argumentative discourse and certain kinds of subject matter. A long tradition of academic parochialism has enforced this sort of discourse through a series of cultural contrasts: light "feminine" novels vs. tough-minded intellectual treatises; domestic "chattiness" vs. serious thinking; and summarily, the "damned mob of scribbling women" vs. a few giant intellects, unappreciated and misunderstood in their time, struggling manfully against a flood of sentimental rubbish.[5]

The inability of twentieth-century critics either to appreciate the complexity and scope of a novel like Stowe's, or to account for its enormous popular success, stems from their assumptions about the nature and function of literature. In modernist thinking, literature is by definition a form of discourse that has no designs on the world. It does not attempt to change things, but merely to represent them, and it does so in a specifically literary language whose claim to value lies in its uniqueness. Consequently, works whose stated purpose is to influence the course of history, and which therefore employ a language that is not only not unique but common and accessible to everyone, do not qualify as works of art. Literary texts, such as the sentimental novel, that make continual and ob-vious appeals to the reader's emotions and use technical devices that are distinguished by their utter conventionality, epitomize the opposite of everything that good literature is supposed to be. "For the literary critic," writes J. W. Ward, summing up the dilemma posed by *Uncle Tom's Cabin*, "the problem is how a book so seemingly artless, so lacking in apparent literary talent, was not only an immediate success but has endured."[6]

How deep the problem goes is illustrated dramatically by George F. Whicher's discussion of Stowe's novel in *The Literary History of the United States*. Reflecting the consensus view on what good novels are made of, Whicher writes: "Nothing attributable to Mrs. Stowe or her handiwork can account for the novel's enormous vogue; its author's resources as a purveyor of Sunday-school fiction were not remarkable. She had at most a ready command of broadly conceived melodrama, humor, and pathos, and of these popular elements she compounded her book."[7] At a loss to understand how a book so compounded was able to "convulse a mighty nation," Whicher concludes—incredibly—that Stowe's own explanation that "God wrote it" "solved the paradox." Rather than give up his bias against "melodrama," "pathos," and "Sunday-school fiction," Whicher takes refuge in a solution that, even according to his lights, is patently absurd.[8] And no wonder. The modernist literary aesthetic cannot account for the unprecedented and persistent popularity of a book like *Uncle Tom's Cabin*, for this novel operates according to principles quite other than those that have been responsible for determining the currently sanctified American literary classics.

It is not my purpose, however, to drag Hawthorne and Melville from their pedestals, nor to claim that the novels of Stowe, Fanny Fern, and Elizabeth Stuart Phelps are good in the same way that *Moby-Dick* and *The Scarlet Letter* are; rather, I will argue that the work of the sentimental writers is complex and significant in ways *other than* those that characterize the established masterpieces. I will ask the reader to set aside some familiar categories for evaluating fiction—stylistic intricacy, psychological subtlety, epistemological complexity—and to see the sentimental novel not as an artifice of eternity answerable to certain formal criteria and to certain psychological and philosophical concerns, but as a political enterprise, halfway between sermon and social theory, that both codifies and attempts to mold the values of its time.

The power of a sentimental novel to move its audience depends upon the audience's being in possession of the conceptual categories that constitute character and event. That storehouse of assumptions includes attitudes toward the family and toward social institutions; a definition of power and its relation to individual human feeling; notions of political and social equality; and above all, a set of religious beliefs that organizes and sustains the rest. Once in possession of the system of beliefs that undergirds the patterns of sentimental fiction, it is possible for modern readers to see how its tearful episodes and frequent violations of probability were invested with a structure of meanings that fixed these works, for nineteenth-century readers, not in the realm of fairy tale or escapist fantasy, but in the very bedrock of reality. I do not say that we can read sentimental fiction exactly as Stowe's audience did—that would be impossible—but that we can and should set aside the modernist prejudices which consign this fiction to oblivion, in order to see how and why it worked for its readers, in its time, with such unexampled effect.

Let us consider the episode in *Uncle Tom's Cabin* most often cited as the epitome of Victorian sentimentalism—the death of little Eva—because it is the kind of incident most offensive to the sensibilities of twentieth-century academic critics. It is on the belief that this incident is nothing more than a sob story that the whole case against sentimentalism rests. Little Eva's death, so the argument goes, like every other sentimental tale, is awash with emotion but does nothing to remedy the evils it deplores. Essentially, it leaves the slave system and the other characters unchanged. This trivializing view of the episode is grounded in assumptions about power and reality so common that we are not even aware they are in force. Thus generations of critics have commented with condescending irony on little Eva's death. But in the system of belief that undergirds Stowe's enterprise, dying is the supreme form of heroism. In *Uncle Tom's Cabin*, death is the equivalent not of defeat but of victory; it brings an access of power, not a loss of it; it is not only the crowning achievement of life, it *is* life, and Stowe's entire presentation of little Eva is designed to dramatize this fact.

Stories like the death of little Eva are compelling for the same reason that the story of Christ's death is compelling; they enact a philosophy, as much political as religious, in which the pure and powerless die to save the powerful and corrupt, and thereby show themselves more powerful than those they save. They enact, in short, a *theory* of power in which the ordinary or "common sense" view of what is efficacious and what is not (a view to which most modern critics are committed) is simply reversed, as the very possibility of social action is made dependent on the action taking place in individual hearts. Little Eva's death enacts the drama of which all the major episodes of the novel are transformations, the idea, central to Christian soteriology, that the highest human calling is to give one's life for another. It presents one version of the ethic of sacrifice on which the entire novel is based and contains in some form all of the motifs that, by their frequent recurrence, constitute the novel's ideological framework.

Little Eva's death, moreover, is also a transformation of a story circulating in the culture at large. It may be found, for example, in a dozen or more versions in the evangelical sermons of the Reverend Dwight Lyman Moody which he preached in Great Britain and Ireland in 1875. In one version it is called "The Child Angel" and it concerns a beautiful golden-haired girl of seven, her father's pride and joy, who dies and, by appearing to him in a dream in which she calls to him from heaven, brings him salvation.[9] The tale shows that by dying even a child can be the instrument of redemption for others, since in death she acquires a spiritual power over those who loved her beyond what she possessed in life.

The power of the dead or the dying to redeem the unregenerate is a major theme of nineteenth-century popular fiction and religious literature. Mothers and children are thought to be uniquely capable of this work. In a sketch entitled "Children," published the year after *Uncle Tom* came out, Stowe writes: "Wouldst thou know, o parent, what is that faith which unlocks heaven? Go not to wrangling polemics, or creeds and forms of theology, but draw to thy bosom thy little one, and read in that clear trusting eye the lesson of eternal life."[10] If children because of their purity and innocence can lead adults to God while living, their spiritual power when they are dead is greater still. Death, Stowe argues in a pamphlet entitled *Ministration of Departed Spirits*, enables the Christian to begin his "real work." God takes people from us sometimes so that their "ministry can act upon us more powerfully from the unseen world."[11]

> The mother would fain electrify the heart of her child. She yearns and burns in vain to make her soul effective on its soul, and to inspire it with a spiritual and holy life; but all her own weaknesses, faults and mortal cares, cramp and confine her till death breaks all fetters; and then, first truly alive, risen, purified, and at rest, she may do calmly, sweetly, and certainly, what, amid the tempest and tossings of her life, she labored for painfully and fitfully.[12]

When the spiritual power of death is combined with the natural sanctity of childhood, the child becomes an angel endowed with salvific force.

Most often, it is the moment of death that saves, when the dying child, glimpsing for a moment the glory of heaven, testifies to the reality of the life to come. Uncle Tom knows that this will happen when little Eva dies, and explains it to Miss Ophelia as follows:

> "You know it says in Scripture, 'At midnight there was a great cry made. Behold the bridegroom cometh.' That's what I'm spectin now, every night, Miss Feely,—and I could n't sleep out o' hearin', no ways."
> "Why, Uncle Tom, what makes you think so?"
> "Miss Eva, she talks to me. The Lord, he sends his messenger in the soul. I must be thar, Miss Feely; for when that ar blessed child goes into the kingdom, they'll open the door so wide, we'll all get a look in at the glory, Miss Feely."[13]

Little Eva does not disappoint them. She exclaims at the moment when she passes "from death unto life": "O, love,—joy,—peace!" And her exclamation echoes those of scores of children who die in Victorian fiction and sermon literature with heaven in their eyes. Dickens' Paul Dombey, seeing the face of his dead mother, dies with the words: "The light about the head is shining on me as I go!" The fair, blue-eyed young girl in Lydia Sigourney's *Letters to Mothers*, "death's purple tinge upon her brow," when implored by her mother to utter one last word, whispers "Praise!"[14]

Of course, it could be argued by critics of sentimentalism that the prominence of stories about the deaths of children is precisely what is wrong with the literature of the period; rather than being cited as a source of strength, the presence of such stories in *Uncle Tom's Cabin* could be regarded as an unfortunate concession to the age's fondness for lachrymose scenes. But to dismiss such scenes as "all tears and flapdoodle" is to leave unexplained the popularity of the novels and sermons that are filled with them, unless we choose to believe that a generation of readers was unaccountably moved to tears by matters that are intrinsically silly and trivial. That popularity is better explained, I believe, by the relationship of these scenes to a pervasive cultural myth which invests the suffering and death of an innocent victim with just the kind of power that critics deny to Stowe's novel: the power to work in, and change, the world.

This is the kind of action that little Eva's death in fact performs. It proves its efficacy not through the sudden collapse of the slave system, but through the conversion of Topsy, a motherless, godless black child who has up until that point successfully resisted all attempts to make her "good." Topsy will not be "good" because, never having had a mother's love, she believes that no one can love her. When Eva suggests that Miss Ophelia would love her if only she were good, Topsy cries out: "No; she can't bar me, 'cause I'm a nigger!—she'd's soon have a toad touch her! There can't nobody love niggers, and niggers can't do nothin'! *I* don't care."

"O, Topsy, poor child, *I* love you!" said Eva, with a sudden burst of feeling, and laying her little thin, white hand on Topsy's shoulder; "I love you, because you have n't had any father, or mother, or friends;—because you've been a poor, abused child! I love you, and I want you to be good. I am very unwell, Topsy, and I think I shan't live a great while; and it really grieves me, to have you be so naughty. I wish you would try to be good, for my sake;—it's only a little while I shall be with you."

The round, keen eyes of the black child were overcast with tears;—large, bright drops rolled heavily down, one by one, and fell on the little white hand. Yes, in that moment, a ray of real belief, a ray of heavenly love, had penetrated the darkness of her heathen soul! She laid her head down between her knees, and wept and sobbed,—while the beautiful child, bending over her, looked like the picture of some bright angel stooping to reclaim a sinner. (XXV, 330–331)

The rhetoric and imagery of this passage—its little white hand, its ray from heaven, bending angel, and plentiful tears—suggest a literary version of the kind of polychrome religious picture that hangs on Sunday-school walls. Words like "kitsch," "camp," and "corny" come to mind. But what is being dramatized here bears no relation to these designations. By giving Topsy her love, Eva initiates a process of redemption whose power, transmitted from heart to heart, can change the entire world. And indeed the process has begun. From that time on, Topsy is "different from what she used to be" (XXVI, 335) (eventually she will go to Africa and become a missionary to her entire race), and Miss Ophelia, who overhears the conversation, is different, too. When little Eva is dead and Topsy cries out "ther an't *nobody* left now," Miss Ophelia answers her in Eva's place:

> "Topsy, you poor child," she said, as she led her into her room, "don't give up! *I* can love you, though I am not like that dear little child. I hope I've learnt something of the love of Christ from her. I can love you; I do, and I'll try to help you to grow up a good Christian girl."
>
> Miss Ophelia's voice was more than her words, and more than that were the honest tears that fell down her face. From that hour, she acquired an influence over the mind of the destitute child that she never lost. (XXVII, 349)

The tears of Topsy and of Miss Ophelia, which we find easy to ridicule, are the sign of redemption in *Uncle Tom's Cabin*; not words, but the emotions of the heart bespeak a state of grace, and these are known by the sound of a voice, the touch of a hand, but chiefly, in moments of greatest importance, by tears. When Tom lies dying on the plantation on the Red River, the disciples to whom he has preached testify to their conversion by weeping.

> Tears had fallen on that honest, insensible face,—tears of late repentance in the poor, ignorant heathen, whom his dying love and patience had awakened to repentance. . . . (XLI, 485)

Even the bitter and unregenerate Cassy, moved by "the sacrifice that had been made for her," breaks down; "moved by the few last words which the affectionate soul had yet strength to breathe, ... the dark, despairing woman had wept and prayed" (XLI, 485). When George Shelby, the son of Tom's old master, arrives too late to free him, "tears which did honor to his manly heart fell from the young man's eyes as he bent over his poor friend." And when Tom realizes who is there, "the whole face lighted up, the hard hands clasped, and tears ran down the cheeks" (XLI, 486). The vocabulary of clasping hands and falling tears is one which we associate with emotional exhibitionism, with the overacting that kills off true feeling through exaggeration. But the tears and gestures of Stowe's characters are not in excess of what they feel; if anything they fall short of expressing the experiences they point to—salvation, communion, reconciliation.

If the language of tears seems maudlin and little Eva's death ineffectual, it is because both the tears and the redemption that they signify belong to a conception of the world that is now generally regarded as naive and unrealistic. Topsy's salvation and Miss Ophelia's do not alter the anti-abolitionist majority in the Senate or prevent southern plantation owners and northern investment bankers from doing business to their mutual advantage. Because most modern readers regard such political and economic facts as final, it is difficult for them to take seriously a novel that insists on religious conversion as the necessary precondition for sweeping social change. But in Stowe's understanding of what such change requires, it is the *modern* view that is naive. The political and economic measures that constitute effective action for us, she regards as superficial, mere extensions of the worldly policies that produced the slave system in the first place. Therefore, when Stowe asks the question that is in every reader's mind at the end of the novel—namely, "what can any individual do?"—she recommends not specific alterations in the current political and economic arrangements, but rather a change of heart.

There is one thing that every individual can do—they can see to it that *they feel right*. An atmosphere of sympathetic influence encircles

every human being; and the man or woman who *feels* strongly, health-
ily and justly, on the great interests of humanity, is a constant ben-
efactor to the human race. See, then, to your sympathies in this
matter! Are they in harmony with the sympathies of Christ? or
are they swayed and perverted by the sophistries of worldly policy?
(XLV, 515)

Stowe is not opposed to concrete measures such as the passage of
laws or the formation of political pressure groups, it is just that,
by themselves, such actions would be useless. For if slavery *were*
to be abolished by these means, the moral conditions that produced
slavery in the first place would continue in force. The choice is
not between action and inaction, programs and feelings; the
choice is between actions that spring from the "sophistries of
worldly policy" and those inspired by the "sympathies of Christ."
Reality, in Stowe's view, cannot be changed by manipulat-
ing the physical environment; it can only be changed by conversion in the spirit because it is the spirit alone that is finally
real.

The notion that historical change takes place only through religious conversion, which is a theory of power as old as Christianity
itself, is dramatized and vindicated in *Uncle Tom's Cabin* by the
novel's insistence that all human events are organized, clarified,
and made meaningful by the existence of spiritual realities.[15] The
novel is packed with references to the four last things—Heaven,
Hell, Death, and Judgment—references which remind the reader
constantly that historical events can only be seen for what they are
in the light of eternal truths. When St. Clare stands over the grave
of little Eva, unable to realize "that it was his Eva that they were
hiding from his sight," Stowe interjects, "Nor was it!—not Eva,
but only the frail seed of that bright, immortal form with which
she shall yet come forth, in the day of the Lord Jesus!" (XVII,
350). And when Legree expresses satisfaction that Tom is dead,
she turns to him and says: "Yes, Legree; but who shall shut up
that voice in thy soul? that soul, past repentance, past prayer, past
hope, in whom the fire that never shall be quenched is already
burning!" (XL, 480). These reminders come thick and fast; they
are present in Stowe's countless quotations from Scripture—intro-

duced at every possible opportunity, in the narrative, in dialogue, in epigraphs, in quotations from other authors; they are present in the Protestant hymns that thread their way through scene after scene, in asides to the reader, apostrophes to the characters, in quotations from religious poetry, sermons, and prayers, and in long stretches of dialogue and narrative devoted to the discussion of religious matters. Stowe's narrative stipulates a world in which the facts of Christ's death and resurrection and coming day of judgment are never far from our minds because it is only within this frame of reference that she can legitimately have Tom claim, as he dies, "I've got the victory!" (XLI, 486).

The eschatological vision, by putting all individual events in relation to an order that is unchanging, collapses the distinctions among them so that they become interchangeable representations of a single timeless reality. Groups of characters blend into the same character, while the plot abounds with incidents that mirror one another. These features are the features, not of classical nineteenth-century fiction, but of typological narrative. It is this tradition rather than that of the English novel that *Uncle Tom's Cabin* reproduces and extends; for this novel does not simply quote the Bible, it rewrites the Bible as the story of a Negro slave. Formally and philosophically, it stands opposed to works like *Middlemarch* and *The Portrait of a Lady* in which everything depends on human action and decision unfolding in a temporal sequence that withholds revelation until the final moment. The truths that Stowe's narrative conveys can only be reembodied, never discovered, because they are already revealed from the beginning. Therefore, what seem from a modernist point of view to be gross stereotypes in characterization and a needless proliferation of incident, are essential properties of a narrative aimed at demonstrating that human history is a continual reenactment of the sacred drama of redemption. It is the novel's reenactment of this drama that made it irresistible in its day.

Uncle Tom's Cabin retells the culture's central religious myth— the story of the crucifixion—in terms of the nation's greatest political conflict—slavery—and of its most cherished social beliefs— the sanctity of motherhood and the family. It is because Stowe is able to combine so many of the culture's central concerns in a narrative that is immediately accessible to the general population that she is able to move so many people so deeply. The novel's typological organization allows her to present political and social situations both as themselves and as transformations of a religious paradigm which interprets them in a way that readers can both understand and respond to emotionally. For the novel functions both as a means of describing the social world and as a means of changing it. It not only offers an interpretive framework for understanding the culture, and, through the reinforcement of a particular code of values, recommends a strategy for dealing with cultural conflict, but it is itself an agent of that strategy, putting into practice the measures it prescribes. As the religious stereotypes of "Sunday-school fiction" define and organize the elements of social and political life, so the "melodrama" and "pathos" associated with the underlying myth of crucifixion put the reader's heart in the right place with respect to the problems the narrative defines. Hence, rather than making the enduring success of *Uncle Tom's Cabin* inexplicable, these popular elements which puzzled Whicher and have puzzled so many modern scholars—melodrama, pathos, Sunday-school fiction—are the *only* terms in which the book's success can be explained.

The nature of these popular elements also dictates the terms in which any full-scale analysis of *Uncle Tom's Cabin* must be carried out. As I have suggested, its distinguishing features, generically speaking, are not those of the realistic novel, but of typological narrative. Its characters, like the figures in an allegory, do not change or develop, but reveal themselves in response to the demands of a situation. They are not defined primarily by their mental and emotional characteristics—that is to say, psychologically—but soteriologically, according to whether they are saved or damned. The plot, likewise, does not unfold according to Aristotelian standards of probability, but in keeping with the logic of a preordained design, a design which every incident is intended, in one way or another, to enforce.[16] The setting does not so much describe the features of a particular time and place as point to positions on a spiritual map. In *Uncle Tom's Cabin* the presence of realistic detail

tends to obscure its highly programmatic nature and to lull readers
into thinking that they are in an everyday world of material cause
and effect. But what pass for realistic details—the use of dialect,
the minute descriptions of domestic activity—are in fact performing a rhetorical function dictated by the novel's ruling paradigm;
once that paradigm is perceived, even the homeliest details show
up not as the empirically observed facts of human existence but
as the expressions of a highly schematic intent.[17]

This schematization has what one might call a totalizing effect
on the particulars of the narrative, so that every character in the
novel, every scene, and every incident, comes to be apprehended
in terms of every *other* character, scene, and incident: all are caught
up in a system of endless cross-references in which it is impossible
to refer to one without referring to all the rest. To demonstrate
what I mean by this kind of narrative organization—a demonstration which will have to stand in lieu of a full-scale reading of the
novel—let me show how it works in relation to a single scene. Eva
and Tom are seated in the garden of St. Clare's house on the
shores of Lake Pontchartrain.

> It was Sunday evening, and Eva's Bible lay open on her knee. She
> read,—"And I saw a sea of glass, mingled with fire."
> "Tom," said Eva, suddenly stopping, and pointing to the lake,
> "there 't is."
> "What, Miss Eva?"
> "Don't you see,—there?" said the child, pointing to the glassy
> water, which, as it rose and fell, reflected the golden glow of the sky.
> "There's a 'sea of glass, mingled with fire.' "
> "True enough, Miss Eva," said Tom; and Tom sang—
>
> > *"O, had I the wings of the morning,*
> > *I'd fly away to Canaan's shore;*
> > *Bright angels should convey me home,*
> > *To the new Jerusalem."*
>
> "Where do you suppose new Jerusalem is, Uncle Tom?" said Eva.
> "O, up in the clouds, Miss Eva."
> "Then I think I see it," said Eva. "Look in those clouds!—they
> look like great gates of pearl; and you can see beyond them—far, far
> off—it's all gold. Tom, sing about 'spirits bright.' "
> Tom sung the words of a well-known Methodist hymn,

> *"I see a band of spirits bright,*
> *That taste the glories there;*
> *They all are robed in spotless white,*
> *And conquering palms they bear."*

"Uncle Tom, I've seen *them*," said Eva. . . .

"They come to me sometimes in my sleep, those spirits;" and Eva's eyes grew dreamy, and she hummed, in a low voice,

"They are all robed in spotless white,
And conquering palms they bear."

"Uncle Tom," said Eva, "I'm going there."

"Where, Miss Eva?"

The child rose, and pointed her little hand to the sky; the glow of evening lit her golden hair and flushed cheek with a kind of unearthly radiance, and her eyes were bent earnestly on the skies.

"I'm going *there*," she said, "to the spirits bright, Tom; *I'm going, before long.*" (XXII, 303–307)

The iterative nature of this scene presents in miniature the structure of the whole novel. Eva reads from her Bible about a "sea of glass, mingled with fire," then looks up to find one before her. She reads the words aloud a second time. They remind Tom of a hymn which describes the same vision in a slightly different form (Lake Pontchartrain and the sea of glass become "Canaan's shore" and the "new Jerusalem") and Eva sees what he has sung, this time in the clouds, and offers her own description. Eva asks Tom to sing again and his hymn presents yet another form of the same vision, which Eva again says she has seen: the spirits bright come to her in her sleep. Finally, Eva repeats the last two lines of the hymn and declares that she is going "there"—to the place which has now been referred to a dozen times in this passage. Stowe follows with another description of the golden skies and then with a description of Eva as a spirit bright, and closes the passage with Eva's double reiteration that she is going "there."

The entire scene itself is a re-presentation of others that come before and after. When Eva looks out over Lake Pontchartrain, she sees the "Canaan of liberty" (VII, 70) Eliza saw on the other side of the Ohio River, and the "eternal shore" (XLIII, 499). Eliza and George Harris will reach when they cross Lake Erie in the end. Bodies of water mediate between worlds: the Ohio runs between the slave states and the free; Lake Erie divides the United States from Canada, where runaway slaves cannot be returned to their masters; the Atlantic Ocean divides the North American continent from Africa, where Negroes will have a nation of their own; Lake Pontchartrain shows Eva the heavenly home to which she is going soon; the Mississippi River carries slaves from the relative ease of the middle states to the grinding toil of the southern plantations; the Red River carries Tom to the infernal regions ruled over by Simon Legree. The correspondences between the episodes I have mentioned are themselves based on correspondences between earth and heaven (or hell). Ohio, Canada, and Liberia are related to one another by virtue of their relationship to the one "bright Canaan" for which they stand; the Mississippi River and the Ohio are linked by the Jordan. (Ultimately, there are only three places to be in this story: heaven, hell, or Kentucky, which represents the earthly middle ground in Stowe's geography.)

Characters in the novel are linked to each other in exactly the same way that places are—with reference to a third term that is the source of their identity. The figure of Christ is the common term which unites all of the novel's good characters, who are good precisely in proportion as they are imitations of him. Eva and Tom head the list (she reenacts the last supper and he the crucifixion), but they are also linked to most of the slaves, women, and children in the novel by the characteristics they all share: piety, impressionability, spontaneous affection—and victimization.[18] In this scene, Eva is linked with the "spirits bright" (she later becomes a "bright, immortal form," XXVII, 350) both because she can see them and is soon to join them, and because she, too, always wears white and is elsewhere several times referred to as an "angel." When Eva dies, she will join her father's mother, who was also named Evangeline, and who herself always wore white, and who, like Eva, is said to be "a direct embodiment and personification of the New Testament" (XIX, 263). And this identification, in its turn, refers back to Uncle Tom who is "all the moral and Christian virtues bound in black morocco, complete" (XIV, 179). The circularity of this train of association is typical of the way the narrative doubles back on itself: later on, Cassy, impersonating the ghost of Legree's saintly mother, will wrap herself in a white sheet.[19]

The scene I have been describing is a node within a network of allusion in which every character and event in the novel has a place. The narrative's rhetorical strength derives in part from the impression it gives of taking every kind of detail in the world into account, from the preparation of breakfast to the orders of the angels, and investing those details with a purpose and a meaning which are both immediately apprehensible and finally significant. The novel reaches out into the reader's world and colonizes it for its own eschatology: that is, it not only incorporates the homely particulars of "Life among the Lowly" into its universal scheme, but it gives them a power and a centrality in that scheme, thereby turning the socio-political order upside down. The totalizing effect of the novel's iterative organization and its doctrine of spiritual redemption are inseparably bound to its political purpose: to bring in the day when the meek—which is to say, women—will inherit the earth.

The specifically political intent of the novel is apparent in its forms of address. Stowe addresses her readers not simply as individuals but as citizens of the United States: "to you, generous, noble-minded men and women, of the South," (XLV, 513) "farmers of Massachusetts, of New Hampshire, of Vermont," "brave and generous men of New York," "and you, mothers of America" (XLV, 514). She speaks to her audience directly in the way the Old Testament prophets spoke to Israel, exhorting, praising, blaming, warning of the wrath to come. "This is an age of the world when nations are trembling and convulsed. A mighty influence is abroad, surging and heaving the world, as with an earthquake. And is America safe? . . . O, Church of Christ, read the signs of the times!" (XLV, 519). Passages like these, descended from the revivalist rhetoric of "Sinners in the Hands of an Angry God," are intended, in the words of a noted scholar, "to direct an imperiled people toward the fulfillment of their destiny, to guide them individually towards salvation, and collectively toward the American city of God."[20]

These words are from Sacvan Bercovitch's *The American Jeremiad*, an influential work of modern scholarship which, although it completely ignores Stowe's novel, makes us aware that *Uncle Tom's Cabin* is a jeremiad in the fullest and truest sense. A jeremiad, in Bercovitch's definition, is "a mode of public exhortation . . . designed to join social criticism to spiritual renewal, public to private identity, the shifting 'signs of the times' to certain traditional metaphors, themes, and symbols."[21] Stowe's novel provides the most obvious and compelling instance of the jeremiad since the Great Awakening, and its exclusion from Bercovitch's book is a striking instance of how totally academic criticism has foreclosed on sentimental fiction; for, because *Uncle Tom's Cabin* is absent from the canon, it isn't "there" to be referred to even when it fulfills a man's theory to perfection. Hence its exclusion from critical discourse is perpetuated automatically, and absence begets itself in a self-confirming cycle of neglect. Nonetheless, Bercovitch's characterization of the jeremiad provides an excellent account of how *Uncle Tom's Cabin* actually worked: among its characters, settings, situations, symbols, and doctrines, the novel establishes a set of correspondences which unite the disparate realms of experience Bercovitch names—social and spiritual, public and private, theological and political—*and*, through the vigor of its representations, attempts to move the nation as a whole toward the vision it proclaims.

The tradition of the jeremiad throws light on *Uncle Tom's Cabin* because Stowe's novel was political in exactly the same way the jeremiad was: both were forms of discourse in which "theology was wedded to politics and politics to the progress of the kingdom of God."[22] The jeremiad strives to persuade its listeners to a providential view of human history which serves, among other things, to maintain the Puritan theocracy in power. Its fusion of theology and politics is not only doctrinal—in that it ties the salvation of the individual to the community's historical enterprise—it is practical as well, for it reflects the interests of Puritan ministers in their bid to retain spiritual and secular authority. The sentimental novel, too, is an act of persuasion aimed at defining social reality; the difference is that the jeremiad represents the interests of Puritan ministers, while the sentimental novel represents the interests of middle-class women. But the relationship between rhetoric and history in both cases is the same. In both cases it is not as if rhetoric and history stand opposed, with rhetoric made up of wish fulfillment and history made up of recalcitrant facts that resist rhetoric's onslaught. Rhetoric *makes* history by shaping reality to the dictates of its political design; it makes history by convincing the people of the world that its description of the world is the true one. The sentimental novelists make their bid for power by positing the kingdom of heaven on earth as a world over which women exercise ultimate control. If history did not take the course these writers recommended, it is not because they were not political, but because they were insufficiently persuasive.

Uncle Tom's Cabin, however, unlike its counterparts in the sentimental tradition, was spectacularly persuasive in conventional political terms: it helped convince a nation to go to war and to free its slaves. But in terms of its own conception of power, a conception it shares with other sentimental fiction, the novel was a political failure. Stowe conceived her book as an instrument for bringing about the day when the world would be ruled not by force, but by Christian love. The novel's deepest political aspirations are expressed only secondarily in its devastating attack on the slave system; the true goal of Stowe's rhetorical undertaking is nothing less than the institution of the kingdom of heaven on earth. Embedded in the world of *Uncle Tom's Cabin*, which is the fallen world of slavery, there appears an idyllic picture, both utopian and Arcadian, of the form human life would assume if Stowe's readers were to heed her moral lesson. In this vision, described in the chapter entitled "The Quaker Settlement," Christian love fulfills itself not in war, but in daily living, and the principle of sacrifice is revealed not in crucifixion, but in motherhood. The form that Stowe's utopian society takes bears no resemblance to the current social order. Man-made institutions—the church, the courts of law, the legislatures, the economic system—are nowhere in sight. The home is the center of all meaningful activity; women perform the most important tasks; work is carried on in a spirit of mutual cooperation; and the whole is guided by a Christian woman who, through the influence of her "loving words," "gentle moralities," and "motherly loving kindness," rules the world from her rocking-chair.

> For why? for twenty years or more, nothing but loving words, and gentle moralities, and motherly loving kindness, had come from that chair;—head-aches and heart-aches innumerable had been cured there,—difficulties spiritual and temporal solved there,—all by one good, loving woman, God bless her! (XIII, 163)

The woman in question *is* God in human form. Seated in her kitchen at the head of her table, passing out coffee and cake for breakfast, Rachel Halliday, the millenarian counterpart of little Eva, enacts the redeemed form of the last supper. This is holy communion as it will be under the new dispensation: instead of the breaking of bones, the breaking of bread. The preparation of breakfast exemplifies the way people will work in the ideal society; there will be no competition, no exploitation, no commands. Motivated by self-sacrificing love, and joined to one another by its cohesive power, people will perform their duties willingly and with pleasure: moral suasion will take the place of force.

> All moved obediently to Rachel's gentle "Thee had better," or more gentle "Hadn't thee better?" in the work of getting breakfast. . . . Everything went on so sociably, so quietly, so harmoniously, in the great kitchen,—it seemed so pleasant to every one to do just what they were doing, there was such an atmosphere of mutual confidence and good fellowship everywhere. . . . (XIII, 169–170)

The new matriarchy which Isabella Beecher Hooker had dreamed of leading, pictured here in the Indiana kitchen ("for a breakfast in the luxurious valleys of Indiana is . . . like picking up the rose-leaves and trimming the bushes in Paradise," [XIII, 169]), constitutes the most politically subversive dimension of Stowe's novel, more disruptive and far-reaching in its potential consequences than even the starting of a war or the freeing of slaves. Nor is the ideal of matriarchy simply a daydream; Catherine Beecher, Stowe's elder sister, had offered a ground plan for the realization of such a vision in her *Treatise on Domestic Economy* (1841), which the two sisters republished in an enlarged version entitled *The American Woman's Home* in 1869.[23] Dedicated "To the Women of America, in whose hands rest the real destinies of the republic," this is an instructional book on homemaking in which a wealth of scientific information and practical advice are pointed toward a millenarian goal. Centering on the home, for these women, is not a way of indulging in narcissistic fantasy, as critics have argued,[24] or a turning away from the world into self-absorption and idle reverie; it is the prerequisite of world conquest—defined as the reformation of the human race through proper care and nurturing of its young. Like *Uncle Tom's Cabin, The American Woman's Home* situates the minutiae of domestic life in relation to their soteriological function: "What, then, is the end designed by the family state which Jesus Christ came into this world to secure? It is to provide for the training of our race . . . by means of the self-sacrificing labors of the wise and good . . . with chief reference to a future immortal existence."[25] "The family state," the authors announce at the beginning, "is the aptest earthly illustration of the heavenly kingdom, and . . . woman is its chief minister."[26] In the body of the text, the authors provide women with everything they need to know for the proper establishment and maintenance of home and family, from the construction of furniture ("The [bed] frame is to be fourteen inches from the floor . . . and three inches in thickness. At the head, and at the foot, is to be screwed a notched two-inch board, three inches wide, as in Fig. 8," [30]), to architectural plans, to chapters of instruction on heating, ventilation, lighting, healthful diet, preparation of food, cleanliness, the making and mending of clothes, the care of the sick, the organization of routines, financial management, psychological health, the care of infants, the managing of young children, home amusement, the care of furniture, planting of gardens, the care of domestic animals, the disposal of waste, the cultivation of fruit, and providing for the "Homeless, the Helpless, and the Vicious" (433). After each of these activities has been treated in detail, they conclude by describing the ultimate aim of

Are women trying to take power?
Or buying into male dominant public sphere thing

the domestic enterprise. The founding of a "truly 'Christian family' " will lead to the gathering of a "Christian neighborhood." This "cheering example," they continue,

> would soon spread, and ere long colonies from these prosperous and Christian communities would go forth to shine as "lights of the world" in all the now darkened nations. Thus the "Christian family" and "Christian neighborhood" would become the grand ministry, as they were designed to be, in training our whole race for heaven.[27]

The imperialistic drive behind the encyclopedism and determined practicality of this household manual flatly contradicts the traditional derogations of the American cult of domesticity as a "mirror-phenomenon," "self-immersed" and "self-congratulatory."[28] *The American Woman's Home* is a blueprint for colonizing the world in the name of the "family state" (19) under the leadership of Christian women. What is more, people like Stowe and Catherine Beecher were speaking not simply for a set of moral and religious values. In speaking for the home, they speak for an economy—a household economy—which had supported New England life since its inception. The home, rather than representing a retreat or a refuge from a crass industrial-commercial world, offers an economic *alternative* to that world, one which calls into question the whole structure of American society which was growing up in response to the increase in trade and manufacturing.[29] Stowe's image of a utopian community as presented in Rachel Halliday's kitchen is not simply a Christian dream of communitarian cooperation and harmony; it is a reflection of the real communitarian practices of village life, practices which depended upon cooperation, trust, and a spirit of mutual supportiveness which characterize the Quaker community of Stowe's novel.

One could argue, then, that for all its revolutionary fervor, *Uncle Tom's Cabin* is a conservative book, because it advocates a return to an older way of life—household economy—in the name of the nation's most cherished social and religious beliefs. Even the emphasis on the woman's centrality might be seen as harking back

to the "age of homespun" when the essential goods were manufactured in the home and their production was carried out and
guided by women. But Stowe's very conservatism—her reliance
on established patterns of living and traditional beliefs—is precisely
what gives her novel its revolutionary potential. By pushing those
beliefs to an extreme and by insisting that they be applied universally, not just to one segregated corner of civil life, but to the
conduct of all human affairs, Stowe means to effect a radical transformation of her society. The brilliance of the strategy is that it
puts the central affirmations of a culture into the service of a vision
that would destroy the present economic and social institutions;
by resting her case, absolutely, on the saving power of Christian
love and on the sanctity of motherhood and the family, Stowe
relocates the center of power in American life, placing it not in
the government, nor in the courts of law, nor in the factories, nor
in the marketplace, but in the kitchen. And that means that the
new society will not be controlled by men, but by women. The
image of the home created by Stowe and Beecher in their treatise
on domestic science is in no sense a shelter from the stormy blast
of economic and political life, a haven from reality divorced from
fact which allows the machinery of industrial capitalism to grind
on; it is conceived as a dynamic center of activity, physical and
spiritual, economic and moral, whose influence spreads out in ever-
widening circles. To this activity—and this is the crucial innovation—men are incidental. Although the Beecher sisters pay lip
service on occasion to male supremacy, women's roles occupy
virtually the whole of their attention and dominate the scene. Male
provender is deemphasized in favor of female processing. Men
provide the seed, but women bear and raise the children. Men
provide the flour, but women bake the bread and get the breakfast.
The removal of the male from the center to the periphery of the
human sphere is the most radical component of this millenarian
scheme, which is rooted so solidly in the most traditional values—
religion, motherhood, home, and family. Exactly what position
men will occupy in the millennium is specified by a detail inserted
casually into Stowe's description of the Indiana kitchen. While the
women and children are busy preparing breakfast, Simeon Halli-

day, the husband and father, stands "in his shirt-sleeves before a little looking-glass in the corner, engaged in the anti-patriarchal operation of shaving" (XIII, 169).

With this detail, so innocently placed, Stowe reconceives the role of men in human history: while Negroes, children, mothers, and grandmothers do the world's primary work, men groom themselves contentedly in a corner. The scene, as critics have noted is often the case in sentimental fiction, is "intimate," the backdrop is "domestic," the tone at times is even "chatty";[30] but the import, as critics have failed to recognize, is world-shaking. The enterprise of sentimental fiction, as Stowe's novel attests, is anything but domestic, in the sense of being limited to purely personal concerns. Its mission, on the contrary, is global and its interests identical with the interests of the race. If the fiction written in the nineteenth century by women whose works sold in the hundreds of thousands has seemed narrow and parochial to the critics of the twentieth century, that narrowness and parochialism belong not to these works nor to the women who wrote them; they are the beholders' share.[31]

VI

The Other
American Renaissance

If the tradition of American criticism has not acknowledged the value of *Uncle Tom's Cabin*, it has paid even less attention to the work of Stowe's contemporaries among the sentimental writers. Although these women wrote from the same perspective that made *Uncle Tom's Cabin* so successful, and although in the nineteenth century their works were almost equally well-known, their names have been entirely forgotten. The writer I am concerned with in particular is Susan Warner, who was born in the same year as Herman Melville, and whose best-selling novel, *The Wide, Wide World*, was published in the same twelve-month period as *Moby Dick*. But I am not interested in Warner's novel for the light it can shed on Melville;[1] I am interested in it because it represents, in its purest form, an entire body of work that this century's critical tradition has ignored.

According to that tradition, the "great" figures of the 1850s, a period known to us now as the "American Renaissance," were a handful of men who refused to be taken in by the pieties of the age. Disgusted by the clichés that poured from the pens of the "scribbling women," these men bore witness to a darker reality, which the mass of readers could not face. While successful female authors told tearful stories about orphan girls whose Christian virtue triumphed against all odds, the truly great writers—Poe, Hawthorne, Melville, Emerson, Thoreau—dared, according to Henry Nash Smith, to "explore the dark underside of the psyche," and to tackle "ultimate social and intellectual issues." And because they repudiated the culture's dominant value system, they were, in Perry Miller's words, "crushed by the juggernaut" of the popular sentimental novel.[2] The sentimental writers, on the other hand, were sadly out of touch with reality. What they produced, says Smith, was a literature of "reassurance," calculated to soothe the anxieties of an economically troubled age. To the "Common Man and Common Woman," fearful of challenge or change, they preached a "cosmic success story," which promised that the practice of virtue would lead to material success. Their subject matter—the tribulations of orphan girls—was innately trivial; their religious ideas were "little more than a blur of good intentions"; they "feared the probing of the inner life"; and above all were committed to avoiding anything that might make the "undiscriminating mass" of their middlebrow readers "uncomfortable."[3]

What about Ellen's Mom.

Those judgments are, in fact, amplified versions of what Hawthorne and Melville said about their sentimental rivals, whom they hated for their popular and critical success. My purpose here is to challenge that description of sentimental novels and to argue that their exclusion from the canon of American literature has been a mistake. For its seems to me that, instead of accepting uncritically the picture Hawthorne and Melville painted—of themselves as victims, of the sentimental novelists as negligible, and of the general public as, in Hawthorne's words, "that great gull, whom we are endeavoring to circumvent"—modern scholars ought to pay attention to a body of work which was so enormously influential and which drew so vehement a response from those who—successfully as it turned out—strove to suppress it.

The publication of Susan Warner's *The Wide, Wide World* in December of 1850, caused an explosion in the literary marketplace that was absolutely unprecedented—nothing like it, in terms of sales, had ever been seen before. Fifteen months later, *Uncle Tom's Cabin*, whose fame is still legendary, broke the records Warner's novel had set. Two years later, Maria Cummins' *The Lamplighter*—the direct literary descendant of *The Wide, Wide World*, and the novel that earned Hawthorne's special contempt—made another tremendous hit.[4] Critics have been at a loss to explain the enormous and long-standing popularity of these books, and one critic, who has devoted an entire study to the influence of popular fiction on classical American writing, dismisses the phenomenon, saying "it is impossible now to determine just what did happen to the market in the early 1850's."[5]

But it is not impossible to determine. The impact of sentimental novels is directly related to the cultural context that produced them. And once one begins to explore this context in even a preliminary way, the critical practice that assigns Hawthorne and Melville the role of heroes, the sentimental novelists the role of villains, and the public the role of their willing dupes, loses its credibility. The one great fact of American life during the period under consideration was, in Perry Miller's words, the "terrific universality" of the revival.[6] Sentimental fiction was perhaps the most influential expression of the beliefs that animated the revival movement and had shaped the character of American life in the years before the Civil War. Antebellum critics and readers did not distinguish sharply between fiction and what we would now call religious propaganda. Warner, for instance, never referred to her books as "novels," but called them stories, because, in her eyes, they functioned in the same way as Biblical parables, or the pamphlets published by the American Tract Society; that is, they were written for edification's sake and not for the sake of art, as we understand it. The highest function of any art, for Warner as for most of her contemporaries, was the bringing of souls to Christ. Like their counterparts among the evangelical clergy, the sentimental novelists wrote to educate their readers in Christian perfection and to move the nation as a whole closer to the city of God. They saw their work as part of a world-historical mission; but in order to understand the nature of their project, one has to have some familiarity with the cultural discourse of the age for which they spoke.[7]

The best place to begin is with a set of documents that, as far as I know, have never made their way into criticism of American Renaissance literature: the publications of the American Tract Society, one of the five great religious organizations of the Evangelical United Front.[8] These organizations were a concrete mobilization of wealth, energy, and missionary fervor designed to convert the entire nation and eventually the entire world to the truths of Protestant Christianity. That monumental effort, though it failed in its original purpose, did provide the nation with that "sameness of views" that, as Lyman Beecher, one of the movement's chief initiators, observed, was essential to the welfare of a nation torn apart by sectional strife.[9] The literature of the American Tract Society, the first organization in America to publish and distribute the printed word on a mass scale, is a testament both to the faith of evangelical Christians—to the shape of their dreams— and to what they experienced as everyday reality. It is only by attempting to see reality as they did that one can arrive at a notion of what gave sentimental fiction its tremendous original force.

I. THE CLOSET

The conception of reality on which the reform movement was based is nowhere more dramatically illustrated than in the activities of the New York City Tract Society which, in 1829, undertook a massive experiment in what we would now call social welfare. The Society divided the city's fourteen wards into districts of about sixty families each and appointed teams of its members to visit every family in each district once a month.[10] The Tract Visiters, as they were called, ministered to the poor in a material way, helping them to find jobs and better homes; but this was not their primary purpose. Their major business was distributing Bibles and religious tracts, organizing prayer meetings, urging church attendance, and talking to people about the state of their souls. The Tract Visiters believed that the only real help one could offer another person, rich or poor, was not material, but spiritual, and the directions that guided them in their work insisted on this: "Be much in prayer," the directions said. "Endeavor to feel habitually and deeply that all your efforts will be in vain unless accompanied by the Holy Ghost. And this blessing you can expect only in answer to prayer. Pray, therefore, without ceasing. Go from your closet to your work and from your work return again to the closet."[11]

If one can understand what made these directions meaningful and effective for the people who carried them out, one is in a position to understand the power of sentimental fiction. For all sentimental novels take place, metaphorically and literally, in the "closet." Sentimental heroines rarely get beyond the confines of a private space—the

kitchen, the parlor, the upstairs chamber—but more important, most
Is this really true of Ellen?
of what they do takes place inside the "closet" of the heart. For what
the word *sentimental* really means in this context is that the arena of
human action, as in the Tract Society directions, has been defined
not as the world, but as the human soul. This fiction shares with the
evangelical reform movement a theory of power that stipulates that
all true action is not material, but spiritual; that one obtains spiritual
power through prayer; and that those who know how, in the privacy
of their closets, to struggle for possession of their souls will one day
possess the world through the power given to them by God. This
theory of power makes itself felt, in the mid-nineteenth century, not
simply in the explicit assertions of religious propaganda, nor in personal declarations of faith, but as a principle of interpretation that
gives form to experience itself, as the records the Tract Visiters left
of their activities show.

The same beliefs that make the directions to Tract Visiters intelligible structured what the Visiters saw as they went about their
work. In one Tract Society report the Visiter records that a young
woman who was dying of pulmonary consumption became concerned at the eleventh hour about the condition of her soul and
asked for spiritual help. The report reads:

> She was found by the Visiter supplied with a number of tracts, and
> kindly directed to the Saviour of sinners. Some of her relatives—they
> cannot be called friends—attempted to impede the visiter's way to
> her bedside, and would often present hinderances which she could
> not remove. God, however, showed himself strong in her behalf.
> . . . For some time clouds hung over her mind, but they were at
> length dispelled by the sun of righteousness. . . . As she approached
> the hour which tries men's souls, her strength failed fast; her friends
> gathered around her; . . . and while they were engaged in a hymn
> her soul seemed to impart unnatural energy to her emaciated and
> dying body. To the astonishment of all, she said to her widowed
> mother, who bent anxiously over her, "Don't weep for me, I shall
> soon be in the arms of my Saviour." She prayed fervently, and fell
> asleep in Jesus.[12]

Like all the fiction we label "sentimental," this narrative blots
out the uglier details of life and cuts experience to fit a pattern of

pious expectation. The anecdote tells nothing about the personality or background of the young woman, fails to represent even the barest facts of her disease or of her immediate surroundings. For these facts, the report substitutes the panaceas of Christian piety— God's mercy on a miserable sinner, the tears and prayers of a deathbed conversion, falling "asleep" in Jesus. Its plot follows a prescribed course from sin to salvation. But what is extraordinary about this anecdote is that it is not a work of fiction, but a factual report. Though its facts do not correspond to what a twentieth-century observer would have recorded, had he or she been at the scene, they faithfully represent what the Tract Society member saw. Whereas a modern social worker would have noticed the furniture of the sick room, the kind of house the woman lived in, her neighborhood, would have described her illness, its history and course of treatment, and sketched in her socio-economic background and that of her relatives and friends, the Tract Visiter sees only a spiritual predicament: the woman's initial "alarm," the "clouds [that] hung over her mind," God's action on her heart, the turn from sin to righteousness. Whereas the modern observer would have structured the events in a downward spiral, as the woman's condition deteriorated from serious to critical, and ended with her death, the report reverses that progression. Its movement is upward, from "thoughtlessness" to "conviction," to "great tranquility, joy, and triumph."[13]

The charge twentieth-century critics have always leveled against sentimental fiction is that it presents a picture of life so oversimplified and improbable, that only the most naive and self-deceiving reader could believe it. But the sense of the real that this criticism takes for granted is not the one that the readers of sentimental novels had. *Their* assumptions are the same as those that structured the events of the report I have just quoted. For what I've been speaking about involves three distinct levels of apprehension: "reality itself" as it appears to people at a given time; what people will accept as an "accurate description" of reality; and novels and stories that, because they seem faithful to such descriptions, therefore seem true. The audience for whom the thoughtless young lady's conversion was a moving factual report, found the tears and prayers of sentimental heroines equally compelling. This is not because they didn't know what good fiction was, nor because their notions about human life were naive and superficial, but because the "order of things" to which both readers and fictions belonged was itself structured by such narratives.

The story of the young woman's death from pulmonary consumption is exactly analogous to the kind of exemplary tale that had formed the consciousness of the nation in the early years of the nineteenth century. Such stories filled the religious publications distributed in unimaginably large quantities by organizations like those of the Evangelical United Front. The American Tract Society alone claims to have published thirty-seven million tracts at a time when the entire population of the country was only eleven million. And the same kind of exemplary narrative was the staple of the McGuffey's readers and primers of a similar type on which virtually the entire nation had been schooled. They appeared in manuals of social behavior, and in instructional literature of every variety, filled the pages of popular magazines, and appeared even in the daily newspapers. As David Reynolds has recently demonstrated, the entire practice of pulpit oratory in this period shifted from an expository and abstract mode of explicating religious doctrine, to a mode in which sensational narratives carried the burden of theological precept.[14] These stories were always didactic in nature— illustrating the importance of a particular virtue such as obedience, faith, sobriety, or patience—and they were usually sensational in content—the boy who plays hooky from school falls into a pond and drowns, the starving widow is saved at the last moment by a handsome stranger who turns out to be her son. But their sensationalism ultimately lies not so much in the dramatic nature of the events they describe as in the assumptions they make about the relation of human events to the spiritual realities that make them meaningful. One of their lessons is that all experience is sensational, when seen in the light of its soteriological consequences: the saving or damning of the soul. In their assumptions about the nature and the purpose of human life, these stories provided a fundamental framework for the ordering of experience. The following typical account of a sick child's conversion provides some sense of how that interpretive system worked.

"Ann Eliza Williams, or the Child an Hundred Years Old, an Authentic Narrative" by the Reverend William S. Plumer, D.D. (New York: American Tract Society, n.d.) records that a young girl of "exquisite nervous sensibility" and "an irascible, obstinate, and ungovernable temper" had become concerned about her soul after two attacks of tuberculosis. During the second attack, she is converted, joins the church, and from that time on becomes a model of Christian deportment. On one particular occasion, the sick child is asked by her doctor and pastor how she feels. But instead of reporting her physical sensations, she "seems to forget all her bodily pain" and gives an answer that ignores the question: "O Jesus is precious, I am happy in him; his favor is life and his loving kindness is better than life."[15] Far from ignoring the question, however, Ann Eliza implicitly rebukes her questioners by putting their question into its proper perspective. Her words can be paraphrased as follows: "My physical condition is not important; what matters is my soul, for that alone is immortal. And since Jesus by his death has redeemed my soul, I am happy because of him." This theological answer seems to deny the practical realities of Ann Eliza's situation—her sickness, her pain, her possible death—but in fact it deals with those realities directly by pointing to the means of overcoming them. The thought of Jesus' love transforms her experience, makes her happy, drives away her pain. Her recognition that God's love is the final fact of existence transforms Ann Eliza's situation: what she experiences now is not pain, but the knowledge of her salvation. And therefore when someone asks her how she feels, "O Jesus is precious" is not a pious evasion, but a truthful reply.

It is extremely difficult for modern readers to hold on to the perspective that makes Ann Eliza's answer seem true, both because its theological assumptions are different from ours and because those assumptions carry with them a correspondingly alien rhetoric. In the twentieth century, materialist notions about the ultimate nature of reality and faith in the validity of scientific method have given rise to strategies of persuasion that require institutionally certified investigators to argue in a technical vocabulary for conclusions based on independently verifiable evidence, gathered according to professionally sanctioned methods of inquiry. (The metaphysical assumptions behind this mode of argumentation are no less powerful for being unstated.) In the same way, a belief that reality is ultimately spiritual, and a conception of Jesus as a personal savior with whom one has a loving and intimate relationship, gave rise in the early nineteenth century to a rhetoric in which an individual (such as the Reverend Plumer) testifies in impassioned language to miraculous or sensational events bearing witness to the truths of religious faith. In this rhetorical tradition, a single representative case, strikingly presented, constitutes the most effective form of evidence because that is the form which the audience *expects* such demonstrations to take. The force of the demonstration, moreover, depends upon the miraculousness of the events it describes, not on their probability—as the subtitle "or the Child an Hundred Years Old" suggests—since the point of the story is to affirm the existence of supernatural powers by pointing to God's intervention in human affairs, and not to chart the course of natural, unregenerate behavior. There is no need, either, for independent verification of the evidence, because supernatural events, by definition, cannot be repeated experimentally. Other "authentic" cases just like this one—of which the tract literature is full—would be the best kind of auxiliary verification. The Reverend Plumer's credentials, moreover, are superb. He is a Christian minister and a doctor of divinity, and therefore can be presumed to have special insight into phenomena of the kind he relates, and he is vouched for by the prestigious American Tract Society, a bastion of the country's religious (and socio-economic) establishment. Finally, the language of his narration gives palpable proof of the spiritual realities he bears witness to, not because it is neutral and detached, but because it is so obviously the product of intense feeling. When the presence of the Holy Ghost is what is in question, spontaneous eloquence, Biblical and oracular in style, is the most persuasive form of rhetoric.

In short, the conditions within which Ann Eliza's story is heard as convincing are just as culturally determined as those that shape its theology. The same network of assumptions that supported the religious beliefs of evangelical Christians shaped their rhetorical and stylistic conventions as well. For a text depends upon its audience's beliefs not just in a gross general way, but intricately and precisely. It depends, to borrow a term from ethnomethodology, upon "the fine power of a culture," which "does not, so to speak, merely fill brains in roughly the same way, but fills them so that they are alike in fine detail."[16] And this means that the cultural conventions that make a narrative convincing inform not only the perception of nonmaterial concerns such as the existence of God or the shape of an argument, they also inform perception of the ordinary facts of existence.

The records people left of their lives in antebellum America suggest that the modes of thought underlying the Tract Society directions and the story of Ann Eliza Williams pervaded people's perceptions of their everyday affairs. The letters they wrote to one another, the diaries they kept, the way they thought about their work, their homes, and their families, reflect the same sense of millenarian purpose that drove the reform movement and inspired writers like Warner and Stowe. The Protestant-Republican ideology, which identified the spreading of the Gospel with the building of a nation, did not distinguish clearly if at all between activities that had a practical aim—such as the straightening of a room, the building of a school, or the starting of a business—and activities that were specifically spiritual—like reading the Bible or attending prayer meetings. The welfare of the nation, conceived in millenarian terms as the bringing of God's kingdom to earth, depended upon the virtue of the individual citizen; any task, no matter how small, could be seen as either helping or hindering the establishment of Christ's kingdom. As John Thompson declared in addressing the American Home Missionary Society's twenty-second annual meeting:

> no nation can either prosper or last without popular virtue— . . . the virtue of the Bible, in all its purity and life, and generous conviction! Religion, Protestant religion, is our great national want, as it is our greatest national security. . . . Our power lies in no gleaming spear,

or gloating admirals; . . . it dwells in the workshops, the manufac-
tories, in the open fields, by the firesides, in the homes and haunts
of our widespread population; and this virtue comes not of nature;
it is a foreign element and must first be implanted.[17]

The implantation of virtue was the primary goal of nearly everything nineteenth-century Americans read: textbooks, novels, poems,
magazine stories, or religious tracts. As David Tyack and Elisabeth
Hansot have recently argued, the entire educational system in this
country was founded on the premise that a democratic republic
depended on the Christian character of its citizens; the men who
built the nation's common schools saw themselves as doing the
Lord's work.[18] When the coming of God's kingdom depended on
the private virtue of every citizen, even deciding when to get up
in the morning, or what time to eat dinner had consequences that
no Christian could afford to overlook. For example, in this time
schedule printed in a child-rearing manual entitled *Thoughts on
Domestic Education, The Result of Experience* by a "Mother,"
the sense of an overriding purpose entwines itself with the
minute-by-minute organization of a young lady's typical
day.

SCHEME
for the distribution of time.

Hours		o'Clock
	To rise, all the year round	—7 A.M.
1	Dressing, washing, bathing	—8
1	Prayer and study	—9
1	Breakfast and conversation	—10
4	Studious occupation	—2 P.M.
2	Walking, riding, or dancing	—4
1	Light reading or drawing	—5
1	Dinner	—6
2	Music, needlework, or reading	—8
1	Tea and conversation	—9
1	Dancing, music, needlework, or reading	—10
	To be in bed by	—11
8	Sleep	—7 A.M.

The last question before going to sleep: What good have I
done today?[19]

The question that ends the day is the key to understanding what the time schedule is for. So that the young lady will never be at a loss as to how to answer it, the Mother appends a table of virtues to her volume, starting with "Obedience," and including others such as "Humility" and "Industry," which the young lady can check off according to whether or not she has performed them. The organization of time into regular blocks of activity, beginning with prayer and ending with a checklist of virtues, provides a miniature example of how people in the antebellum era thought about their daily lives, and indeed about the whole of life. The cultivation of social skills like conversation, and of artistic accomplishments like drawing and needlework, the pursuit of "studious occupation" and of physical fitness through "walking, riding, or dancing" were conceived not as ends in themselves, but as part of the practice of virtue which had to be learned through conscious self-discipline. One had a "scheme" for the distribution of time the better to serve God and one's fellow man. The time schedule and the checklist of virtues were ways of building Christian character, the foundation stone of a democratic republic.[20] And this sort of instructional material was not merely theoretical in its consequences; people did not simply *talk* about virtue, they lived it. Just as whole families in the slums of New York wept and asked to be instructed in the Scriptures when they heard Visiters read aloud the story of "Bob, the Cabin Boy," so young ladies really did organize their days according to the principles the Mother recommended.[21] The best example I have found of how totally the evangelical movement had saturated American culture is this time schedule found in the pocket of a girl's dress. Mrs. Lydia Sigourney reprints it in her biography of Margaret Flower, who died in Hartford, Connecticut, in 1834, at the age of fourteen.

> Rise at half past five. Take care of the rooms. Sew until two hours from that time. Practice my piano one hour, then study one hour. Work till three in the afternoon, then practice an hour, and study an hour, reserving time for exercise.[22]

Margaret Flower's schedule (composed, as Sigourney notes, when she was *on vacation*) shows that directions such as those that the Mother offered her readers, and which the Tract Society distributed to its members, really worked. They had traction because the readers they addressed already understood life according to the principles that these directions are attempting to inculcate. Margaret Flower follows the instructions she finds in a manual because she already wishes to make herself into a more effective agent of God's will. The didactic literature of the antebellum era was not an abstract set of standards designed to *force* life into a predetermined shape; rather, it helped its original audience to put into practice the aims they already had at heart.[23] As Robert Wiebe observed, the leaders of the reform movement "believed that they spoke *for* the nation rather than to it"; assuming that their audience "shared the same ethical system, the same dedication to public service," they attempted "not to convince people but simply to rouse them."[24] For Margaret Flower, as for the author of *Thoughts on Domestic Education*, taking care of the rooms, practicing an hour, then studying an hour were activities that had to be regulated because they were understood in the light of a great purpose: the saving of one's soul and the bringing of all souls to Christ.

When you turn from the tract society reports, religious narratives, educational manuals, and autobiographical documents to the fiction of writers like Stowe and Warner, you find the same assumptions at work. Those novels are motivated by the same millennial commitment; they are hortatory and instructional in the same way; they tell the same kinds of stories; they depend upon the same rhetorical conventions; and they take for granted the same relationship between daily activities and the forging of a redeemer nation. When critics dismiss sentimental fiction because it is out of touch with reality, they do so because the reality *they* perceive is organized according to a different set of conventions for constituting experience. For while the attack on sentimental fiction claims for itself freedom from the distorting effects of a naive religious perspective, the real naiveté is to think that that attack is launched from no perspective whatsoever, or that its perspective is disinterested and not culture-bound in the way the sentimental novelists were. The popular fiction of the American Renaissance has been dismissed primarily because it follows from assumptions about the shape and meaning of existence that we no longer hold. But once one has a grasp of the problems these writers were trying to solve, their solutions do not seem hypocritical or shallow, unrealistic or naive; on the contrary, given the social circumstances within which they had to work, their prescriptions for living seem at least as heroic as those put forward by the writers who said, "No, in thunder."

II. POWER

If the general charge against sentimental fiction has been that it is divorced from actual human experience, a more specific form of that charge is that these novels fail to deal with the brute facts of political and economic oppression, and therefore cut themselves off from the possibility of truly affecting the lives of their readers. Tremaine McDowell, writing in *The Literary History of the United States*, dismisses Mrs. Lydia Sigourney—who epitomizes the sentimental tradition for modern critics—by saying that while she "knew something of the humanitarian movements of the day, all . . . she did for Negroes, Indians, the poor, and the insane was to embalm them in her tears."[25] Such cutting remarks are never made about canonical authors of the period, though they, too, did nothing for "Negroes, Indians, the poor," and wrote about them considerably less than their female rivals. But what this sort of commentary reveals, beyond an automatic prejudice against sentimental writers, is its own failure to perceive that the great subject of sentimental fiction is preeminently a social issue. It is no exaggeration to say that domestic fiction is preoccupied, even obsessed, with the nature of power. Because they lived in a society that celebrated free enterprise and democratic government but were excluded from participating in either, the two questions these female novelists never fail to ask are: what is power, and where is it located? Since they could neither own property, nor vote, nor speak at a public meeting if both sexes were present, women had to have a way of defining themselves which gave them power and status nevertheless, in their own eyes and in the eyes of the world.[26] That is the problem sentimental fiction addresses.

In his characterization of American women, Tocqueville accurately described the solution to this problem as it appeared to an outsider. He noted that the interests of a "Puritanical" and "trading" nation lead Americans to require "much abnegation on the part of women, and a constant sacrifice of her pleasures to her duties." But, he continues, "I never observed that the women of America consider conjugal authority as a usurpation of their rights. . . . It appeared to me, on the contrary, that they attach a sort of pride to the voluntary surrender of their own will and make their boast to bend themselves to the yoke, not to shake it off."[27] The ethic of sentimental fiction, unlike that of writers like Melville, Emerson, and Thoreau, was an ethic of submission. But the relation of sentimental authors to their subservient condition and to the dominant beliefs about the nature and function of women was more complicated than Tocqueville supposed. The fact is that American women simply could not assume a stance of open rebellion against the conditions of their lives for they lacked the material means of escape or opposition. They had to stay put and submit. And so the domestic novelists made that necessity the basis on which to build a power structure of their own. Instead of rejecting the culture's value system outright, they appropriated it for their own use, subjecting the beliefs and customs that had molded them to a series of transformations that allowed them both to fulfill and transcend their appointed roles.

The process of transformation gets underway immediately in Warner's novel when the heroine, Ellen Montgomery, a child of ten, learns that her mother is about to leave on a long voyage for the sake of her health and that she will probably never see her mother again. The two have been weeping uncontrollably in one another's arms, when Mrs. Montgomery recollects herself and says: "Ellen! Ellen! Listen to me, . . . my child—This is not right. Remember, my darling, who it is that brings this sorrow upon us,—though we *must* sorrow, we must not rebel" (I, 12).[28] Ellen's mother, who has been ordered to go on this voyage by her husband

and her physician, makes no attempt to change the situation. She accepts the features of her life as fixed and instructs her daughter to do the same. The message of this scene, and of most sentimental fiction, is that "though we *must* sorrow, we must not rebel." This message can be understood in one of two ways. The most obvious is to read it as an example of how this fiction worked to keep women down. This reading sees women as the dupes of a culture that taught them that disobedience to male authority was a "sin against heaven."[29] When mothers teach their daughters to interpret the commands of husbands and fathers as the will of God, they make rebellion impossible, and at the same time, hold out the false hope of a reward for suffering, since, as Mrs. Montgomery says, "God sends no trouble upon his children but in love" (I, 13). In this view, religion is nothing but an opiate for the oppressed and a myth which served the rulers of a "Puritanical" and "trading nation." In this view, the sentimental novelists, to use Ann Douglas' phrase, did "the dirty work" of their culture by teaching women how to become the agents of their own subjection.[30]

The problem with this reading is that it is too simplistic. The women in these novels make submission "their boast" not because they enjoyed it, but because it gave them another ground on which to stand, a position that, while it fulfilled the social demands placed upon them, gave them a place from which to launch a counter-strategy against their worldly masters that would finally give them the upper hand. Submission, as it is presented throughout *The Wide, Wide World*, is never submission to the will of a husband or father, though that is what it appears to be on the surface; submission is first of all a self-willed act of conquest of one's own passions. Mrs. Montgomery tells Ellen that her tears of anger are "not right," that she must "command" and "compose" herself, because, she says, "you will hurt both yourself and me, my daughter, if you cannot" (I, 12). Ellen will hurt herself by failing to submit because her submission is not capitulation to an external authority, but the mastery of herself, and therefore, paradoxically, an assertion of autonomy.[31] In its definition of power relations, the domestic novel operates here, and elsewhere, according to a principle of reversal whereby what is "least" in the world's eyes

[margin annotations: "Feminization of Am. Culture" with arrow; "I don't know if I buy this"]

becomes "greatest" in its perspective. So "submission" becomes "self-conquest" and doing the will of one's husband or father brings an access of divine power. By conquering herself in the name of the highest possible authority, the dutiful woman merges her own authority with God's. When Mrs. Montgomery learns that her husband and doctor have ordered her to part from Ellen, she says to herself, "not my will, but thine be done" (I, 31). By making themselves into the vehicles of God's will, these female characters become nothing in themselves, but all-powerful in relation to the world. By ceding themselves to the source of all power, they bypass worldly (male) authority and, as it were, cancel it out. The ability to "submit" in this way is presented, moreover, as the special prerogative of women, transmitted from mother to daughter. As the women in these novels teach one another how to "command" themselves, they bind themselves to one another and to God in a holy alliance against the men who control their material destinies. Thus, when Mr. Montgomery refuses his wife the money to buy Ellen a parting gift, it is no accident that she uses her own mother's ring to make the purchase; the ring symbolizes the tacit system of solidarity that exists among women in these books. Nor is it an accident that the gift Mrs. Montgomery gives her daughter is a Bible. The mother's Bible-gift, in sentimental literature, is invested with supernatural power because it testifies to the reality of the spiritual order where women hold dominion over everything by virtue of their submission on earth.[32]

The bypassing of worldly authority ultimately produces a feminist theology in which the godhead is refashioned into an image of maternal authority. When Mrs. Montgomery teaches Ellen what it means to trust in God, she asks her to describe her feelings toward herself:

> "Why, mamma:—in the first place, I trust every word you say— entirely—I know nothing could be truer; if you were to tell me black is white, mamma, I should think my eyes had been mistaken. Then everything you tell or advise me to do, I know it is right, perfectly. And I always feel safe when you are near me, because I know you'll take care of me. And I am glad to think I belong to you, and you have the management of me entirely, and I needn't manage myself,

because I know I can't; and if I could, I'd rather you would, mamma."
(I, 18)

Mrs. Montgomery replies:

"My daughter, it is just so; it is *just* so: that I wish you to trust in
God. He is truer, wiser, stronger, kinder, by far, than I am, . . . and
what will you do when I am away from you:—and what would you
do, my child, if I were to be parted from you forever?" (I, 18)

Mrs. Montgomery's words produce a flood of tears from Ellen,
but nevertheless Ellen has learned that when her mother dies she
will not really be bereft, for God, who is just like her mother, will
take her mother's place in her life; and conversely, the novel seems
to suggest, Mrs. Montgomery will take the place of God. When
the moment of parting comes, she writes in the flyleaf of Ellen's
Bible:

" 'I love them that love Me; and they that seek Me early shall find
Me.' "
This was for Ellen; but the next words were not for her; what made
her write them?—
" 'I will be a God to thee, and to thy seed after thee.' "
They were written almost unconsciously, and, as if bowed by an
unseen force, Mrs. Montgomery's head sank upon the open page.
. . . (I, 49)

There are two ways of understanding this passage which parallel
the double meaning of "submission" in the politics of sentimental
fiction. We can read Mrs. Montgomery's inscriptions so that the
"I" in "I love them that love Me" and "I will be a God to thee"
are spoken by God, whose words she is just repeating. Or, we can
read the inscriptions so that the words are spoken by Mrs. Montgomery herself. Indeed, it is this interpretation that is borne out
by subsequent events in which Ellen's goodness, her devotion to
duty, her piety, and Christian deportment are all attributed to the
influence of her mother. The definition of the mother as the chan-
nel of God's grace, the medium through which he becomes known
to mankind, locates the effective force of divinity in this world in

women. Doing the will of God finally becomes identical with doing what one's mother wants. And if one is a woman, doing the will of God means obeying a divinity that comes to look more and more like oneself. Scene after scene in *The Wide, Wide World* ends with Ellen weeping in the arms of a kind mother-figure—a representative of God in human form. As Ellen matures, and her spiritual counselors grow closer to her in age—she calls them "sister" and "brother"—she finally learns to control her passions on her own and becomes her own mother. Not coincidentally, the one completely happy, whole, and self-sufficient character in this novel is an elderly woman who lives alone on a mountaintop and is, so to speak, a God unto herself. This is the condition toward which the novel's ethic of submission strives. While outwardly conforming to the exigencies of her social role, inwardly the heroine becomes master of her fate and subject to no one outside herself.

Read within the context of nineteenth-century American culture, the scene between Ellen and her mother reconciles women's need for power and status with a condition of economic and political subservience. This fiction presents an image of people dominated by external authorities and forced to curb their own desires; but as they learn to transmute rebellious passion into humble conformity to others' wishes, their powerlessness becomes a source of strength. These novels teach the reader how to live without power while waging a protracted struggle in which the strategies of the weak will finally inherit the earth.

Ellen is not weak, meek

III. TRIFLES

But while women were attempting to outflank men in a struggle for power by declaring that it was not the world that was important to conquer but one's own soul, they did in fact possess a territory of their own that was not purely spiritual, and they made maximum use of the one material advantage they possessed. The territory I am referring to is, of course, the home, which operates in these novels as the basis of a religious faith that has unmistakably worldly dimensions. The religion of the home does not situate heaven in the afterlife, but locates it in the here and now, offering its disciples the experience of domestic bliss. Just as the practice of submission, which looks like slavery to us, became, in the context of evangelical Christianity, the basis for a claim to mastery, so confinement to the home, which looks to us like deprivation, became a means of personal fulfillment.

Social historians have tended to take a dim view of the domestic ideology, regarding its promises of happiness as illusory and the accompanying restrictions as impossible to bear.[33] In the course of illustrating how women had to abandon any ambitions of their own, accommodating themselves to their husband's position in society, Barbara Epstein quotes a tale from a textbook for young girls about a man who had lost his fortune and was forced to move to a humble cottage in the country. As he walks home one evening with a friend, he worries aloud about his wife's state of mind. He is afraid she may not be able to cope with poverty, the fatigue of housework, and the absence of elegant appointments. But when the men arrive at the cottage, the wife

came tripping forth . . . in a pretty rural dress of white; a few wild flowers were twisted in her fine hair; a fresh bloom was on her cheek; her whole countenance beamed with smiles . . . "My dear George," cried she, "I am so glad you are home! I've set out a table under a beautiful tree behind the cottage; and I've been gathering some of the most delicious strawberries, for I know you are fond of them and we have such excellent cream, and everything is so sweet and still here.—"Oh!" said she, putting her arm within his, and looking up brightly into his face, "Oh! we shall be so happy."[34]

Epstein comments that although domesticity protected women from the harsh economic world, "in real life drudgery and isolation were more prominent than strawberries and cream."[35] Epstein's sarcasm here is understandable, but it misses something important. Of course homelife was mostly drudgery, but the women who wrote scenes like the one I have just quoted knew that. The religion of domesticity could never have taken hold if it had not had something real to offer. And what it had to offer was an extraordinary com-

bination of sensual pleasures, emotional fulfillment, spiritual aspirations, and satisfaction in work accomplished.

Of all the characters in *The Wide, Wide World*, the one who has
achieved the greatest spiritual victory is old Mrs. Vawse, who lives
in a house built into a cleft of rock on a windswept mountaintop.
Though she has no one to lean on—her husband, children, and
former mistress are all dead—she says "I am never alone . . . I
have nothing to fear" because "my home is in heaven, and my
Savior is there preparing a place for me" (XVIII, 201, 197). Though
Mrs. Vawse says her home is in heaven, everything that the novel
says about her goes to show how well she lives in her earthly one.
Though deprivation is ostensibly the defining feature of this woman's existence—she has no money, no property, no relatives—her
house is warm and comfortable, her surroundings are pleasant,
she works at odd jobs to earn money when she needs it, and she
obviously enjoys the company of her friends. She is always, says
Warner, "cheerful and happy, as a little girl" (XIX, 203). While
Mrs. Vawse claims that the secret of her contentment is "letting
go of earthly things . . . for they that seek the Lord shall not want
any good thing," (XVIII, 197) she in fact has everything she wants.
Mrs. Vawse is the most completely happy and fulfilled person in
the novel because economically, socially, and emotionally she is
the most independent. When Ellen asks her why she lives so far
away from everyone, she answers, "I can breathe better here than
on the plain. I feel more free" (XVIII, 201). Autonomy and freedom, exactly what the lives of antebellum American women lacked,
are the defining features of Mrs. Vawse's existence. Heaven, as it
is figured in Warner's novel, is a place of one's own where one
can be "happy, as a little girl" but without the dependency of
childhood, or of most Victorian women.

Despite the novel's emphasis on Mrs. Vawse's spirituality as the
source of her contentment, it is the physical features of her one-
room house that, rightly understood, provide a lesson to those who
would emulate her success. Everything in Mrs. Vawse's house
shines with the consequences of her labor. The floor is "beautifully
clean and white," the windows are "clean and bright as panes of
glass can be," "the hearth was clean swept up," "the cupboard

doors . . . unstained and unspoiled, though fingers had worn the paint off" (XVIII, 198). The work of scrubbing and polishing—women's work—has produced a spiritual purity and a physical beauty in which holiness and pleasure are combined, a combination repeated in the juxtaposition of her "large Bible" and "cushioned armchair" (XVIII, 198). Ellen and her friend, Alice, have come to Mrs. Vawse to "get a lesson in quiet contentment" (XVIII, 196). The lesson that they get—in addition to the one that Mrs. Vawse explicitly gives them—is that piety and industry, both activities over which a woman has control, can set you free. Mrs. Vawse's home presents an ideal of fulfillment toward which the readers of sentimental fiction could strive. It is full of material pleasures—cleanliness, attractive surroundings, warmth and good food (Mrs. Vawse gives Ellen and Alice delicious cheese, bread, and "fine tea" [XVIII, 200])—and it offers spiritual and emotional nourishment as well—Mrs. Vawse gives religious counsel and affection to her friends, and sends them on their way fortified in every sense. While the ethic of submission required a stifling of aggression, a turning inward of one's energies to the task of subduing the passions, the home provided an outlet for constructive effort, for *doing* something that could bring tangible results.

At the same time that the domestic ideal gave women a concrete goal they could work toward and enjoy the possession of, it gave them a way of thinking about their work that redeemed the particularities of daily existence and conferred on them a larger meaning. The triviality of sentimental fiction has, along with its morality and its tears, traditionally been the object of critical derision. But this triviality is the effect of a critical perspective that regards household activity as unimportant. Women writers of the nineteenth century, having been allotted one small corner of the material universe as their own, could hardly allow that area to be defined as peripheral or insignificant. Besides making the home into an all-sufficient basis for satisfaction and fulfillment in the present, they wrote about domestic routines in such a way that everything else appeared peripheral. Just as "submission" is transformed into "self-command," and the extinction of self into the assumption of a god-like authority, so the routines of the fireside acquire sacramental power in the novels of this period; the faithful performance of household tasks becomes not merely a reflection or an expression of celestial love but, as in this scene from Warner's novel, its point of origin and consummation:

> To make her mother's tea was Ellen's regular business. She treated it as a very grave affair, and loved it as one of the pleasantest in the course of the day. She used in the first place to make sure that the kettle really boiled; then she carefully poured some water into the tea-pot and rinsed it, both to make it clean and to make it hot; then she knew exactly how much tea to put in the tiny little tea-pot, which was just big enough to hold two cups of tea, and having poured a very little boiling water to it, she used to set it by the side of the fire while she made half a slice of toast. How careful Ellen was about that toast! The bread must not be cut too thick, nor too thin; the fire must, if possible, burn clear and bright, and she herself held the bread on a fork, just at the right distance from the coals to get nicely browned without burning. When this was done to her satisfaction (and if the first piece failed she would take another), she filled up the little tea-pot from the boiling kettle, and proceeded to make a cup of tea. She knew, and was very careful to put in, just the quantity of milk and sugar that her mother liked; and then she used to carry the tea and toast on a little tray to her mother's side, and very often held it there for her while she ate. All this Ellen did with the zeal that love gives, and though the same thing was to be gone over every night of the year, she was never wearied. It was a real pleasure; she had the greatest satisfaction in seeing that the little her mother could eat was prepared for her in the nicest possible manner; she knew her hands made it taste better; her mother often said so. (I, 13–14)

The making of tea as it is described here is not a household task, but a religious ceremony. It is also a strategy for survival. The dignity and potency of Ellen's life depend upon the sacrality she confers on small duties, and that is why the passage I have quoted focuses so obsessively and so reverentially on minute details. Ellen's preparation of her mother's tea has all the characteristics of a religious ritual: it is an activity that must be repeated ("the same thing was to be gone over every night of the year"); it must be repeated correctly ("she knew exactly how much tea to put in the tiny little tea-pot," "the bread must not be cut too thick, nor too

thin," "and if the first piece failed she would take another"); it
must be repeated in the right spirit ("all this Ellen did with the
zeal that love gives"); and it must be repeated by the right person
(Ellen "knew her hands made it taste better; her mother often
said so"). Ellen's hands make the tea and toast taste better because
the ritual has worked, but it works not only because it has been
performed correctly, but because Ellen and her mother believe in
it. The creation of moments of intimacy like this through the making of a cup of tea is what their lives depend on. What the ritual
effects is the opening of the heart in an atmosphere of closeness,
security, and love. The mutual tenderness, affection, and solicitude
made visible in the performance of these homely acts are the values
sacred to sentimental fiction and the reward it offers its readers
for that other activity which must also be performed within the
"closet"—the control of rebellious passion. While Ellen and her
mother must submit to the will of God, expressed through the
commands of husbands and doctors, they compensate for their
servitude by celebrating daily their exclusive, mutually supportive
love for one another.

That is why this ritual, although it resembles the Christian sac-
rament of holy communion, does not merely *promise* fulfillment;
it offers consummation in the present moment. The tea and toast
are real food, and the feelings that accompany them, like those
that characterize the soul's relation to Christ in evangelical hymns,
are feelings living human beings share with one another.[36] The
exigencies of a Puritanical and trading nation had put women in
the home and barred the door; and so in order to survive, they
had to imagine their prison as the site of bliss. In this respect, the
taking of tea is no different from hoeing a bean patch on the shores
of Walden Pond, or squeezing case aboard a whaling ship; they
are parallel reactions against pain and bondage, and a means of
salvation and grace. The spaces that American Renaissance writing
marks out as the site of possible transcendence are not only the
forest and the open sea. The hearth, in domestic fiction, is the site
of a "movement inward," as far removed from the fetters of land-
locked existence as the Pacific Ocean is from Coenties Slip.

The happiness that women engender in the home is their prerogative and their compensation. But this felicity is not limited in its effects to women, although they alone are responsible for it. Like prayer, which must be carried on in solitude and secrecy in order to change the world, the happiness that women create in their domestic isolation finally reaches to the ends of the earth. "Small acts, small kindnesses, small duties," writes the Reverend Peabody, "bring the happiness or misery . . . of a whole generation. Whatever of happiness is enjoyed . . . beyond the circle of domestic life, is little more than an offshoot from that central sun."[37] The domestic ideology operates in this, as in every other respect, according to a logic of inversion whereby the world becomes "little more than an offshoot" of the home. Not only happiness, but salvation itself is seen to depend upon the performance of homely tasks. "Common daily duties," says the Reverend Peabody, "become sacred and awful because of the momentous results that depend upon them. Performed or neglected, they are the witnesses that shall appear for or against us at the last day."[38] By investing the slightest acts with moral significance, the religion of domesticity makes the destinies of the human race hang upon domestic routines. Margaret Flower makes out a time schedule when she is on vacation, and Ellen Montgomery treats the making of her mother's tea as "a very grave affair" because they know that "momentous results" depend upon these trifles. The measuring out of life in coffee spoons, a modernist metaphor for insignificance and futility, is interpreted in sentimental discourse as a world-building activity. When it is done exactly right, and "with the zeal that love gives," it can save the world.

It is easy and may be inevitable at this point to object that such claims are pathetic and ridiculous—the fantasies of a disenfranchised group, the line that society feeds to members whom it wants to buy off with the illusion of strength while denying them any real power. But what is at stake in this discussion is precisely what constitutes "real" power. From a modern standpoint, the domestic ideal is self-defeating because it ignores the realities of political and economic life. But those were not the realities on which Americans in the nineteenth century founded their conceptions of the world. As Lewis Saum has written: "In popular thought of the

pre–Civil War period, no theme was more pervasive or philosophically fundamental than the providential view. Simply put,
that view held that, directly or indirectly, God controlled all things."[39]
Given this context, the claims the domestic novel made for the
power of Christian love and the sacred influence of women were
not in the least exaggerated or illusory. The entire weight of Protestant Christianity and democratic nationalism stood behind them.
The notion that women in the home exerted a moral force that
shaped the destinies of the race had become central to this country's vision of itself as a redeemer nation. The ethic of submission
and the celebration of domesticity were not losing strategies in an
age dominated by the revival movement. They were a successful
bid for status and sway. Even as thoroughgoingly cosmopolitan a
man as Tocqueville became convinced of this as a result of his visit
to the United States from 1830 to 1831. "As for myself," he said,
concluding his observations on American women, "I do not hes-
itate to avow that, although the women of the United States are
confined within a narrow circle of domestic life, and their situation
is in some respects one of extreme dependence, I have nowhere
seen woman occupying a loftier position; and if I were asked, now
that I am drawing to the close of this work, in which I have spoken
of so many important things done by the Americans, to what the
singular prosperity and growing strength of that people ought mainly
to be attributed, I should reply—to the superiority of their women."[40]

IV. PAIN

The claims that sentimental fiction made for the importance of
the spiritual life and for women's crucial role in the salvation of
the race were not spurious or self-deceiving, because they were
grounded in and appealed to beliefs that had already organized
the experience of most Americans. But while the sense of power
and feelings of satisfaction that the religion of domesticity afforded
were real, not just imagined, they were bought and paid for at an
almost incalculable price. The pain of learning to conquer her own
passions is the central fact of the sentimental heroine's existence.
For while a novel like *The Wide, Wide World* provides its readers

with a design for living under drastically restricted conditions, at the same time it provides them with a catharsis of rage and grief that registers the cost of living according to that model. When Melville writes that Ahab "piled upon the white whale's hump the sum of all the general rage and hate felt by his whole race from Adam down, and then, as if his chest had been a mortar . . . burst his hot heart's shell upon it," he describes the venting of a rage that cannot be named as such in Warner's novel, but whose force is felt nevertheless in the deluge of the heroine's tears.[41] The force of those passions that must be curbed at all costs pushes to the surface again and again in her uncontrollable weeping. For although these novels are thought to have nothing to say about the human psyche, and to be unaware of "all the subtle demonisms of life and thought" which preoccupied greater minds, in fact they focus exclusively on the emotions, and specifically on the psychological dynamics of living in a condition of servitude. The appeal of Warner's novel lay in the fact that it grappled directly with the emotional experience of its readership; it deals with the problem of powerlessness by showing how one copes with it hour by hour and minute by minute. For contrary to the long-standing consensus that sentimental novelists "couldn't face" the grim facts of their lives, their strength lay precisely in their dramatization of the heroine's suffering as she struggles to control each new resurgence of passion and to abase herself before God. It is a suffering which, the novelists resolutely insist, their readers, too, must face or else remain unsaved. And they force their readers to face it by placing them inside the mind of someone whose life is a continual series of encounters with absolute authority.

Warner's novel pulls the reader immediately into such a situation. As the novel opens, Ellen Montgomery is sitting quietly at the window of her parents' New York townhouse, watching the evening close in on a partially deserted street. Her invalid mother is resting and has asked her to be still. (Characteristically, the heroine is trapped in an enclosed space, is under an injunction *not* to do anything, has no direct access to the world she can see from her limited vantage point, and must make the best of her situation.) Ellen studies the scene outside the window with great concentra-

tion. It is pouring rain. She watches the last foot passengers splash-
ing through the water, horses and carriages making their way through
the mud, until finally, at the far end of the street, one by one,
lights begin to appear. "Presently," Warner writes, "Ellen could
see the dim figure of the lamplighter crossing the street from side
to side with his ladder;—then he drew near enough for her to
watch him as he hooked his ladder on the lamp irons, ran up and
lit the lamp, then shouldered the ladder and marched off quick,
the light glancing on his wet oil-skin hat, rough great-coat and
lantern, and on the pavement and iron railings" (I, 10). When the
lamplighter has finally disappeared, Ellen sets herself to straightening the room: she adjusts the curtains, stirs the fire, arranges
the chairs, puts some books and her mother's sewing-box back in
their places. Finally, having done everything she can think of, Ellen
kneels down and lays her head next to her mother's on the pillow
and after a moment gently strokes her cheek. "And this succeeded," says Warner, "for Mrs. Montgomery arrested the little
hand as it passed her lips and kissed it fondly" (I, 10).

What makes this scene work is the way it draws the reader into
its own circuit of attention. Forced into the dark parlor with Ellen,
the reader has to pay attention to what Ellen pays attention to—
the tiny details of the lamplighter's progress down the street, parlor
furniture, books, sewing-boxes, the moment of suspense when she
lays her hand on her mother's cheek. These things become the all-
engrossing features of the reader's world. The circumscribed materials of Warner's novel do not seem at all lacking in importance
when seen from the heroine's perspective; instead, the restricted
focus, which one might have supposed to be a disastrous limitation,
works to intensify the emotional force of what takes place. At
times, the vulnerability of the child, forced to live within the boundaries authority prescribes and constantly under the pressure of a
hostile supervision, becomes almost too painful to bear.

Warner's refusal to mitigate the narrow circumstances of her
heroine's existence is particularly striking when one compares this
novel to the opening of *Huckleberry Finn*. When Huck is trapped
by his drunken father near the beginning of Twain's novel, he
concocts an elaborate ruse that allows him to escape. He kills a

hog, scatters its blood around the cabin, drags a sack of meal across the threshhold to imitate the imprint of a body, and disappears, hoping that his father and the townspeople will think he has been murdered—and of course they do. *The Adventures of Huckleberry Finn* has for a long time stood as a benchmark of American literary realism, praised for its brilliant use of local dialects and its faithfulness to the texture of ordinary life. Twain himself is famous for his scoffing attacks on the escapism of sentimental and romantic fiction. But if one compares his handling of a child's relation to authority with Warner's, the events of *Huckleberry Finn* enact a dream of freedom and autonomy that goes beyond the bounds of the wildest romance. The scenario whereby the clever and deserving Huck repeatedly outwits his powerful adversaries along the riverbank acts out a kind of adolescent wish fulfillment that Warner's novel never even glances at. When Ellen is sent by her father to live with a sadistic aunt in New England, when she is deeded by him a second time to an even more sinister set of relatives, there is absolutely nothing she can do. Ellen is never for a moment out of the power of her guardians and never will be, as long as she lives. While the premise of Twain's novel is that, when faced by tyranny of any sort, you can simply run away, the problem that Warner's novel sets itself to solve is how to survive, given that you can't.

In the light of this fact, it is particularly ironic that novels like Warner's should have come to be regarded as "escapist." Unlike their male counterparts, women writers of the nineteenth century could not walk out the door and become Mississippi riverboat captains, go off on whaling voyages, or build themselves cabins in the woods. Nevertheless, modern critics, as we have seen, persist in believing that what sentimental novelists offered was an easy way out: a few trite formulas for the masses who were too cowardly to face the "blackness of darkness," too lazy to wrestle with moral dilemmas, too stupid to understand epistemological problems, and too hidebound to undertake "quarrels with God." But "escape" is the one thing that sentimental novels never offer; on the contrary, they teach their readers that the only way to overcome tyranny is through the practice of a grueling and inexorable discipline. Ellen Montgomery says to her aunt early in the novel that if she were free to do what she wanted she would run away—and spends the rest of the novel learning to extirpate that impulse from her being. For not only can you not run away, in the world of sentimental fiction, you cannot protest the conditions under which you are forced to remain. Ahab's cosmic protest "I'd strike the sun if it insulted me" epitomizes the revolutionary stance of the heroes of classical American fiction; sentimental heroines practice a heroism of another sort.

Learning to renounce her own desire is the sentimental heroine's vocation, and it requires, above all else, a staggering amount of work. Since self-suppression does not come naturally, but is a skill that can only be acquired through practice, the taking apart and putting back together of the self must be enacted over and over again, as each new situation she meets becomes the occasion for the heroine's ceaseless labor of self-transformation. It is, as Ellen often says to her spiritual mentors, "hard." And since, in any individual instance, crushing the instinct for self-defense and humbling oneself before God can only be accomplished through protracted effort, the scenes that enact this process are long and tortuous. Over and over again the heroine must overcome the impulse to rebel and justify herself, must throw herself on the mercy of the Lord and ask his help in forgiving those who have wronged her.

In a sense, these novels resemble, more than anything else, training narratives: they are like documentaries and made-for-TV movies that tell how Joe X, who grew up on the streets of Chicago, became a great pitcher for the White Sox, or how Kathy Y overcame polio and skated her way to stardom. They involve arduous apprenticeships in which the protagonist undergoes repeated failures and humiliations in the course of mastering the principles of her vocation. They always involve, prominently, a mentor-figure who initiates the pupil into the mysteries of the art, and enunciates the values the narrative is attempting to enforce. The trainer, who is simultaneously stern and compassionate, loves the protagonist most when she is being hardest on her. In sentimental fiction, the vocation to be mastered is Christian salvation, which, translated into social terms, means learning to submit to the authorities society has placed over you. In Ellen's case, her Aunt Fortune (a literal representative of fate), and later her Scottish relatives, are the authorities whom Ellen must learn to obey without a murmur. And her mentors are first her mother, then Alice Humphries, a young woman who befriends Ellen in her first exile, and then Alice's brother John, who takes over when Alice dies.

The role Ellen's mentors play in administering the novel's disciplinary program is a complicated and crucial one. Though they are her refuge and her loving saviors, it is they who put the "rock" in Ellen's soul by refusing to let her give way to her rebellious feelings. Whereas her Aunt Fortune exerts control over Ellen's life externally, her mentors control her inmost being; they alter her behavior at its source by teaching her how to interpret her feelings. Anger and indignation—no matter what the cause—are a disease of which she must be cured, and in order to be cured she must not "shrink" from her "physician." "No hand but His," they tell her, "can touch that sickness you are complaining of (XV, 158). Relentless in their determination that Ellen shall learn to humble herself before God, her mentors make demands of her that are excruciatingly intimate and exacting.

It is hard for people who have not read Warner's novel to understand the nature of the heroine's relation to her mentors. The claustrophobic atmosphere of the novel, its concentration on the moral consequences of even the smallest pieces of behavior, and above all the sense it conveys of someone utterly at the mercy of implacable authorities, trap the reader into the heroine's cycle of frustration, humiliation, and striving. The immediacy and force of her emotions invest the tiniest incidents with an intensity that a simple account of their features cannot recapture. What most eludes the attempt to portray these scenes is the passion that fills them— a passion that erupts continually and inarticulately in the flood of her tears, as repeatedly she is made to bare her soul to the gaze of her superiors.

When Ellen runs to her friend Alice, after her Aunt Fortune has treated her cruelly, at first Alice is all sympathy and affection. But what Ellen learns from Alice, comforting and solicitous as she is, is that her protests are all pride and selfishness, and that she must learn not to stand up to her aunt even to *herself*. "For," as Alice says, "the heart must be set right before the life can be" (XVI, 173). The only way to set the heart right is through total self-abnegation, and the only way to achieve that is by praying to the "dear Savior." When Ellen asks "what shall I do to set it right?" Alice's answer is "Pray," (XVI, 173) and this will always be her answer. When Ellen says "But, dear Miss Alice, I have been praying all morning that I might forgive Aunt Fortune and yet I cannot do it," Alice's answer is still the same, "Pray still, my dear, . . . pray still. If you are in earnest the answer will come" (XVI, 173). Alice never gives an inch in these exchanges because her job is to teach Ellen that the self must *never* have its way, for "God resisteth the proud, but giveth grace unto the humble" (XVI, 174). When Ellen bursts into tears at such sayings, and cries out "but it is so hard to forgive," Alice is unmoved. "Hard, yes, it is hard when our hearts are so, but there is little love to Christ and no just sense of his love to us in the heart that finds it hard. Pride and selfishness make it hard. The heart full of love to the dear Savior cannot lay up offenses against itself" (XVI, 174).

Tears and prayers are the heroine's only recourse against injustice; the thought of injustice itself is implicitly forbidden. The anger that such a thought would arouse is Ellen's worst enemy and her besetting sin; that anger must be transmuted into humility and love for "the hand that has done it" (XLII, 461). And so, Ellen's mentors are immitigable in their insistence that Ellen turn to Christ for help when she is in distress. If she wants to be happy, she must learn to seek him. "Remember Him, dear Ellen," they always say, "remember your best Friend. Learn more of Christ, our dear Savior, and you can't help but be happy" (XVII, 183). When Ellen thanks Miss Alice for befriending her, exclaiming, "Oh, Miss Alice, what would have become of me without you!" Alice gently rebuffs her: "Don't lean upon me, dear Ellen," says Alice, "remember you have a better Friend than I always near you. . . . Whenever you feel wearied and sorry, flee to the shadow of that great rock" (XVI, 174; XVII, 183). Through constant and repeated reminders, Ellen's mentors establish Christ in Ellen's mind as an all-powerful internal "Friend" who watches everything she does. Thanks to her mentors, when Ellen goes to her room in tears, she is not retreating to a safe place any longer because, once in the privacy of her room, she must abase herself before the authority she has internalized.

Ellen's self-command increases as she learns to turn more frequently to prayer, to her Bible, to hymns, and to religious books for strength and solace. And from time to time, Warner notes with satisfaction the "progress" of the "little pilgrim" (XXXV, 368);[42] "solitude and darkness saw many a tear of hers," says Warner, as she "struggled . . . to get rid of sin and to be more like what would please God" (XXXI, 331). But despite her constant progress in the business of self-renunciation, Ellen always needs more inner strength than she can muster. She is constantly being caught in some attitude of incomplete surrender which earns her the devastatingly mild rebukes of Miss Alice or Mr. John. The faintest signs of irritation or self-concern tell them that her devotion to Christ is not yet absolute. "Is seeking His face your first concern?" they ask, "be humbled in the dust before Him" (XLV, 489; XXVIII, 309).

But the massive tests of Ellen's faith are still before her. Ellen learns that her mother has died, and is inconsolable. She goes into a decline from which she is rescued only by Mr. John's tutelage and affection. Then Alice dies, and Ellen is desolate. But this time "she knew the hand that gave the blow and did not raise her own against it. . . . Her broken heart crept to His feet and laid its burden there" (XLI, 446). The final blow is separation from Mr. John. Her father dies and deeds her to some rich relatives in Scotland; Ellen is cast upon the wide world a second time, and this time she will have no mentors to rely on. Like all true Christians, she must learn to live on faith alone.

The final chapters of *The Wide, Wide World* require of the heroine an extinction of her personality so complete that there is literally nothing of herself that she can call her own. Whereas Ellen's aunt had subjected her to constant household drudgery and frequently hurt her feelings, she made no attempt to possess her soul. But Ellen's Scottish relatives are spiritual tyrants; they look upon Ellen as a "dear plaything, to be taught, governed, disposed of." "They would do with her and make of her precisely what they pleased" (XLVII, 524). What they please is that she give up her identity. Under their rule, in which the "hand that pressed her cheek," though "exceeding fond," is also the "hand of power," (XLVII, 530) submission reaches its acutest manifestations. The store of loyalties and affections that Ellen has garnered during her first exile is stripped from her methodically and completely. The Lindsays' authority will brook no appeal. Her uncle makes Ellen call him "father," changes her name from Montgomery to Lindsay, orders her to forget her nationality, forces her to drink wine, forbids her to speak of her former friends, refuses to let her talk of religion, and insists that she give up her sober ways and act "cheerful." After prolonged internal struggles, many prayers and tears, and much consulting of her Bible, Ellen bends submissively to every one of these commands; her time, her energies, her name, her nationality, her conversation, her friends are not hers to dispose of. "God will take care of me if I follow Him," she says to herself, "it is none of my business." "God giveth grace to the humble, I will humble myself" (XLVIII, 546). Absolutely friendless, with no one to understand and comfort her, Ellen (who is about thirteen years old by now) has only God to turn to. When the Lindsays try to take God away from her, it marks the turning point in her Christian education. Up to now, Ellen's Christian duty has required her to submit silently to every assault on her personal desires; the final test of her obedience will require that she disobey, because it is an attack not on herself but on "Him."

Ellen has been in the habit of spending an hour every morning in Bible reading and prayer; it is this hour that enables her to maintain her humble bearing in the face of the Lindsays' demands. When her grandmother learns of it, she forbids Ellen to continue, but this time Ellen says to her grandmother, "there is One I must obey even before you" (L, 563). Although it looks as though, in disobeying, Ellen has gone against everything she has been taught, in fact, the novel's lesson here is the same as it has been throughout: obey the Lord and He will provide. In her distress, Ellen behaves exactly as her mentors had instructed her—she "flees to the shadow of that great rock." She goes to her room, and cries, and then begins to sing:

> *When I draw this fleeting breath,—*
> *When my eyelids close in death,—*
> *When I rise to worlds unknown,*
> *And behold Thee on Thy throne,—*
> *Rock of Ages, cleft for me,*
> *Let me hide myself in Thee.* (L, 566)

Because Ellen has not asked anything for herself, her will, which is one with the will of God, prevails. Ellen's uncle overhears her singing, and, won over by her meekness and humility, intercedes for her with her grandmother; he arranges for her to have her precious hour alone if she will promise to be more cheerful and keep her "brow clear." Ellen keeps the promise. "Her cheerfulness," says Warner, "was constant and unvarying." Her "unruffled brow," "clear voice," and "ready smile" are the product of a pure heart and a broken will, for though "tears might often fall that nobody knew of," Ellen had "grasped the promises 'He that cometh to Me shall never hunger,' and 'Seek and ye shall find' " (L, 569).

To Warner's audience, steeped in the Christian tradition of self-denial and submission to God's will, Ellen's suffering, as she gradually gives up the right to *be* herself, is necessary. It is not only necessary; it is desirable. Ellen's mentors express their love for her in their willingness to inflict pain as God, in the Protestant tradition, loves those whom he chastises. After her mother has died, John asks Ellen, "do you love Him less since He has brought you into this great sorrow?" "No," Ellen replies, sobbing, "*more*" (XXXIV, 363). But the embrace of pain and the striving for self-abandonment that characterize the heroines of sentimental fiction have, for the modern reader, psycho-sexual overtones that are inescapable and should at least be mentioned here. When Mr. John says to Ellen, "be humbled in the dust before Him—the more the better," (XXVIII, 309) his words, harsh and titillating at the same time, suggest the relationship between punishment and sex-

ual pleasure, humiliation and bliss. The intimate relation between
love and pain that Warner's novel insists on calls to mind nothing
so much as *The Story of O*, another education in submission in
which the heroine undergoes ever more painful forms of sexual
humiliation and self-effacement, until finally she asks "permission"
to die. In each case, when the heroine has learned to submit totally
to one authority, she is passed on to a more demanding master,
or set of masters, who will exact submissions that are even more
severe.

The end point of the disciplinary process is the loss of self: either
through physical death, as in O's case or Uncle Tom's, or psychological death, as in Ellen's, a sloughing off of the unregenerate
self. By the end of Warner's novel, Ellen does not exist for herself
any more, but only for others. Sanctified by the sacrifice of her
own will, she becomes a mentor by example, teaching lessons in
submissiveness through her humble bearing, downcast eyes, unruffled brow, and "peculiar grave look" (XLV, 494). Even the joy
that Ellen gives her elders is not her own doing, but God in her.
She is a medium through which God's glory can show itself to men.
Like Alice, Ellen becomes a person who "supplied what was
wanting everywhere; like the transparent glazing which painters
use to spread over the dead color of their pictures; unknown, it
was she gave life and harmony to the whole" (XX, 213). The ideal
of behavior to which the novel educates its readers is the opposite
of self-realization; it is to become empty of self, an invisible transparency that nevertheless is miraculously responsible for the life
in everything.

Given the amount of pain that sentimental heroines endure, it
is almost inconceivable that their stories should have been read as
myths of "reassurance." But perhaps this reading, insofar as it
arises from anything that is really in these novels, is based on the
way they end. At the end of *The Wide, Wide World*, Ellen is
rewarded for her suffering, like Job—to whom she is twice com-
pared. Having given up everything, she now has everything re-
stored to her a hundredfold. That restoration takes the form of
Mr. John, whom Ellen loves, to whom she has "given herself,"
and who, Warner intimates, will marry her when she comes of

age. In Mr. John the various authorities in Ellen's life are finally merged. Whereas before, the authorities over her had been divided into three separate realms—the earthly authority of her father, Aunt Fortune, and the Lindsays; the transcendent authority of God; and the authority of her spiritual mentors who mediated between the two—now they are all contained in a single person. Since, as Warner observes, Mr. John's commands are always "on the side of right," there will never again for Ellen be a conflict between duty and obedience. The male figure, representing both divine and worldly authority, who marries the heroine in the end, is the alternative to physical death in sentimental fiction; he provides her with a way to live happily and obediently in this world while obeying the dictates of heaven. He is the principle that joins self-denial with self-fulfillment, extending and enforcing the disciplinary regimen of the heroine's life, giving her the love, affection, and companionship she had lost when she was first orphaned, providing her with material goods and social status through his position in the world.

The union with Mr. John looks at first exactly like the sort of fairy-tale ending that sentimental fiction is always accused of fobbing off on its readers: Cinderella rescued by Prince Charming. One can see Aunt Fortune as the wicked stepmother who makes Ellen sweep and churn butter when she would rather be studying French, and Alice as the fairy godmother who provides supernatural help and leads her to the prince. But the real analogues to Warner's novel are not fairy tales, though they do have happy endings. The narratives that lie behind *The Wide, Wide World* are trials of faith—the story of Job and *Pilgrim's Progress*—spiritual "training" narratives in which God is both savior and persecutor and the emphasis falls not on last-minute redemption, but on the toils and sorrows of the "way." These narratives, like Warner's novel, teach the reader, by example, how to live. And their lesson, like Warner's, is that the only thing that really matters in this world is faith in God and doing his will: nothing else counts. Although Ellen will be united eventually with Mr. John, her submissiveness has become so complete that it hardly matters who is her master now. Through prolonged struggle, she has taught herself to be the perfect extension of another's will; because her real self is inviolate, having become one with God, she can accept whatever fate deals out. And in fact, Warner gives her "three or four more years of Scottish discipline" before restoring her to the "friends and guardians she best loved" (LII, 592). The education of the sentimental heroine is no more a fairy story than the story of Job or *Pilgrim's Progress*. Rather, it is an American Protestant *bildungsroman*, in which the character of the heroine is shaped by obedience, self-sacrifice, and faith. Warner's language in summing up her heroine's career makes this plain:

> The seed so early sown in little Ellen's mind, and so carefully tended by sundry hands, grew in course of time to all the fair stature and comely perfection it had bid fair to reach—storms and winds that had visited it did but cause the root to take deeper hold;—and at the point of its young maturity it happily fell into those hands that had of all been most successful in its culture. (LII, 592)

In an unfriendly review of Warner's book, Charles Kingsley quipped that it should have been called "The Narrow, Narrow World" because its compass was so small.[43] And in a sense he was right. Although the frontispiece of the first illustrated edition shows a ship tossing on a stormy sea, with the sun breaking through clouds in the background, all of the heroine's adventures take place indoors, in small enclosed spaces that are metaphors for the heart. Warner tells the reader as much in the novel's epigraph:

> *Here at the portal thou dost stand,*
> *   And with thy little hand*
> *Thou openest the mysterious gate*
> *   Into the future's undiscovered land.*
> *   I see its valves expand*
> *As at the touch of Fate*
> *   Into those realms of Love and Hate.*

The realms of love and hate are no less turbulent and suspenseful than those Kingsley described in *Westward, Ho!*, and considerably less given to the playing out of adolescent fantasies. The storms and winds of Warner's novel are those that nineteenth-century readers actually encountered in their lives. The wideness of this world is to be measured not by geographical or sociological standards, but by the fullness with which the novel manages to account for the experience of its readers. That experience, as I have argued, was shaped conclusively by the revival movement and by the social and economic condition of American women in the antebellum years. That is the condition that Ellen Montgomery's story represents, and it is "narrow" only in the sense of being confined to a domestic space, like most of Henry James' fiction, or Jane Austen's. But unlike Austen or James, the sentimental writers had millennial aims in mind. For them the world could be contracted to the dimensions of a closet because it was in the closet that one received the power to save the world. As the Reverend Dr. Patton, addressing the fifteenth annual meeting of the American Home Missionary Society, said:

> The history of the world . . . is the history of prayer. For this is the power that moves heaven. Yet it is the power which may be wielded by the humblest and obscurest saint. It will doubtless be found in the great day, that many a popular and prominent man will be set aside; whilst the retired but pleading disciple, will be brought forth to great honor, as having alone in her closet, wrestled with the angel and prevailed.[44]

VII
"But Is It Any Good?": The Institutionalization of Literary Value

People often object, when presented with the arguments I have made above, that while one may affirm the power or centrality of a novel on the grounds that it intersects with widely-held beliefs and grapples with pressing social problems, that affirmation does not prove anything one way or another about the literary value of the text, and does nothing to guarantee its status as a work of art. This objection seems particularly trenchant in the present context because while it grants the validity of my argument on one level and even suggests that the point is obvious—*of course* best-sellers reflect the concerns of the passing moment—it denies the relevance of the argument to literary criticism. For criticism, the objection goes, concerns itself with the specifically *literary* features of American writing. And what distinguishes a work *as literature* is the way it separates itself from transitory issues of the kind I have been discussing—revolution (Brockden Brown), consolidation (Cooper), revival (Warner), and abolition (Stowe). The fact that a work engages such issues, in this view, is an index not of its greatness, but of its limitation; the more directly it engages purely local and temporal concerns, the less literary it will be, not only because it is captive to the fluctuations of history, but also because in its attempt to mold public opinion it is closer to propaganda than to art, and hence furnishes material for the historian rather than the literary critic.

The objection, as I have phrased it, is never put in exactly this way, but usually takes the form of a question like: but are these works really any *good*? or, what about the *literary* value of *Uncle Tom's Cabin*? or, do you really want to defend Warner's *language*? These questions imply that the standards of judgment to which they refer are not themselves challengeable, but are taken for granted among qualified readers. "You and I know what a good novel is," the objection implies, "and we both know that these novels fall outside that category." But the notion of good literature that the question invokes is precisely what we are arguing about. That tacit sense of what is "good" cannot be used to determine the value of these novels because literary value *is* the point at issue. At this juncture, people will frequently attempt to settle the question empirically by pointing to one or another indisputably "great" work, such as *Moby-Dick* or *The Scarlet Letter*, and asking whether *The Wide, Wide World* is as good as *that*.

But the issue cannot be settled by invoking apparently unquestionable examples of literary excellence such as these as a basis of comparison, because these texts already represent one position in the debate they are being called upon to decide. That is, their value, their identity, and their constituent features have been made available for description by the very modes of perception and evaluation that I am challenging. It is not from any neutral space that we have learned to see the epistemological subtleties of Melville or Hawthorne's psychological acuity. Those characteristics have been made available by critical strategies that have not always been respectable, but had to be explained, illustrated, and argued for (as I am arguing now) against other critical assumptions embodied in other masterpieces that seemed just as invincible, just as unquestionably excellent as these now do. Such strategies do not remain stable and do not emerge in isolation, but are forged in the context of revolutions, revivals, periods of consolidation or reform—in short, in the context of all those historical circumstances by which literary values are supposed to remain unaffected. Even in the last sixty years, the literary canon has undergone more than one major shift as the circumstances within which critics evolved their standards of judgment changed.

The evidence for this assertion becomes dramatically available when one examines the history of literary anthologies.[1] Between the time that Fred Pattee made selections for *Century Readings for a Course in American Literature* (1919) and the time that Perry Miller and his coeditors decided whom to include in *Major Writers of America* (1962), the notion of who counted as a major writer and even the concept of the "major writer" had altered dramatically. Whereas Pattee's single volume, compiled at the close of World War I, contained hundreds of writers, Miller's much larger two-volume work, published at the close of the Cold War, contained only twenty-eight.[2] Three years earlier, Gordon Ray's *Masters of American Literature* had reduced the number to eighteen; the Macmillan anthology, published in the same year as Miller's, had pared the number to twelve; and in 1963, a Norton anthology edited by Norman Foerster and Robert Falk had reduced it to only eight.[3] "In choosing Emerson, Thoreau, Hawthorne, Poe, Melville, Whitman, Mark Twain, James, Emily Dickinson, Frost, Eliot, and Faulkner," the Macmillan editors write, "we can imagine little dispute."[4] But if they had looked back at the literary anthologies published since Pattee's, they might have been less sure about the absence of debate. Howard Mumford Jones and Ernest Leisy, in the preface to *Major American Writers* (1935), state categorically that "there can be no question that Franklin, Cooper, Irving, Bryant, Emerson, Hawthorne, Longfellow, Whittier, Lincoln, Poe, Thoreau, Lowell, Melville, Whitman, and Mark Twain constitute the heart of any course in American literary history."[5]

The contradiction that emerges when one places these statements side by side springs from a contradiction internal to the project of anthology-making as these editors conceive it. The difference between the two lists of "central" authors stems from the fact that the editors are active shapers of the canon, whose differing aims and assumptions determine what will seem central and what peripheral. This fact emerges clearly in the prefaces, where the editors anxiously justify their choices, defend them against other possible selections, and apologize for significant omissions. But the editors' beliefs about the nature of literary value—i.e., that it is "inherent in the works themselves," timeless, and universal—prevent them from recognizing their own role in determining which are the truly great works.[6] In describing their own activity, therefore, they speak as if they themselves had played virtually no part in deciding which authors deserved to be included, but were simply codifying choices about which there could be "no question." This mode of self-characterization is most explicitly illustrated by Perry Miller, who pictures the authors in his anthology as forcing themselves upon him and his coeditors. We were free, he says, from the obligation to cleave to a " 'party-line,' " but adds, "this is not to say that the American *writers* represented in the pages which follow left their editors alone. Quite the contrary. In fact, *Major Writers of America* may best be taken as a varied testimony to the force that the literature continues to exert over and against time. Such attraction at such a distance is what signalizes a major writer."[7] But if it is the literature that governs a critic's choices, and not the critic himself, or a "line" imposed upon him, then it is hard to explain the drastic alterations that took place in literary anthologies between 1919 and 1962. It is not just a question of disagreement over exactly which authors are to be considered major; the whole character of the anthologies changes in the interval.

Indeed, if we take Pattee and Miller as representative, we can see that in addition to a sharp narrowing in the range and number of authors, there has been a virtual rewriting of literary history, as entire periods, genres, and modes of classification disappear. Between 1919 and 1962 more than a dozen authors have dropped away in the Colonial period alone, while in the Revolutionary period, only one out of seven makes it through; the Revolutionary songs and ballads are missing entirely. The Federalist period disappears altogether and so does most of the first half of the nineteenth century. Gone are the *fin-de-siècle* poets—John Trumbull, Timothy Dwight, Joel Barlow—and with them the lyricists of the early century—Richard Henry Dana, Edward Coate Pinckney, Richard Henry Wilde, and John Howard Payne. None of the songwriters survive—George Pope Morris, Samuel Woodworth, Thomas Dunn English, Phoebe Cary, Stephen Foster. The selections from D. G. Mitchell's *Reveries of a Bachelor* disappear, along with the orations of John C. Calhoun and Daniel Webster. The historians of the mid-nineteenth century, W. H. Prescott, John Lothrop Motley, and Francis Parkman vanish, as do the southern writers (Simms,

Timrod, Paul Hamilton Hayne) and the antislavery writers—Whittier and Stowe. Gone are Abraham Lincoln and all the songs and ballads of the Civil War. Out of six western humorists, only Twain survives; of the "transition poets"—Bayard Taylor, Edmund Clarence Stedman, Thomas Bailey Aldrich, Sidney Lanier, Thomas Buchanan Read, George Henry Boker, Richard Henry Stoddard, and Celia Leighton Thaxter—not one. Of the late nineteenth-century nature writers, not one. Out of a dozen poets of the same period, only Crane and Dickinson. The local colorists—Bret Harte, General Lewis Wallace, Edward Eggleston, John Hay, Joaquin Miller, Helen Hunt Jackson, Henry Grady, Hamlin Garland, George Washington Cable, Joel Chandler Harris, Sarah Orne Jewett, Mary Wilkins Freeman, Mary Noialles Murfree, Charles Dudley Warner—cede their places to Henry James, Henry Adams, and Theodore Dreiser. The critics are wiped out in toto, along with Edward Everett Hale, Ambrose Bierce, Henry Cuyler Bunner, and Frank Stockton. The "feminine novelists" of the twentieth century whom Pattee added to his 1932 edition—Willa Cather and Edith Wharton—give way to Faulkner, Fitzgerald, and Hemingway, and, with the exception of Frost, all of the twentieth-century poets—Robinson, Lindsay, Masters, Sandburg, Lowell, Sterling, and Millay—disappear.

The emphases have also changed. In 1919 Emma Lazarus is represented by four poems and Emily Dickinson by six. Henry James and Constance Fenimore Woolson are allotted two stories apiece; Bret Harte is represented by five selections, Mark Twain by one. Pattee includes just as many Civil War songs as poems by Walt Whitman, and in his introduction mentions "Poe or Lowell or Whitman or Burroughs" in a single breath, implying that they are all of similar stature; but hardly anyone knows who Burroughs is anymore (he wrote eighteen volumes of essays on nature in the late nineteenth century), and today Lowell is not considered the equal of Whitman and Poe.[8]

I have listed these excisions and revisions at length because they show in a detailed and striking manner that "literature" is not a stable entity, but a category whose outlines and contents are variable. The anthologies of the 1930s, midway between Pattee and

Miller, show unmistakably that this variability is a function of the political and social circumstances within which anthologists work.[9] The thirties' anthologies include items that had not appeared in such collections before and have seldom appeared there since— cowboy songs, Negro spirituals, railroad songs, southwestern yarns, and, in translation, the songs and prayers of Native Americans. They include letters, extracts from journals, passages from travel literature, and a large number of political speeches—Woodrow Wilson's "Address to Newly Naturalized Citizens," Lee's "Farewell to the Army of Northern Virginia." There are essays by Margaret Fuller and Sophia Ripley from *The Dial*, excerpts from Henry George's *Progress and Poverty* and *Social Problems*, William James' "What Pragmatism Means," and John Fiske's "Darwinism Verified." There are descriptions of America written by European writers, and a great deal of writing about, as well as by, Abraham Lincoln. One anthology, prepared by teachers from New York City, even turns the last forty pages into a sort of "melting pot" selection from the literatures of Europe and the Orient—passages from the Egyptian Book of the Dead; the sayings of Confucius and Gautama Buddha; an excerpt from Lady Murasaki; Greek, Hebrew, and Latin poetry; and translations from the literatures of Germany, Scandinavia, France, Spain, Italy, and Russia.[10]

In their introductions, the editors of these anthologies seem to be trying to reformulate their notions of what an anthology should represent, and of what literature itself should do. They say that "ethical as well as aesthetic ideals have been kept in mind in making this volume."[11] They say they want to combine "selections which embody reflections of the political and social history of the age with those which embody their authors' best literary art."[12] They speak of presenting a "variety of reactions" to "our great political experiment—democracy," by including writers "of recognized importance often overlooked by anthologists."[13] In all of their remarks, the editors evince a need to show the "connection" between "our literature and American life and thought," as if somehow literature had been delinquent in its responsibility to society.[14] In short, the social and political consciousness of the thirties changes anthologists' sense of their aims as literary critics.

That sense changes again in the fifties and early sixties. *Major Writers of America, Masters of American Literature*, and Macmillan's *Twelve American Writers*, coming at the end of the McCarthy era, the Cold War, and the heyday of New Criticism, are a response to the conservative temper of the post-war years, just as the collections of the thirties are to the Depression. Miller is not concerned to demonstrate literature's relation to social change, "democracy," or "American life"; on the contrary, he insists that "we must vindicate the study of literature primarily because the matter is *literature* and only secondarily because it is American."[15] He concerns himself not with the social relevance of literature, but with evaluation, or, as he puts it, making clear "which are the few peaks and which the many low-lying hills."[16] Miller's agenda, as I will demonstrate in a moment, belongs to the Eisenhower years, just as the thirties anthologies did to the New Deal. The different conceptions of literature these two kinds of anthologies represent—one seeing literature as a "voice of the people," emphasizing its relation to historical events, the other preoccupied with questions of aesthetic excellence and the formal integrity of individual works—show up in the split that develops within the anthology-making tradition. From about 1950 forward, three different types of anthologies are discernible: the "major masters" type represented by Perry Miller, Pochman and Allen, Gordon Ray, and Gibson and Arms; the "rich variety" type represented by Leon Howard, and Edwin Cady; with texts like the new Norton and the 1980 Macmillan falling somewhere in between.[17]

Yet even though anthologists characterize their projects differently, and although the contents of their volumes vary drastically, the one element that, ironically, remains unchanged throughout them all is the anthologists' claim that their *main* criterion of selection has been literary excellence. But, as has by now become abundantly clear, while the *term* "literary excellence" or "literary value" remains constant over time, its *meaning*—what literary excellence turns out to be in each case—does not. Contrary to what Miller believed, great literature does not exert its force over and against time, but changes with the changing currents of social and political life.

Still, someone might object that Miller's theory, whatever its abstract merits, justifies itself on practical grounds. Surely the authors represented in his anthology *are* the major writers of America, give or take a few names, while the works the anthology excludes are minor works at best. Most educated people today, if asked to say which was better, a poem by Stedman or a poem by Dickinson, would choose the latter without hesitation. And this fact would seem to bear out the rightness of Miller's intuitions about which writers ought to be considered great. But our conviction that Miller's choice was correct does not prove anything about the intrinsic superiority of the texts he chose; it proves only that we were introduced to American literature through the medium of anthologies similar to his. The general agreement about which writers are great and which are minor that exists at any particular moment in the culture creates the impression that these judgments are obvious and self-evident. But their obviousness is not a natural fact; it is constantly being produced and maintained by cultural activity: by literary anthologies, by course syllabi, book reviews, magazine articles, book club selections, radio and television programs, and even such apparently peripheral phenomena as the issuing of commemorative stamps in honor of Hawthorne and Dickinson, or literary bus tours of New England stopping at Salem and Amherst. The choice between Stedman and Dickinson, Stowe and Hawthorne, is never made in a vacuum, but from within a particular perspective that determines in advance which literary works will seem "good."

In saying that judgments of literary value are always perspectival, and not objective or disinterested, I do not wish to be understood as claiming that there is no such thing as value or that value judgments cannot or should not be made. We are always making choices, and hence value judgments, about which books to read, teach, write about, recommend, or have on our shelves. The point is not that these discriminations are baseless; the point is that the grounds on which we make them are not absolute and unchanging but contingent and variable. As Barbara Smith has recently argued, our tastes, emphases, preferences, and priorities, literary or otherwise, do not exist in isolation, but emerge from within a dynamic system of values which determines what, at a given moment, will be considered best.[18] Thus, for example, when the anthology editors of the late fifties and early sixties decided to limit their selection of American writers to a handful, they did so within a framework of critical beliefs that were themselves embedded in a larger cultural context. The notion that fullness and depth of representation are preferable to variety was already implicit in the New Critical insistence on studying "wholes" rather than "parts"; and that insistence, in turn, was implicit in the premium that formalism placed on making judgments about the aesthetic as opposed to the historical significance of works of art. Moreover, the formalist doctrines that stood behind the exclusivity of these anthologies did not take shape in isolation either, but were themselves implicated in a web of political, legislative, demographic, and institutional circumstances, and of disciplinary rivalries, that affected the way critics articulated and carried out their aims.

The New Critics' emphasis on the formal properties of literary discourse was part of a struggle that literary academicians had been waging for some time to establish literary language as a special mode of knowledge, so that criticism could compete on an equal basis with other disciplines, and particularly with the natural sciences, for institutional support. That struggle, whose nature had been determined by the growing prestige of science in the twentieth century, was intensified in the fifties by the arms race and especially by the launching of Sputnik, which added impetus to the rivalry between the sciences and the humanities and urgency to the claims that critics made for the primacy of form in understanding "how poems mean."[19] At the same time, the emphasis on formal properties accommodated another feature of the academic scene in the 1950s, namely, the tripling of the college population, brought about by the GI Bill, postwar affluence, and an increasing demand for people with advanced degrees.[20] The theory of literature that posited a unique interrelation of form and content justified close reading as an analytic technique that lent itself successfully to teaching literature on a mass scale. These connections between the contents of literary anthologies and historical phenomena such as the Depression, the GI Bill, and the arms race, show that *literary* judgments of value do not depend on literary considerations alone, since the notion of what is literary is defined by and nested within changing historical conditions of the kind I have outlined here. Thus, the emphasis on "major" writers did not come about in response to a sudden perception of the greatness of a few literary geniuses; it emerged from a series of interconnected circumstances that moved the theory, teaching, and criticism of literature in a certain direction.

But in arguing that criteria of literary judgment depend upon an array of fluctuating historical conditions, I do not mean to imply that "historical conditions" are a root cause from which everything else can be derived or that literature and criticism are always finally interpretable in the light of "brute facts" that exist independently of our systems of valuation. I do not wish to exempt descriptions of "historical context" from the variability and contingency to which I have said literary values are subject. "Historical conditions" are not external to the systems of valuation that they modify, but are themselves articulated within them. Thus, for example, the economic conditions of the Depression that called attention to working class, immigrant, and minority experience, and altered the contents of literary anthologies accordingly, could have been seen and described as they were only from within a value system that already insisted on the importance of the common man and took seriously the sufferings of ordinary people. The democratic tradition of values enabled certain "events" or "conditions" to be noticed and to assume a shape and significance such that they assumed priority in people's thinking and provided a basis for deciding what kind of experience a selection of American writing ought to represent. American literature itself, as represented in literary anthologies, affects the way people understand their lives and hence becomes responsible for defining historical conditions. Thus, if literary value judgments respond to changing historical conditions, the reverse is also true.

You will recall that the entire argument thus far has been a response to the question "but is it any good?" which implies that the works I have discussed are not really literary and are therefore not worth discussing. My tactic has been to show that the assumptions behind this question—namely, that literary values are fixed, independent, and demonstrably present in certain master-works—are mistaken, and I have used the evidence of the literary anthologies to challenge these notions one by one. But at this point someone might observe that despite changes in the contents of the anthologies, there are some authors and some works that do persist from one decade to the next and that therefore, although the perimeters of the canon may vary, its core remains unchanged, a testimony to the enduring merits of a few great masterpieces. To this objection I would reply that the evidence of the anthologies demonstrates not only that works of art are not selected according to any unalterable standard, but that their very essence is always changing in accordance with the systems of description and eval-uation that are in force. Even when the "same" text keeps turning up in collection after collection, it is not really the same text at all.

Let us take as an example Hawthorne's short story "The May-pole of Merrymount," which appears in the 1932 edition of *Century Readings in American Literature* along with "Sights from a Stee-ple," "The White Old Maid," "David Swan," and "The Old Manse." The other selections Pattee has chosen signal immediately that, although its title may be the same, this is not the tale Hershel Parker has included in the 1979 Norton anthology. For the context in which "The Maypole of Merrymount" appears in the Norton anthology is entirely different. I will come to that context in a moment; but first, let us look at how the tale is framed in 1932.

Pattee's introduction places all the emphasis on Hawthorne's personality and habits and has very little to say about the tales themselves. His biographical sketch depicts Hawthorne as "shy and solitary," "writing, dreaming, wandering about the city at night," a writer whose Puritanism was a "pale night flower" that bloomed amidst the "old decay and ruin" of a town whose mold-ering docks conveyed a sense of "glory departed."[21] The roman-ticism of this portrait stands in sharp contrast to Pattee's dry, taxonomic approach to Hawthorne's work. Pattee tells us he has chosen these pieces because they illustrate five of the eight "types" into which he has divided Hawthorne's shorter writings.[22] Thus for

Pattee's readers, Hawthorne's story emerges as an object to be identified and catalogued within a highly articulated system of classification. For not only is the tale one of four types within a subgroup (tales) within the classification "shorter writings," which is contrasted to another classification, "major romances," under the rubric "Hawthorne"; the author himself is identified as the member of a group, "The Concord Group" (made up of Hawthorne, Emerson, and Thoreau), which is one of six such groups— "The Mid-Century Historians" (Prescott, Motley, and Parkman), "The Cambridge Scholars" (Longfellow, Holmes, and Lowell), "Melville and Dana" in a category of their own, "The Southern Group" (Poe, Simms, and Hayne), and "The Anti-Slavery Movement" (Whittier, Stowe, Lincoln, and songs and ballads of the Civil War)—all of which constitute the category "The Mid-Nineteenth Century" that in its turn is one of the six historical periods into which Pattee divides all of American literature. This classificatory scheme, with its geographical and chronological bias, reproduces itself inevitably in the anthologist's only comment on "The Maypole of Merrymount," namely, that it is a "New England legend." Given his taxonomic approach to literary texts, there is little else that it could be.

This approach to Hawthorne reverses itself dramatically when one turns to the 1979 Norton anthology. Here it is the biography that is matter-of-fact; Hershel Parker's introduction gives us the "healthy" Hawthorne of Randall Stewart's revisionist biography, the Hawthorne who loved "tramping," drinking, smoking, and cardplaying, who socialized, flirted, and traveled "as far as Detroit."[23] Parker doesn't get excited until he starts talking about the tales, and then the fascination with morbidity and introversion that had animated Pattee's discourse on the "pale night flower" reappears. The tales Parker reprints along with "The Maypole"— "My Kinsman, Major Molineux," "Young Goodman Brown," "Rappaccini's Daughter," "Wakefield," "The Minister's Black Veil,"—are all, according to him, concerned with the "futility," "difficulty," and "impossibility" of dealing with the problems of "sin," "guilt," and "isolation."[24] These are the somber Freudian texts that mid-twentieth-century critics have created, texts that "muse obsessively over a small range of psychological themes," are full of "curiosity about the recesses of . . . men's . . . hearts," tales by "a master of psychological insight," whose "power of psychological burrowing" was nevertheless a source of "ambivalence" because of its invasive and prurient nature.[25] Thus, when the reader comes to "The Maypole of Merrymount" in the context provided by the Norton anthology, the tale is no longer a "New England legend"; it is a probe into the depths of the human heart. Parker's reading of the tale as "a conflict between lighthearted and sombre attitudes towards life" springs directly from an interpretive framework that sees literary texts as vehicles of "psychological insight," just as Pattee's definition sprang from an interpretive framework that classified texts according to historical, geographical, and generic categories.

The context within which "The Maypole of Merrymount" appears in each case frames the story so differently that the story itself changes. Neither its meaning nor its value remains constant from 1932 to 1979 because the strategies through which editors and their readers construct literary texts have changed in the intervening years. We may feel that the Norton editor is right, and that Hawthorne really was the "master of psychological insight" he is represented as here. But that is because our sense of Hawthorne's art, like Parker's, has been influenced by books such as Frederick Crews' *The Sins of the Fathers*,[26] and by an entire tradition of describing and interpreting human behavior that arose after psychoanalysis took root in the United States.

It is worth dwelling a moment longer on this example because it illustrates something important about the influence criticism has on the canon and what it represents. Crews' reading of Hawthorne reinforced the psychological perspective on his work and helped to determine *which* of Hawthorne's tales would be read by hundreds of thousands of Norton readers, and also *the way* those tales would be interpreted. The critical strategy that guides Crews' reading in effect constructs a new Hawthorne, who becomes for a time *the* Hawthorne—the only one that many students will ever know. As Crews' book is to "Hawthorne," so other broad-gauge and highly influential critical works are to "American literature." Books like

R. W. B. Lewis' *The American Adam* and Richard Chase's *The American Novel and its Tradition* have become responsible for the way we understand entire genres and whole periods of literary history, determining which authors are important, which texts are read, what vocabulary critics use to discuss them, and so on. These authors, texts, and issues are now regarded as permanent features of the literary landscape, and seem, like Perry Miller's "mountain peaks," to have been there always.

It is important to recognize that criticism creates American literature in its own image because American literature gives the American people a conception of themselves and of their history. As a spectacular example of this phenomenon, consider F. O. Matthiessen's *American Renaissance*, of which perhaps the most important sentences are these:

> The half-decade of 1850–55 saw the appearance of *Representative Men* (1850), *The Scarlet Letter* (1850), *The House of the Seven Gables* (1851), *Moby-Dick* (1851), *Pierre* (1852), *Walden* (1854), and *Leaves of Grass* (1855). You might search all the rest of American literature without being able to collect a group of books equal to these in imaginative vitality.[27]

With this list Matthiessen determined the books that students would read and critics would write about for decades to come. More important, he influenced our assumptions about what kind of person can be a literary genius, what kinds of subjects great literature can discuss, our notions about who can be a hero and who cannot, notions of what constitutes heroic behavior, significant activity, central issues. Matthiessen, who believed that criticism should "be for the good and enlightenment of all the people, and not for the pampering of a class," believed that the books he had chosen were truly representative of the American people, for these works, more than any others, called "the whole soul of man into activity."[28]

But from the perspective that has ruled this study, Matthiessen's list is exclusive and class-bound in the extreme. If you look at it carefully, you will see that in certain fundamental ways the list does not represent what most men and women were thinking about between 1850 and 1855, but embodies the views of a very small, socially, culturally, geographically, sexually, and racially restricted elite. None of the works that Matthiessen names is by an orthodox Christian, although that is what most Americans in the 1850s were, and although religious issues pervaded the cultural discourse of the period. None deals explicitly with the issues of abolition and temperance which preoccupied the country in this period, and gave rise to such popular works as *Uncle Tom's Cabin* and T. S. Arthur's *Ten Nights in a Barroom*. None of the works on the list achieved great popular success, although this six-year period saw the emergence of the first American best-sellers. The list includes no works by women, although women at that time dominated the literary marketplace. The list includes no works by males not of Anglo-Saxon origin, and indeed, no works by writers living south of New York, north of Boston, or west of Stockbridge, Massachusetts. From the point of view that has governed the foregoing chapters, these exclusions are a more important indicator of the representativeness of literary works than their power to engage "the whole soul of man."

What I want to stress is that the present study and Matthiessen's are competing attempts to constitute American literature. This book makes a case for the value of certain novels that Matthiessen's modernist critical principles had set at a discount. Instead of seeing such novels as mere entertainment, or as works of art interpretable apart from their context, which derive their value from "imaginative vitality" and address themselves to transhistorical entities such as the "soul of man," I see them as doing a certain kind of cultural work within a specific historical situation, and value them for that reason. I see their plots and characters as providing society with a means of thinking about itself, defining certain aspects of a social reality which the authors and their readers shared, dramatizing its conflicts, and recommending solutions. It is the notion of literary texts as doing work, expressing and shaping the social context that produced them, that I wish to substitute finally for the critical perspective that sees them as attempts to achieve a timeless, universal ideal of truth and formal coherence. The American Renaissance, as we now know it, provides people with an image of themselves and of their history, with conceptions of justice and of human nature, attitudes towards race, class, sex, and nationality. The literary canon, as codified by a cultural elite, has power to influence the way the country thinks across a broad range of issues. The struggle now being waged in the professoriate over which writers deserve canonical status is not just a struggle over the relative merits of literary geniuses; it is a struggle among contending factions for the right to be represented in the picture America draws of itself.

Notes

NOTES TO CHAPTER I

1. Samuel Johnson, *Preface to Shakespeare*, in *The Great Critics*, ed. James Harry Smith and Edd Winfield Parks, 3rd ed. (New York: W. W. Norton & Co., 1951), pp. 444–445.

2. Matthew Arnold, "The Study of Poetry," in *Essays in Criticism, Second Series* (London: Macmillan, 1958), pp. 2–3; Matthew Arnold, *Culture and Anarchy*, in *Lectures and Essays in Criticism*, ed. R. H. Super (Ann Arbor: University of Michigan Press, 1962), p. 13; Percy Bysshe Shelley, *A Defense of Poetry*, in *The Great Critics*, ed. Smith, pp. 563–564, 575.

3. T. S. Eliot, "What Is Minor Poetry?," in *On Poets and Poetry* (New York: Farrar, Straus & Cudahy, 1957), pp. 34–51; T. S. Eliot, "What Is a Classic?," in *On Poets and Poetry*, pp. 52–74. Frank Kermode devotes an entire chapter to Hawthorne's work without ever raising the question of why Hawthorne should be considered a classic author. *The Classic: Literary Images of Permanence and Change* (New York: Viking, 1975), pp. 90–114.

4. Bertha Faust, *Hawthorne's Contemporaneous Reputation: A Study of Literary Opinion in America and England, 1828–1864* (New York: 1968), a reprint of the 1939 University of Pennsylvania dissertation, p. 16.

5. Faust, pp. 16–17.

6. See Frank Luther Mott, *A History of American Magazines, 1741–1850* (New York: D. Appleton, 1930), I, for characterizations of *Graham's* (pp. 544–555); *Godey's Lady's Book* (pp. 580–594); and the *Southern Literary Messenger* (pp. 629–657).

7. Faust, pp. 12, 15, 17.

8. Faust, pp. 16, 24, 25.

9. Faust, p. 27.

10. Joseph Donald Crowley, ed., *Hawthorne, The Critical Heritage* (New York: Barnes & Noble, Inc., 1970), p. 55.

11. Henry Wadsworth Longfellow, *North American Review*, 45 (July 1837), pp. 59–73, as reprinted in *Hawthorne*, ed. Crowley, pp. 56, 55.

12. See, for example, Charles Fenno Hoffman, *American Monthly Magazine*, n.s., 5 (March 1838), pp. 281–283, as reprinted in *Hawthorne*, ed. Crowley, p. 61; Longfellow, as reprinted in Crowley, pp. 58–59; and Andrew Peabody, *Christian Examiner*, 25 (November 1838), pp. 182–190, as reprinted in Crowley, pp. 64–65.

13. *Major Writers of America*, ed. Perry Miller (New York: Harcourt, Brace & World, 1962), I, p. 465.

14. *Graham's Magazine*, (May 1842), as reprinted in *The Complete Works of*

Edgar Allan Poe, ed. James A. Harrison (New York: Thomas Y. Crowell, 1902), XI, p. 105.

15. *Godey's Lady's Book*, (November 1847), as reprinted in Harrison, XIII, pp. 154–155.

16. "Hawthorne and His Mosses," in *The Works of Herman Melville*, ed. Raymond Weaver (London: Constable & Co., 1922), XIII, pp. 123–143.

17. *The Works of Melville*, pp. 136, 131, 127, 125.

18. Peabody, as reprinted in *Hawthorne*, ed. Crowley, p. 66.

19. For an excellent discussion of the cult of domesticity, see Kathryn Kish Sklar, *Catherine Beecher, A Study in American Domesticity* (New York: W. W. Norton and Co., 1976), pp. 151–167; Peabody, as reprinted in *Hawthorne*, ed. Crowley, p. 64.

20. See Bernard Wishy, *The Child and the Republic* (Philadelphia: University of Pennsylvania Press, 1968).

21. Richard P. Adams, "Hawthorne's *Provincial Tales*," *The New England Quarterly*, 30 (March 1957), p. 50.

22. Adams, p. 50.

23. Of course, Adams' reading of "The Gentle Boy" may seem to *us* a willful imposition of his own ideas, and just as far off the mark, in its way, as Peabody's response. But what I am attempting to show is not that either critic is right or wrong, but that their readings of the tale flow naturally from their critical presuppositions.

24. As reprinted in *Hawthorne*, ed. Crowley, pp. 66, 56, 60.

25. F. O. Matthiessen, *American Renaissance: Art and Expression in the Age of Emerson and Whitman* (New York: Oxford University Press, 1941), pp. 274–275; *Hawthorne*, ed. Crowley, p. 58.

26. Samuel W. S. Dutton, "Nathaniel Hawthorne," *New Englander*, 5 (January 1847), pp. 56–69, as reprinted in *Hawthorne*, ed. Crowley, p. 138; Carolyn Kirkland, "Novels and Novelists," *North American Review*, 76 (1853), p. 114. See also two reviews of *Queechy*, one from *Tait's Magazine*, the other from the *New York Evening Post*, reprinted in *Littel's Living Age*, 34 (July–September 1852), pp. 57–58.

27. Henry F. Chorley, in a review of *The Blithedale Romance, Athenaeum*, 10 (July 1852), pp. 741–743, as reprinted in *Hawthorne*, ed. Crowley, p. 247 (the remark is typical); Kirkland, p. 121.

28. Kirkland, p. 121; the *Literary World*, 7 (December 1850), p. 525; Amory Dwight Mayo, "The Works of Nathaniel Hawthorne," *Universalist Quarterly*, 8 (July 1851), pp. 272–293, as reprinted in *Hawthorne*, ed. Crowley, pp. 219, 223.

29. Kirkland, p. 221. Most of Hawthorne's reviewers make this point in one way or another.

30. Evert Augustus Duyckinck, *Arcturus*, 1 (January 1841), pp. 125–126, as quoted in Faust, pp. 37–38.

31. Evert Augustus Duyckinck, the *Literary World*, 8 (April 1851), pp. 334–335, as reprinted in *Hawthorne*, ed. Crowley, p. 194; an unsigned review in the *Christian Examiner*, 50 (May 1851), pp. 508–509, as reprinted in Crowley, p. 195.

32. These characterizations of Hawthorne are drawn from reviews by Edgar Allan Poe, Anne W. Abbott, Rufus Griswold, Henry Tuckerman, E. P. Whipple, R. H. Stoddard, Samuel W. S. Dutton, Evert Duyckinck, Charles Wilkins Webber,

Amory Dwight Mayo, and George Loring. All are reprinted in *Hawthorne*, ed. Crowley.

33. These characterizations of Melville came from reviews in *The Spectator*, the Boston *Post*, the *Literary World*, the *Democratic Review*, the London *New Monthly Magazine*, the *Southern Quarterly*, the *Albion*, the *Atlas*, the *Athenaeum*, *Today*, and *Petersen's Magazine*, as cited by Hugh Hetherington, "Early Reviews of *Moby-Dick*," in *Moby-Dick Centennial Essays*, ed. Tyrus Hillway and Luther S. Mansfield (Dallas: Southern Methodist University Press, 1953), pp. 89–122.

34. Though critics used the terms "original" and "deep" to praise both writers, Hawthorne's reviewers liked to characterize him as "gentle," "tasteful," "quiet," "delicate," "subtle," "graceful," and "exquisite," while Melville's admirers constantly used words such as "racy," "wild," "extravagant," "brilliant," "eccentric," "outrageous," and "thrilling."

35. Mayo, as reprinted in *Hawthorne*, ed. Crowley, p. 223; Donald A. Ringe, "Hawthorne's Psychology of the Head and Heart," *PMLA*, 65 (1950), p. 120.

36. Ringe, pp. 121, 122, 125.

37. Mayo, as reprinted in *Hawthorne*, ed. Crowley, p. 223.

38. Mayo, as reprinted in *Hawthorne*, ed. Crowley, p. 221.

39. George Bailey Loring, *Massachusetts Quarterly Review*, 3 (September 1850), p. 484–500, as reprinted in *Hawthorne*, ed. Crowley, pp. 168–175. The critics in question are Bertha Faust; Joseph Donald Crowley; and Bernard Cohen, ed., *The Recognition of Nathaniel Hawthorne* (Ann Arbor: University of Michigan Press, 1969).

40. Anne W. Abbott, in *Hawthorne*, ed. Crowley, pp. 165, 166.

41. Loring, in *The Recognition of Hawthorne*, ed. Cohen, p. 48.

42. Loring, in *The Recognition of Hawthorne*, ed. Cohen, p. 48; Henry Nash Smith's characterization of Hawthorne's subject matter in "The Scribbling Women and the Cosmic Success Story," *Critical Inquiry*, 1 (September 1974), p. 58.

43. Loring, in *Hawthorne*, ed. Crowley, p. 173.

44. For one of the other famous attacks on *The Scarlet Letter*, see Orestes Brownson, *Brownson's Quarterly Review*, n.s., 5 (October 1850), pp. 528–532, as reprinted in *Hawthorne*, ed. Crowley, p. 175.

45. Loring, in *Hawthorne*, ed. Crowley, p. 171.

46. Conrad Wright, "Introduction," *A Stream of Light, A Sesquicentennial History of American Unitarianism*, ed. Conrad Wright (Boston: Unitarian Universalist Association, 1975).

47. Theodore Parker, "Discourse of the Transient and Permanent in Christianity," reprinted in *The Transcendentalists*, ed., introd. Perry Miller (Cambridge, Mass.: Harvard University Press, 1950), pp. 278, 277.

48. See Miller's headnote to Loring's review, reprinted in *The Transcendentalists*, ed. Miller, pp. 476.

49. Frank Luther Mott, *A History of American Magazines, 1850–1865* (Cambridge, Mass.: Harvard University Press, 1957), II, p. 241.

50. Mott, *American Magazines* (1930), I, pp. 775–779.

51. For the main outlines of the controversy, see *A Stream of Light*, ed. Wright.

52. Charles Feidelson, Jr., *Symbolism and American Literature* (Chicago: University of Chicago Press, 1953), p. 15.

53. C. E. Frazer Clark, Jr., "Posthumous Papers of a Decapitated Surveyor:

The Scarlet Letter in the Salem Press," *Studies in the Novel*, 2 (1970), pp. 395–419.

54. What happened was that Hawthorne, who had gotten the job through the influence of his old college friends and not through local connections or service to the party, lost his post when the Whigs took office. Because he was accused, in the process, of using his office for partisan ends, he became angry enough to stir up his friends on his behalf—hence the heated exchanges in the Salem and Boston papers. See George Woodberry, *Nathaniel Hawthorne* (Boston: Houghton Mifflin, 1902), pp. 163–177, and Arlin Turner, *Nathaniel Hawthorne, A Biography* (New York: Oxford University Press, 1980), pp. 177–187.

55. Longfellow, *North American Review*, 56 (April 1842), pp. 496–499, as reprinted in *Hawthorne*, ed. Crowley, p. 83.

56. Sydney E. Ahlstrom, *A Religious History of the American People* (New Haven: Yale University Press, 1972), p. 398. Ahlstrom's account of the emergence of Unitarianism is instructive for understanding the literary history of the period.

57. Lewis P. Simpson, *The Man of Letters in New England and the South* (Baton Rouge: Louisiana State University Press, 1973).

58. Simpson, p. 22.

59. Simpson, p. 22.

60. Robert E. Spiller et al., eds., *Literary History of the United States*, 3rd ed., rev. (London: Macmillan, 1963), pp. 286–287.

61. Mott, *American Magazines* (1930), I, pp. 253–255.

62. Mott, *American Magazines* (1957), II, p. 32.

63. Caroline Ticknor, *Hawthorne and His Publisher* (Boston: Houghton Mifflin, 1913), p. 7.

64. Mott, *American Magazines* (1957), II, pp. 33, 494, 496.

65. Turner, pp. 392–393.

66. *Literary History*, ed. Spiller, p. 888; Mott, *American Magazines* (1957), II, pp. 493 ff.

67. Edwin Cady, " 'The Wizard Hand': Hawthorne, 1864–1900," in *Hawthorne Centenary Essays*, ed. Roy Harvey Pearce (Columbus: Ohio State University Press, 1964), pp. 324 ff.

68. Cady, p. 331.

69. Much of this interesting social information is contained in Julian Hawthorne, *The Memoirs of Julian Hawthorne*, ed. Edith Garrigue Hawthorne (New York: Macmillan, 1938).

70. Cady, p. 334.

71. Anna Warner, *Susan Warner* (New York: G. P. Putnam Sons, 1909), p. 126.

72. Henry James, writing in *The Nation* in 1865, says that in its depiction of rural scenes *The Wide, Wide World* is superior to the realism of Flaubert. But later in the review he expresses exactly that critical doctrine which would eventually disqualify Warner's fiction from serious consideration as art. In reviewing *The Schönberg-Cotta Family*, he says that novels written for both parents and children, "frequently contain . . . an infusion of religious and historical information, and they in all cases embody a moral lesson. This latter fact is held to render them incompetent as novels; and doubtless, after all, it does, for of a genuine novel the meaning and the lesson are infinite; and here they are carefully narrowed down to a special precept." (*The Nation* [September 14, 1865], pp. 344–345). It is interesting

to compare James' comment with Brownson's review of *The Scarlet Letter* attacking the novel for failing to be Christian and moral enough.

73. Faust, p. 72; *Hawthorne*, ed. Crowley, p. 21; Faust, p. 141.

74. Henry James, *Hawthorne* (Ithaca: Cornell University Press, 1956), pp. 90–92.

75. Roy R. Male, in *American Literary Scholarship, An Annual, 1969* (Durham, North Carolina: Duke University Press, 1971), pp. 19–20.

NOTES TO CHAPTER II

1. Charles Brockden Brown, *Wieland; or The Transformation, An American Tale*, ed. Sydney J. Kraus et al. (Kent, Ohio: Kent State University Press, 1977), p. 3. All quotations from *Wieland* will be from this edition; chapter and page numbers will be given in parentheses in the text.

2. Paul Witherington, "Benevolence and the 'Utmost Breach': Charles Brockden Brown's Narrative Dilemma," *Criticism*, 14 (1972), pp. 175–191, sees Carwin as representing the destructive force of art; Michael Bell, " 'The Double-Tongued Deceiver': Sincerity and Duplicity in the Novels of Charles Brockden Brown," *Early American Literature*, 9 (Fall 1974), p. 143, also associates Carwin's villainy with literature and contends that for Brown literary order is threatened by the sources of its own energy; in *The Development of American Romance* (Chicago: University of Chicago Press, 1980), pp. 143–163, Bell broadens his interpretation to include psychological, and, in the later novels, political issues; A. Carl Bredahl, Jr., "Transformation in *Wieland*," *Early American Literature*, 12 (1977), pp. 77–191, expanding on Bell's idea, attributes the transformations of the novel to a demonic energy associated with the imagination, and life in the New World; Robert Ferguson, "Literature and Vocation in the Early Republic: The Example of Charles Brockden Brown," *Modern Philology*, 78 (November 1980), pp. 139–152, argues that Brown pictured himself as a Romantic artist whose sensibilities were threatened by a philistine world and whose fiction is therefore dominated by vocational anxieties; and Mark Seltzer, "Saying Makes It So: Language and Event in Brown's *Wieland*," *Early American Literature*, 13, (1978), pp. 81–91, picking up on Bell's notion that the imagination is duplicitous, extends that to cover "an equivocation regarding the process of uttering," and "an uncertain causal relation between speech" and its effects.

3. Because Brown's settings are, relatively speaking, so empty, there is a strong tendency for critics to see him as dealing in universal symbols. Leslie Fiedler, *Love and Death in the American Novel* (New York: The World Publishing Company, 1962) p. 142, sees Brown as a mythopoeic novelist who projected our "deepest fears and guilts" into "symbolic actions" taking place in a "symbolic landscape"; Dieter Schultz, "*Edgar Huntly* as Quest Romance," *American Literature*, 43 (1971), pp. 323–335, and Philip R. Hughes, "Archetypal Patterns in *Edgar Huntly*," *Studies in the Novel*, 5, pp. 176–190, read *Edgar Huntly* as, respectively, a quest romance and a Jungian Myth of the Hero; Carl Nelson, Jr., "Brown's Manichaean Mock-Heroic: The Ironic Self in a Hyperbolic World," *West Virginia University Philological Papers*, 20 (1975), pp. 26–42, argues that the "true substance of [Brown's]

work" lies in "the psychological polarities of the human mind"; David Lyttle, "The Case Against Carwin," *Nineteenth Century Fiction*, 26 (1971), pp. 257–269, maintains that Carwin, using Clara and Wieland as surrogate parents, acts out an Oedipal revolt against his own father; and Donald A. Ringe, *Charles Brockden Brown* (New York: Twayne Publishers, 1966) p. 66, concludes somewhat weakly that in *Wieland* "human beings are much more complex than the contemporary psychology assumed and . . . their motives and actions are not so simply explained." In a recent psychological interpretation of *Wieland*, which makes an elaborate case that Clara herself is mad, James F. Russo, "The Chimeras of the Brain," *Early American Literature*, 16 (1981), pp. 60–88, claims that *Wieland* "ultimately . . . deals with the complex issue of epistemology," and that the real problem is that "Man is incapable of perceiving things correctly." The most recent book on Brown's fiction, Alan Axelrod, *Charles Brockden Brown, An American Tale* (Austin, Texas: University of Texas Press, 1983), p. 64, also takes this line, though it attributes Brown's epistemological skepticism to his "uneasy command of both Old and New World sources."

4. Larzer Ziff, "A Reading of *Wieland*," *PMLA*, 77 (1962), pp. 51–57, was the first to recognize Brown's critique of the enlightenment's optimistic psychology; William Hedges, "Charles Brockden Brown and the Culture of Contradictions," *Early American Literature*, 9 (1974), pp. 107–142, emphasizes the need to pay attention to Brown's political and philosophical ideas and to his cultural milieu, but concentrates his own analysis on the cultural contradictions of *Edgar Huntly* and *Arthur Mervyn*. Those critics whose reading of *Wieland* most resembles my own are Jay Fliegelman, *Prodigals and Pilgrims, The American Revolution Against Patriarchal Authority, 1750–1800* (Cambridge: Cambridge University Press, 1982), pp. 237–240, and David Brion Davis, *Homicide in American Fiction, 1789–1860: A Study in Social Values* (Ithaca, N.Y.: Cornell University Press, 1957). While Fliegelman and I developed almost identical approaches to *Wieland* independently, I am indebted to Davis for indicating that *Wieland* might be read as a socio-political allegory.

5. Joseph Katz, "Analytical Bibliography and Literary History: The Writing and Printing of *Wieland*," *Proof*, I (1971), pp. 8 ff., provides a sampling of the chorus of complaints over Brown's "unprofessionalism," but then goes on to acknowledge their justice by explaining that Brown was writing the novel while it was being printed, had no opportunity to revise, and wrote the final chapters as a way of reconciling the narrative's "changing directions."

6. Nina Baym, "A Minority Reading of *Wieland*," in *Critical Essays on Charles Brockden Brown*, ed. Bernard Rosenthal (Boston: G. K. Hall, 1981), pp. 87–103. The quotation is on p. 91.

7. Baym, pp. 88, 92, 95.

8. Joseph Ellis, *After the Revolution: Profiles of Early American Culture* (New York: W. W. Norton & Co., 1979), pp. 25, 24.

9. Neither of two very informative and interesting analyses of Brown's political ideas, Charles C. Cole, Jr., "Brockden Brown and the Jefferson Administration," *Pennsylvania Magazine of History and Biography*, 72 (July 1948), pp. 253–263, and Warner Berthoff, "Brockden Brown: The Politics of the Man of Letters," *The Serif*, 3, No. 4 (December 1966), pp. 3–11, sees Brown's novels as vehicles for his

politics. Cole never discusses Brown's fiction, and Berthoff, pp. 3–4, reflecting the standard critical consensus, has this to say:

> From the metaphysics of spiritual "transformation" (the subtitle of *Wieland*) he turned to the mechanics of practicable social compromise. It is this latter interest that finds expression in Brown's political writings, the great bulk of which was produced after 1801. His preoccupations as a writer cease now to resemble those of a Poe or Hawthorne and approach those of a Fenimore Cooper. For Cooper's studied methods of advancing political opinions and social judgments in fiction, however, Brown had neither talent nor interest. He simply changed his métier.

Both Cole and Berthoff, moreover, date Brown's opposition to Jefferson from the period when Brown gave up writing fiction. Cole, pp. 253, 254, dates the beginning of a transition to conservatism from "after 1798," with the "change of heart" registering finally in 1803, and Berthoff seems to concur.

10. This and the following account of the relationship between literature and politics in the period surrounding the American Revolution are drawn chiefly from Kenneth Silverman, *A Cultural History of the American Revolution* (New York: Thomas Y. Crowell Company, 1976), pp. 484–536.

11. Silverman, p. 520.

12. Silverman, p. 513. For an interesting discussion of the Federalist satirists, who exemplify the interpenetration of literature and politics in Brown's day, see Linda Kerber, "Journey to Laputa: The Federalist Era as an Augustan Age," in *Federalists in Dissent: Imagery and Ideology in Jeffersonian America* (Ithaca N.Y.: Cornell University Press, 1970), pp. 1–22.

13. Silverman, p. 487.

14. Joel Barlow, *The Works of Joel Barlow*, ed. and introd. William K. Bottorff and Arthur L. Ford (Gainesville, Fla.: Scholars' Facsimiles and Reprints, 1970), p. 99.

15. Charles Brockden Brown, "Walstein's School of History," in *The Rhapsodist and Other Uncollected Writings*, ed. Harry Warfel (New York: Scholars' Facsimiles and Reprints, 1943), p. 150.

16. As quoted by David Lee Clark, *Charles Brockden Brown, Pioneer Voice of America* (Durham, North Carolina: Duke University Press, 1952), p. 163.

17. Brown, "Walstein's School," pp. 151–152.

18. Brown, "Walstein's School," p. 150.

19. Brown, "Walstein's School," p. 154.

20. William Godwin, *The Adventures of Caleb Williams, or Things As They Are*, ed. George Sherburne (New York: Holt, Rinehart & Winston, 1960), p. xxiii.

21. *Great Issues in American History: A Documentary Record, 1765–1865*, ed. Richard Hofstadter (New York: Vintage Books, 1958), I, pp. 64–65.

22. *Tracts of the American Revolution, 1763–1776*, ed. Merrill Jensen (Indianapolis: Bobbs-Merrill, 1967), p. 488.

23. As quoted by Howard Mumford Jones, *O Strange New World, American Culture: The Formative Years* (New York: The Viking Press, 1952) p. 295.

24. Jones, pp. 276–292.

25. Gordon S. Wood, "Introduction," *The Rising Glory of America, 1760–1820*, ed. Gordon S. Wood (New York: George Braziller, 1971), p. 10.

26. This account is based on Lawrence Friedman, *Inventors of the Promised Land* (New York: Alfred A. Knopf, 1975), pp. 3–78.

27. Thomas Jefferson, Letter to Charles Bellini, Sept. 30, 1785. As quoted by Howard Mumford Jones, p. 297.

28. St. Jean de Crèvecoeur, "What Is an American?" in *Letters from an American Farmer*, ed. W. P. Trent and Ludwig Lewisohn (New York: E. P. Dutton, 1906), p. 40.

29. These are the words of James Otis, quoted by John Eliot to Jeremy Belknap, *Belknap Papers* (January 12, 1777), p. 104, as quoted by Gordon S. Wood, *The Creation of the American Republic, 1776–1787* (New York: W. W. Norton & Co., 1969), p. 477. On this phenomenon Wood himself makes the following pronouncement, which accords well with Brown's picture of the post-Revolutionary era: "The most pronounced social effect of the Revolution was not harmony or stability but the sudden appearance of new men everywhere in politics and business."

30. For the Republican vs. the Federalist view of the efficacy of education in promoting good government, see Wood, *Creation*, pp. 426–428.

31. John Dickinson, *The Letters of Fabius, in 1788, on the Federal Constitution*, as quoted by Wood, *Creation*, p. 475. "Whenever any disorder happens in any government," wrote supporters of the Constitution, "it must be ascribed, to a fault in some of the institutions of it," as quoted by Wood, *Creation*, p. 429.

32. Axelrod, p. 57. Axelrod makes very little of this point, which seems to me crucial in understanding what *Wieland* is about.

33. Brown's combination of conservative politics and epistemological skepticism parallels Hume's, although for Brown the inability to perceive and judge accurately is a consequence of political and social instability, and not a separate philosophical issue. Humean skepticism, according to Henry F. May, *The Enlightenment in America* (New York: Oxford University Press, 1976), pp. 112–114, defined one of the two main forms of enlightenment thought in America, although Hume's political and religious notions (as contained in his *History of England* and the *Essays*) were better known than his epistemology. Two of the passages that May quotes from Hume seem particularly relevant to the views Brown seems to adopt in *Wieland*. Speaking of popular turbulence that arises from religious fanaticism, Hume says:

> Popular rage is dreadful, from whatever motive derived: But must be attended with the most pernicious consequences, when it arises from a principle, which disclaims all controul by human law, reason, or authority. ("Of the Coalition of Parties," *Philosophical Works*, III, p. 469.)

Hume, according to May, p. 119, blamed the English Civil War on Puritan fanaticism, and believed that illegal violence always ends, as it did in this case, in despotism. Brown's critique of antinomianism in *Wieland* parallels Hume's, and Clara's mystification at Wieland's "divine" revelation resembles Hume's agnosticism on the question of religious faith:

> The whole is a riddle, an aenigma, an inexplicable mystery. Doubt, uncertainty, suspense of judgment appear the only result of our most accurate scrutiny, concerning this subject. ("The Natural History of Religion," *Philosophical Works*, IV, p. 363.)

Whether or not Brown knew Hume isn't known, but, according to May, pp. 233–235, the members of the Friendly Club, to which Brown belonged, had read Hume, and, distressed by the popular turbulence of New York politics in the 1790s, became politically more conservative, despite their enthusiasm for Godwin, in an effort to distinguish themselves from the masses, whom they deemed ignorant and prejudiced.

34. Davis is the first person to suggest reading the history of the Wielands as an allegory of the coming of civilization to the New World. His interpretation, pp. 88–94, which is highly schematic and concentrates on the second and third generations of Wielands, is the basis of my own reading.

35. Joseph Ridgely, "The Empty World of *Wieland*," in *Individual and Community: Variations on a Theme in American Fiction* (Durham, North Carolina: Duke University Press, 1975), pp. 3–16. Ridgely, p. 16, at the end of his essay, broaches the line of thought I have developed at length here. "Brown himself," he writes, "was experiencing the deprivation of a fostering social order, of those traditional institutions by which the individual self attempts to gauge its proper role. . . . The terrible emptiness of the world of *Wieland* . . . suggest[s] that Brown perceived America's need for . . . some replacement for severed parental ties."

36. Jones, p. 434, cites the following works as providing accounts of the "stirring effect" the American Revolution had on European countries; Jacques Godechot, *Les Révolutions (1770–1799)*, and Durand Echeverria, *Mirage in the West: A History of the French Image of American Society to 1815*. He also provides, p. 275, a dramatic account of the precariousness of American civil life in the post-Revolutionary era, which he sums up as follows:

Instability was of the essence of the American nation. The rickety though threatening republic was born in civil war among the members of the British Empire and had tried to conquer or lure other parts of that empire into rebellion. Operating after 1776 under a bad constitution that was not even adopted until 1781, the nation had replaced this by another constitution in 1789. It had been threatened by a monarchical counter-revolution and a military putsch in 1782. It had had to put down treason in 1777, 1780, and 1804–5. It had, since the treaty of 1789, fought one war in 1798, a second in 1801, a third in 1812, and it carried on incessant excursions over its vague borders into the Indian country. It had confronted insurrection in 1786 and again in 1794, and threats of secession in 1784 [the "State of Franklin"], in 1789, and in 1814.

37. These quotations are from the *New-England Palladium* (1801), as cited by Kerber, pp. 193–194.

38. Kerber, p. 194. According to Kerber, Federalists constantly cited the decline of the Roman and Athenian republics as examples of what might happen here, adducing as evidence Aristotle's warning that the standard fate of a democracy was demagoguery. See especially chapter 6, pp. 173–215.

39. Fred Lewis Pattee, "Introduction," *Wieland, or the Transformation, Together with Memoirs of Carwin the Biloquist, A Fragment*, by Charles Brockden Brown (New York: Harcourt Brace Jovanovich, 1926), p. xlii.

40. The tale of seduction fascinated American audiences both before and after the Revolution (*Charlotte Temple* was the great best-seller and *Clarissa* extremely popular) partly because it offered a displaced account of what it means to disobey authority. In popular versions, the seduction ends in death for the fallen woman,

as in *Wieland*, but it produces a religious conversion in the victim, making it possible to interpret her disobedience as a "fortunate fall"—a comforting interpretation for American audiences who wanted to feel that their own disobedience had been justified and could be redeemed. This "American" reading of the seduction fable was first developed by Fliegelman. But no Christian act of repentance mitigates the death of Louisa Conway *mère*; her case and that of her daughter function in Brown's novel in exactly the opposite way from the one Fliegelman ascribes to *Clarissa*, namely, as an indictment of, rather than as an apology for, transgression.

41. Baym, p. 91.
42. Baym, p. 91.
43. Baym, p. 91.

NOTES TO CHAPTER III

1. Charles Brockden Brown, *Arthur Mervyn; or, Memoirs of the Year 1793*, ed. Sydney J. Krause et al. (Kent, Ohio: Kent State University Press, 1980), p. 133, 134. All further quotations from *Arthur Mervyn* will be from this edition; part, chapter, and page numbers will be given in parentheses in the text.

2. Norman Grabo, *The Coincidental Art of Charles Brockden Brown* (Chapel Hill: University of North Carolina Press, 1981), pp. ix–xii. But Grabo's thesis, p. x, unlike mine, is that these coincidences reflect Brown's "sense of design" and "sophisticated art."

3. James H. Justus, "Arthur Mervyn, American," *American Literature*, 42 (1970), pp. 304–324, sees the novel as a homiletic *bildungsroman*; Patrick Brancaccio, "Studied Ambiguities: *Arthur Mervyn* and the Problem of the Unreliable Narrator," *American Literature*, 42 (1970), pp. 18–27, reads it as the story of a young man on the make in a competitive, moralistic business culture; Carl W. Nelson, Jr., "A Method for Madness: The Symbolic Patterns in *Arthur Mervyn*," *West Virginia University Philological Papers*, 22 (1975), pp. 29–50, reads the novel as a kind of failed psychological *bildungsroman*; Donald A. Ringe, *American Gothic* (Lexington, Ky.: University of Kentucky Press, 1982) discusses the Gothicism of Brown's depictions of the plague. Several articles address the question of Mervyn's trustworthiness and sincerity, pointing in various ways to the novel's alleged moral ambiguity: Warner Berthoff, "Adventures of a Young Man: An Approach to Charles Brockden Brown," *American Quarterly*, 9 (Winter 1957), pp. 421–434; Kenneth Bernard, "Arthur Mervyn: The Ordeal of Innocence," *Texas Studies in Literature and Language*, 6 (1965), pp. 441–459; Donald Ringe, *Charles Brockden Brown* (New York: Twayne Publishers, 1966); Brancaccio; John Cleman, "Ambiguous Evil: A Study of Villains and Heroes in Charles Brockden Brown's Major Novels," *Early American Literature*, 11 (Fall 1975), pp. 190–217; and more recently, Norman Grabo, "Historical Essay," in the Kent State edition of *Arthur Mervyn*, pp. 447–475. On the other hand, James F. Russo, "The Chameleon of Convenient Vice: A Study of the Narrative of *Arthur Mervyn*," *Studies in the Novel*, 11 (1979), pp. 381–405, sees Mervyn as an out-and-out scoundrel, a conscious liar, seducer, imposter, and murderer—and no ambiguity about it.

4. Grabo, "Historical Essay," p. 473, notes that this tradition began as early as 1824 in a long *Retrospective Review*, 9 (1824), pp. 322–323, which states, "Brown

. . . was defective, generally speaking, in the construction of his plots. His story turns too entirely on one character, and the events are sometimes improbable." And he cites John Neal as remarking that Brown was essentially a writer out of control, a suggestion which, Grabo notes, p. 473, "still haunts criticism of *Arthur Mervyn*."

5. Warner Berthoff, "Introduction," *Arthur Mervyn or, Memoirs of the Year 1793* (New York: Holt, Rinehart, & Winston, 1962), p. vii.

6. Charles Brockden Brown, "Walstein's School of History," in *The Rhapsodist and Other Uncollected Writings*, ed. Harry Warfel (New York: Scholars' Facsimiles and Reprints, 1943), p. 151. Future quotations from "Walstein's School" will be from this edition; page numbers will be given in parentheses in the text. Grabo, "Historical Essay," p. 463, is the only critic of note who takes Brown's pronouncements in "Walstein's School" seriously, pointing to parallel assertions in the preface to *Arthur Mervyn* itself, where Brown speaks of the plague as "fertile of instruction to the moral observer" and as affording an opportunity "of inculcating on mankind the lessons of justice and humanity"(p. 3). But he suspects Brown of "devious purposes" here, given the "sensational events" and "moral ambiguities" that fill the novel.

7. Warner Berthoff, " 'A Lesson on Concealment': Brockden Brown's Method in Fiction," *Philological Quarterly*, 37 (1958), pp. 45–57, gives an account of Brown's plot structure that is similar to this one, but his attitude toward the phenomenon he describes seems on the whole critical. Certainly his criticisms of the "haphazardness" and "discontinuities" in *Arthur Mervyn*'s plot (Rinehart edition, "Introduction," pp. vii, xiv) suggest that he saw this feature of Brown's fiction as a flaw.

8. Whether Brown assumed his readers were male or female or of both sexes is a complex issue beyond the scope of this essay.

9. J. G. A. Pocock, *The Machiavellian Moment: Florentine Political Thought and the Atlantic Tradition* (Princeton: Princeton University Press, 1975), p. 507. I am grateful to Michael Warner for pointing out the relevance of Pocock's great study to my reading of *Arthur Mervyn*.

10. My account of Federalist economic policy is based on Curtis P. Nettels, *The Emergence of a National Economy, 1775–1815*, Vol. II of *The Economic History of the United States* (New York: Holt, Rinehart & Winston, 1962).

11. See Albert O. Hirschmann, "Money-Making and Commerce as Innocent and *Doux*," in *The Passions and the Interests* (Princeton: Princeton University Press, 1977) for a fascinating account of the origin of this notion of commerce. Hirschmann, pp. 56–66, explains that the notion of commerce as a softening and refining activity begins in France in the seventeenth century; that its most influential spokesman was Montesquieu in *The Spirit of the Laws*; that it became linked with the idea of "good" or "calm" passions, as opposed to violent ones, as elaborated by Shaftesbury and Hutcheson; and that the "calm" passion of money-making became associated in turn with the notion of "interest" as a restrainer of violent passion.

12. William Robertson, *View of the Progress of Society in Europe* (1769), ed., introd. Felix Gilbert (Chicago: University of Chicago Press, 1972), p. 67.

13. On Hamilton's economic program, see Nettels, pp. 104–108.

14. On the shortage of currency after the Revolution, see Nettels, pp. 48 ff., 75 ff. One of the effects of the plague noted by Matthew Carey, *A Short Account of*

the Malignant Fever which Prevailed in Philadelphia, in the Year 1793 (Philadelphia: Carey and Lea, 1830), is that the cessation of trade caused a severe shortage of currency.

15. James Henretta, *The Evolution of American Society, 1700–1815* (Lexington, Mass.: D. C. Heath and Co., 1973). My description of the American economy in the period after the Revolution is based on Henretta's account.

16. Henretta, p. 80.

17. See Gordon Fite and Jim Reese, *An Economic History of the United States* (Boston: Houghton Mifflin, 1973).

18. Fite and Reese, p. 115.

19. Hirschmann, p. 61.

20. Berthoff, "Introduction," p. xiv.

21. Carey, pp. 26–27.

22. Carey, p. 27.

23. Pocock, pp. 527–528.

24. Thomas Jefferson, *Notes on the State of Virginia*, ed., introd. Thomas Perkins Abernethy (New York: Harper and Row, 1964), pp. 157–158.

25. Pocock, p. 508, notes that the "Court" ideology in British politics from which Federalist thinking derives "was based not on a simple antithesis between virtue and commerce, but on an awareness that the two interpenetrated one another as did land and currency, authority and liberty."

NOTES TO CHAPTER IV

1. James Fenimore Cooper, *The Last of the Mohicans; A Narrative of 1757*, introd. James Franklin Beard, ed. James A. Sappenfield and E. N. Feltskog (Albany: State University of New York Press, 1983), chap. XXXII, pp. 336–337. All quotations from the novel will be from this edition; chapter and page numbers will be given in parentheses in the text.

2. I refer here to criticism of the Leatherstocking tales and not to criticism of either Cooper's other adventure fiction or his "social" novels.

3. Robert E. Spiller et al., ed., *Literary History of the United States*, I, 4th ed., rev. (New York: Macmillan, 1974), pp. 261, 257.

4. Eric Sundquist, *Home as Found: Authority and Genealogy in Nineteenth-Century American Literature* (Baltimore: The Johns Hopkins University Press, 1979), p. 1.

5. Richard Slotkin, *Regeneration Through Violence* (Middletown, Conn.: Wesleyan University Press, 1973), p. 466. Slotkin, p. 467, goes on to exonerate Cooper from the charge of oversimplification by arguing that "conscious artists," such as Cooper, used stereotypes merely as a "point of creative departure," extracting from them "more . . . moral, social, and metaphysical meaning than . . . [their] purely commercial colleagues."

6. Richard W. B. Lewis, *The American Adam* (Chicago: University of Chicago Press, 1955), p. 104; A. N. Kaul, *The American Vision* (New Haven: Yale University Press, 1963), p. 121.

7. Lewis, p. 102; Kaul, p. 121; Michael D. Butler, "Narrative Structure and

Historical Process in *The Last of the Mohicans*," *American Literature*, 48 (1976), p. 122.

8. James Fenimore Cooper, *The Prairie*, afterword J.W. Ward (New York: New American Library, 1964), p. 405.

9. D. H. Lawrence, *Studies in Classic American Literature* (New York: Thomas Seltzer, 1923). The key passage in the essay, p. 78, is one that describes the relationship between Natty and Chingachgook as "deeper than the deeps of sex. Deeper than property, deeper than fatherhood, deeper than marriage, deeper than love."

10. Yvor Winters, "Fenimore Cooper, or The Ruins of Time," in *In Defense of Reason*, 3rd ed. (Denver: Swallow Press, 1964), p. 197.

11. Henry Nash Smith, *Virgin Land: The American West as Symbol and Myth* (Cambridge: Harvard University Press, 1960), pp. 60–61.

12. Lewis, pp. 100–101.

13. Claude Lévi-Strauss, *Totemism*, trans. Rodney Needham (Boston: Beacon Press, 1963); Lévi-Strauss, "The Story of Asdiwal," in *The Structural Study of Myth and Totemism*, ed. Edmund Leach (London: Tavistock, 1967), pp. 1–47; Lévi-Strauss, *The Raw and the Cooked*, trans. John and Doreen Weightman (New York: Harper and Row, 1969).

14. Lewis, p. 101.

15. D. H. Lawrence established the pattern for this strain of Cooper criticism, which has been the dominant one in the twentieth century. It has been taken up in various forms and with various emphases by such critics as Leslie Fiedler, R. W. B. Lewis, Richard Chase, Joel Porte, and, more recently, Richard Slotkin and Stephen Railton.

16. *The American Novel and Its Tradition* (Baltimore: The Johns Hopkins University Press, 1957). Rpt. of the 1st ed. published by Doubleday, Garden City, N.Y.

17. I am referring to the tradition of Cooper criticism initiated by Robert Spiller in *Fenimore Cooper: Critic of His Times* (New York: Minton, Balch & Co., 1931), and continued by James Grossman, Kay House, and John McWilliams.

18. Lewis, pp. 102–104, for instance, bases his discussion of Cooper's myth of the American hero largely on an analysis of the scene from *The Deerslayer* in which Natty Bumppo kills his first Indian.

19. Timothy Dwight, *Travels in New England and New York*, ed. Barbara M. Solomon (Cambridge, Mass: Harvard University Press, 1969), I, p. xxxiv, as quoted by Moses Rischin, "Creating Crevecoeur's 'New Man': He had a Dream," *Journal of American Ethnic History*, I (1981, 1982), pp. 26–42.

20. Thomas J. Archdeacon, *Becoming American* (New York: The Free Press, 1983), p. 24.

21. Dwight, as quoted by Rischin, I, p. xxxiv.

22. James Fenimore Cooper, *The Pioneers, or the Sources of the Susquehanna; A Descriptive Tale*, introd. and notes James Franklin Beard, ed. Lance Schachterle and Kenneth M. Anderson, Jr. (Albany: State University of New York Press, 1980), chap. III, p. 43.

23. The epigraphs of the novels focus on the theme of "kinds" in a way that points to the difference between the two works. The epigraph of *The Pioneers* is:

"Extremes of habits, manners, time and space,
Brought close together, here stood face to face,
And gave at once a contrast to the view,
That other lands and ages never knew."
Paulding, *The Backwoodsman*, II, 517–574.

And of *The Last of the Mohicans*:

"Mislike me not, for my complexion,
The shadowed livery of the burnished sun."
The Merchant of Venice, II.i.1–2.

24. Richard Drinnon, *Facing West: The Metaphysics of Indian-Hating and Empire-Building* (New York: New American Library, 1980), p. 99.

25. Winthrop Jordan, *White Over Black: American Attitudes Towards the Negro, 1550–1812* (New York: W. W. Norton & Co., 1968), p. xiii.

26. Archdeacon, p. xvi.

27. But the idea of Indian removal had been broached by Jefferson in his plans for the Louisiana territory as early as 1803, according to Drinnon, pp. 83–85.

28. Lawrence Friedman, *Inventors of the Promised Land* (New York: Alfred A. Knopf, 1975), pp. 180 ff.

29. Drinnon, pp. 115–116, points out that the Indian removal policy and Monroe's foreign policy, which arrogated to the United States alone the right to expand in the western hemisphere, mirrored and reinforced one another. "Both provided *prospective* justification for the rapid multiplication of citizens of the United States and for their expansion onto the lands of nonwhites." And the colonization idea, in its turn, was the mirror image of the Indian removal policy. "Blacks . . . could be sent 'back,' to some such place as Sierra Leone, the Indians should move 'on' beyond the horizon of the Great Desert."

30. Jordan, p. xiv.

31. Jordan, p. xiv.

32. See Louise Barnett, *The Ignoble Savage: American Literary Racism, 1790–1890* (Westport, Conn.: Greenwood Press, 1975), pp. 21 ff.

33. Barnett, p. 54.

34. Barnett, p. 67.

35. Michael Bell, *Hawthorne and the Historical Romance of New England* (Princeton: Princeton University Press, 1971), pp. 93 ff., observes that novelists of this period who emphasized America's progress toward religious tolerance used Indians to represent natural piety, which they contrasted to the narrow dogmatism and legalistic mentality of the Puritans. In these narratives, the Puritans' intolerance is illustrated by their burning of witches and by their victimization of the Indians.

36. Benjamin Rush, *The Selected Writings of Benjamin Rush*, ed. Dagobert Runes (New York: Philosophical Library, 1947), pp. 21–22.

NOTES TO CHAPTER V

This chapter is a slightly revised version of the essay that originally appeared in *Glyph, 8*. I would like to thank Sacvan Bercovitch for his editorial suggestions.

1. Johanna Johnston, *Runaway to Heaven* (Garden City, N.Y.: Doubleday and Co., 1963).

2. Edward Halsey Foster, for example, prefaces his book-length study *Susan and Anna Warner* (Boston: Twayne Publishers, n.d.), p. 9, by saying: "If one searches nineteenth-century popular fiction for something that has literary value, one searches, by and large, in vain." At the other end of the spectrum stands a critic like Sally Mitchell, whose excellent studies of Victorian women's fiction contain statements that, intentionally or not, condescend to the subject matter. For example, in "Sentiment and Suffering: Women's Recreational Reading in the 1860's," *Victorian Studies*, 21, No. 1 (Autumn 1977), p. 34, she says: "Thus, we should see popular novels as emotional analyses, rather than intellectual analyses, of a particular society." The most typical move, however, is to apologize for the poor literary quality of the novels and then to assert that a text is valuable on historical grounds.

3. Ann Douglas is the foremost of the feminist critics who have accepted this characterization of the sentimental writers, and it is to her formulation of the anti-sentimentalist position, *The Feminization of American Culture* (New York: Alfred A. Knopf, 1977), that my arguments throughout are principally addressed. Although her attitude toward the vast quantity of literature written by women between 1820 and 1870 is the one that the male-dominated tradition has always expressed—contempt—Douglas' book is nevertheless extremely important because of its powerful and sustained consideration of this long-neglected body of work. Because Douglas successfully focused critical attention on the cultural centrality of sentimental fiction, forcing the realization that it can no longer be ignored, it is now possible for other critics to put forward a new characterization of these novels and not be dismissed. For these reasons, it seems to me, her work is important.

4. These attitudes are forcefully articulated by Douglas, p. 9.

5. The phrase, "a damned mob of scribbling women," coined by Hawthorne in a letter he wrote to his publisher, in 1855, and clearly the product of Hawthorne's own feelings of frustration and envy, comes embedded in a much-quoted passage that has set the tone for criticism of sentimental fiction ever since. As quoted by Fred Lewis Pattee, *The Feminine Fifties* (New York: D. Appleton-Century Co., 1940), p. 110, Hawthorne wrote:

> America is now wholly given over to a d****d mob of scribbling women, and I should have no chance of success while the public taste is occupied with their trash—and should be ashamed of myself if I did succeed. What is the mystery of these innumerable editions of *The Lamplighter*, and other books neither better nor worse? Worse they could not be, and better they need not be, when they sell by the hundred thousand.

6. J. W. Ward, *Red, White, and Blue; Men, Books, and Ideas in American Culture* (New York: Oxford University Press, 1961), p. 75.

7. George F. Whicher, "Literature and Conflict," in *The Literary History of the United States*, ed. Robert E. Spiller et al., 3rd ed., rev. (London: Macmillan, 1963), p. 583.

8. Whicher, in *Literary History*, ed. Spiller, p. 586. Edmund Wilson, despite his somewhat sympathetic treatment of Stowe in *Patriotic Gore: Studies in the Literature of the American Civil War* (New York: Oxford University Press, 1966), pp. 5, 32, seems to concur in this opinion, reflecting a characteristic tendency of commentators on the most popular works of sentimental fiction to regard the success of these

women as some sort of mysterious eruption, inexplicable by natural causes. Henry James gives this attitude its most articulate, though perhaps least defensible, expression in a remarkable passage from *A Small Boy and Others* (New York: Charles Scribner's Sons, 1913), pp. 159–160, where he describes Stowe's book as really not a book at all but as "a fish, a wonderful 'leaping' fish"—the point being to deny Stowe any role in the process that produced such a wonder:

> Appreciation and judgment, the whole impression, were thus an effect for which there had been no process—any process so related having in other cases *had* to be at some point or other critical; nothing in the guise of a written book, therefore, a book printed, published, sold, bought and "noticed," probably ever reached its mark, the mark of exciting interest, without having at least groped for that goal *as* a book or by the exposure of some literary side. Letters, here, languished unconscious, and Uncle Tom, instead of making even one of the cheap short cuts through the medium in which books breathe, even as fishes in water, went gaily roundabout it altogether, as if a fish, a wonderful "leaping" fish, had simply flown through the air.

9. Reverend Dwight Lyman Moody, *Sermons and Addresses*, in *Narrative of Messrs. Moody and Sankey's Labors in Great Britain and Ireland with Eleven Addresses and Lectures in Full* (New York: Anson D. F. Randolph and Co., 1975).

10. Harriet Beecher Stowe, "Children," in *Uncle Sam's Emancipation; Earthly Care, a Heavenly discipline; and other sketches* (Philadelphia: W. P. Hazard, 1853), p. 83.

11. Harriet Beecher Stowe, *Ministration of Departed Spirits* (Boston: American Tract Society, n.d.), pp. 4, 3.

12. Stowe, *Ministration*, p. 3.

13. Harriet Beecher Stowe, *Uncle Tom's Cabin; or, Life among the Lowly* ed. Kathryn Kish Sklar (New York: Library of America, 1982), p. 344. All future references to *Uncle Tom's Cabin* will be to this edition; chapter and page numbers are given in parentheses in the text.

14. Charles Dickens, *Dombey and Son* (Boston: Estes and Luriat, 1882), p. 278; Lydia H. Sigourney, *Letters to Mothers* (Hartford: Hudson and Skinner, 1838).

15. Religious conversion as the basis for a new social order was the mainspring of the Christian evangelical movement of the mid-nineteenth century. The emphasis on "feeling," which seems to modern readers to provide no basis whatever for the organization of society, was the key factor in the evangelical theory of reform. See Sandra Sizer's discussions of this phenomenon in *Gospel Hymns and Social Religion* (Philadelphia: Temple University Press, 1978), pp. 52, 59, 70–71, 72. "It is clear from the available literature that prayer, testimony, and exhortation were employed to create a *community* of intense *feeling*, in which individuals underwent similar experiences (centering on conversion) and would thenceforth unite with others in matters of moral decision and social behavior." "People in similar states of feeling, in short, would 'walk together,' would be agreed." "Conversion established individuals in a particular kind of relationship with God, by virtue of which they were automatically members of a social company, alike in interests and feelings." Good order would be preserved by "relying on the spiritual and moral discipline provided by conversion, and on the company of fellow Christians, operating without the coercive force of government."

16. Angus Fletcher, *Allegory, The Theory of a Symbolic Mode* (Ithaca, N.Y.:

Cornell University Press, 1964), discusses the characteristic features of allegory in such a way as to make clear the family resemblance between sentimental fiction and the allegorical mode. See particularly, his analyses of character, pp. 35, 60, symbolic action, pp. 150ff., 178, 180, 182, and imagery, p. 171.

17. Fletcher's comment on the presence of naturalistic detail in allegory, pp. 198–199, is pertinent here:

> The apparent surface realism of an allegorical agent will recede in importance, as soon as he is felt to take part in a magical plot, as soon as his causal relations to others in that plot are seen to be magically based. This is an important point because there has often been confusion as to the function of the naturalist detail of so much allegory. In terms I have been outlining, this detail now appears not to have a journalistic function; it is more than mere record of observed facts. It serves instead the purposes of magical containment, since the more the allegorist can circumscribe the attributes, metonymic and synecdochic, of his personae, the better he can shape their fictional destiny. Naturalist detail is "cosmic," universalizing, not accidental as it would be in straight journalism.

18. The associations that link slaves, women, and children are ubiquitous and operate on several levels. Besides being described in the same set of terms, these characters occupy parallel structural positions in the plot. They function chiefly as mediators between God and the unredeemed, so that, e.g., Mrs. Shelby intercedes for Mr. Shelby; Mrs. Bird for Senator Bird; Simon Legree's mother (unsuccessfully) for Simon Legree; little Eva and St. Clare's mother for St. Clare; Tom Loker's mother for Tom Loker; Eliza for George Harris (spiritually, she is the agent of his conversion), and for Harry Harris (physically, she saves him from being sold down the river); and Tom for all the slaves on the Legree plantation (spiritually, he converts them) and for all the slaves of the Shelby plantation (physically, he is the cause of their being set free).

19. For a parallel example, see Alice Crozier's analysis of the way the lock of hair that little Eva gives Tom becomes transformed into the lock of hair that Simon Legree's mother sent to Simon Legree. *The Novels of Harriet Beecher Stowe* (New York: Oxford University Press, 1969), pp. 29–31.

20. Sacvan Bercovitch, *The American Jeremiad* (Madison: University of Wisconsin Press, 1978), p. 9.

21. Bercovitch, p. xi.

22. Bercovitch, p. xiv.

23. For an excellent discussion of Beecher's *Treatise* and of the entire cult of domesticity, see Kathryn Kish Sklar, *Catherine Beecher, A Study in American Domesticity* (New York: W. W. Norton and Co., 1976). For other helpful discussions of the topic, see Barbara G. Berg, *The Remembered Gate: Origins of American Feminism, The Woman and the City, 1800–1860* (New York: Oxford University Press, 1978); Sizer; Ronald G. Walters, *The Antislavery Appeal, American Abolitionism after 1830* (Baltimore: The Johns Hopkins University Press, 1976); and Barbara Welter, "The Cult of True Womanhood, 1820–1860," *American Quarterly*, 18 (Summer 1966), pp. 151–174.

24. For Douglas' charges of narcissism against Stowe and her readers, see *The Feminization of American Culture*, pp. 2, 9, 297, and 300.

25. Catherine Beecher and Harriet Beecher Stowe, *The American Woman's*

Home: or, Principles of Domestic Science; Being a Guide to the Formation and Maintenance of Economical, Healthful, Beautiful, and Christian Homes (New York: J. B. Ford and Co., 1869), p. 18.

26. Beecher and Stowe, *The American Woman's Home*, p. 19.

27. Beecher and Stowe, *The American Woman's Home*, pp. 458–459.

28. These are Douglas' epithets, p. 307.

29. For a detailed discussion of the changes referred to here, see Christopher Clark, "Household Economy, Market Exchange and the Rise of Capitalism in the Connecticut Valley, 1800–1860," *Journal of Social History*, 13, No. 2 (Winter 1979), pp. 169–189; and Nancy F. Cott, *The Bonds of Womanhood: "Woman's Sphere" in New England, 1780–1835* (New Haven: Yale University Press, 1977).

30. Douglas, p. 9.

31. In a helpful article in *Signs*, "The Sentimentalists: Promise and Betrayal in the Home," 4, No. 3 (Spring 1979), pp. 434–446, Mary Kelley characterizes the main positions in the debate over the significance of sentimental fiction as follows: (1) the Cowie-Welter thesis, which holds that women's fiction expresses an "ethics of conformity" and accepts the stereotype of the woman as pious, pure, submissive, and dedicated to the home, and (2) the Papashvily-Garrison thesis, which sees sentimental fiction as profoundly subversive of traditional ideas of male authority and female subservience. Kelley locates herself somewhere in between, holding that sentimental novels convey a "contradictory message": "they tried to project an Edenic image," but their own tales "subverted their intentions" by showing how often women were frustrated and defeated in the performance of their heroic roles. My own position is that the sentimental novelists are both conformist and subversive, but not, as Kelley believes, in a self-contradictory way. They used the central myth of their culture—the story of Christ's death for the sins of mankind— as the basis for a new myth which reflected their own interests. They regarded their vision of the Christian home as the fulfillment of the Gospel, "the end . . . which Jesus Christ came into this world to secure," in exactly the same way that the Puritans believed that their mission was to found the "American city of God," and that Christians believe the New Testament to be a fulfillment of the Old. Revolutionary ideologies, typically, announce themselves as the fulfillment of old promises or as a return to a golden age. What I am suggesting here, in short, is that the argument over whether the sentimental novelists were radical or conservative is a false issue. The real problem is how we, in the light of everything that has happened since they wrote, can understand and appreciate their work. See Alexander Cowie, "The Vogue of the Domestic Novel, 1850–1870," *South Atlantic Quarterly*, 41 (October 1942), p. 420; Welter; Helen Waite Papashvily, *All the Happy Endings: A Study of the Domestic Novel in America, the Women Who Wrote It, the Women Who Read It, in the Nineteenth Century* (New York: Harper and Bros., 1956); and Dee Garrison, "Immoral Fiction in the Late Victorian Library," *American Quarterly*, 28 (Spring 1976), pp. 71–80.

NOTES TO CHAPTER VI

1. That is how twentieth-century critics have usually treated this work. See, for example, Henry Nash Smith, "The Scribbling Women and the Cosmic Success

Story," *Critical Inquiry*, 1 (September 1974), pp. 47–49; John T. Frederick, "Hawthorne's 'Scribbling Women,' " *New England Quarterly*, 48 (1975), pp. 231–240; Ramona T. Hull, "Scribbling Females and Serious Males: Hawthorne's Comments from Abroad on Some American Authors," *Nathaniel Hawthorne Journal*, 5 (1975), pp. 35–38.

2. Smith, p. 58; Henry Nash Smith, *Democracy and the Novel* (New York: Oxford University Press, 1978), p. 12; Perry Miller, "The Romance and the Novel," in *Nature's Nation* (Cambridge, Mass.: Harvard University Press, 1967), pp. 255–256.

3. Smith, *Democracy and the Novel*, pp. 13–15.

4. James D. Hart, *The Popular Book: A History of America's Literary Taste* (Berkeley: University of California Press, 1950), pp. 93, 94, 111; Frank Luther Mott, *Golden Multitudes* (New York: Macmillan, 1947), pp. 122–125.

5. Smith, *Democracy and the Novel*, p. 8.

6. Perry Miller, *The Life of the Mind in America from the Revolution to the Civil War* (New York: Harcourt Brace and World, 1965), p. 7.

7. Kenelm Burridge, *New Heaven, New Earth: A Study of Millenarian Activities* (New York: Schocken Books, 1969), provides a valuable account of the social content of millenarianism which has been crucial to my own thinking concerning the assumptions about power implicit in all kinds of evangelical writing, including Warner's novel.

Burridge's definition of religion makes sense in the context of nineteenth-century social thought, which was so intimately bound up with religious beliefs.

"For not only are religions concerned with the truth about power, but the reverse also holds: a concern with the truth about power is a religious activity" (p. 7). "Religious activities will change when the assumptions about the nature of power, and hence the rules which govern its use and control, can no longer guarantee the truth of things" (p. 7).

"The rules which govern the use of power can be determined. Both emerge from the ways in which individuals discharge or evade their obligations, what they do to counter or meet the consequences of evasion, how they cope with a pledge redeemed, what they say the consequences will or might be." "Salvation equals redemption equals unobligedness" (p. 8).

" 'Feeling themselves oppressed' by current assumptions about power, participants in millenarian activities set themselves the task of reformulating their assumptions so as to create, or account for and explain, a new or changing material and moral environment within which a more satisfactory form of redemption will be obtained" (p. 10).

"An adequate or more satisfactory way of gaining prestige, of defining the criteria by which the content of manhood is to be measured, stands at the very heart of a millennarian or messianic movement. And these criteria relate on the one hand to gaining or retaining self-respect, status, and that integrity which is implied in the approved retention of a particular status; and on the other hand to an acknowledged process whereby redemption may be won" (p. 11). "The redemptive process, and so redemption, bears significantly on the politico-economic process, particularly the prestige system" (p. 13). "A prestige system is based upon particular measurements of manhood which relate to gaining or retaining self-respect and integrity, and which refer back to the politico-economic process, the redemptive process, and assumptions about power" (p. 13). "Indeed, all religions are basically concerned with power. They are concerned with the discovery, identification, moral relevance and ordering of different kinds of power, whether these manifest themselves as thunder, or lightning, atomic fission, untramelled desire, arrogance, impulse, apparitions, visions, or persuasive words. . . . And all that is meant by a belief in the supernatural is the belief that there do exist kinds of power whose manifestations and effects are observable, but whose natures are not yet fully comprehended" (p. 5).

"Religions, let us say, are concerned with the systematic ordering of different kinds of power, particularly those seen as significantly beneficial or dangerous" (p. 5).

8. This is the term given to the movement by Charles Foster in his excellent account, *An Errand of Mercy: The Evangelical United Front, 1790–1837* (Chapel Hill: University of North Carolina Press, 1960).

9. As quoted by Foster, p. 273.

10. In March of 1829, for example, a pamphlet entitled *Institution and Observance of the Sabbath* was distributed to 28,383 New York families. See Foster, p. 187.

11. New York City Tract Society, *Eleventh Annual Report* (New York: New York City Tract Society, 1837), back cover.

12. New York City Tract Society, pp. 51–52.

13. New York City Tract Society, pp. 51, 52.

14. David Reynolds, "From Doctrine to Narrative: The Rise of Pulpit Story-Telling in America," *American Quarterly*, 32 (Winter, 1980), pp. 479–498.

15. Reverend William S. Plumer, "Ann Eliza Williams, or the Child an Hundred Years Old, an Authentic Narrative," in *Narratives of Little Henry and His Bearer; The Amiable Louisa; and Ann Eliza Williams* (New York: American Tract Society, n.d.), pp. 4, 11.

16. Harvey Sacks, "On the Analysability of Stories by Children," in *Ethnomethodology*, ed. Roy Turner (Middlesex, England: Penguin, 1974), p. 218.

17. American Home Missionary Society, *Twenty Second Report* (New York: William Osborn, 1848), p. 103.

18. David Tyack and Elisabeth Hansot, *Managers of Virtue: Public School Leadership in America, 1820–1980* (New York: Basic Books, Inc., 1982), pp. 15–104.

19. *Thoughts on Domestic Education, The Result of Experience*, by a Mother (Boston: Carter and Hendee, 1829), p. 106.

20. For a comparable example, see Lydia Maria Child, *The Mother's Book* (Boston: Carter and Hendee, 1829), which devotes an entire chapter to the "Value of Time."

21. New York City Tract Society, p. 158.

22. Mrs. Lydia H. Sigourney, *Margaret and Henrietta* (New York: American Tract Society, 1852), pp. 12–13.

23. The expectation that children should order their lives for the furthering of God's kingdom is commonplace. See, for instance, Lydia Maria Child's New Year's message to children, *The Juvenile Miscellany*, I, 3 (January 1827), pp. 103–105, which urges children to "make a regular arrangement of time" and to be "always employed."

24. Robert Wiebe, "The Social Functions of Schooling," *American Quarterly*, 21 (1969), pp. 147–150.

25. Tremaine McDowell, "Diversity and Innovation in New England," in *The Literary History of the United States*, ed. Robert E. Spiller et al., 3rd ed., rev. (London: Macmillan, 1963), p. 289.

26. In the first half of the nineteenth century, single women could own real property but married women could not. "Essentially," writes Lawrence Friedman, *A History of American Law* (New York: Simon and Schuster, 1973), p. 184, "husband and wife were one flesh; but the man was the owner of that flesh." For a good discussion of the growing discrepancy, from the seventeenth century onward, between anti-patriarchal theories of government and the reinforcement of patriarchal family structure, see Susan Miller Okin, "The Making of the Sentimental Family," *Philosophy and Public Affairs*, 11 (Winter 1982), pp. 65–88.

27. Alexis de Tocqueville, *Democracy in America*, trans. Henry Reive, rev., 2 vols. (New York: Vintage Books, 1957), II, p. 223.

28. Chapter and page references to *The Wide, Wide World* are to the undated, one-volume "Home Library" edition of the novel (New York: A. L. Burt).

29. Reverend Orville Dewey, *A Discourse Preached in the City of Washington, on Sunday, June 27th, 1852* (New York: Charles S. Francis and Company, 1852), p. 13. Dewey's sermon on obedience is characteristic of a general concern that a democratic government was breeding anarchy in the behavior of its citizens, and that obedience therefore must be the watchword of the day. In European society, Dewey argues, where the law of caste still reigns, there is a natural respect for order and authority. But *"here* and *now,"* he continues, pp. 4–5, "all this is changed. . . . With no *appointed* superiors above us, we are liable enough to go to the opposite extreme; we are liable to forget that any body is to be obeyed—to forget even, that God is to be obeyed. . . . Only let every man, every youth, every child, think that he has the right to speak, act, do any where and every where, whatever any body else has the right to do; that he has as much right to his will as any body; and there is an end of society. That is to say, let there be an end of obedience in the world, and there is an end of the world." Since, in Dewey's eyes, pp. 13–14, the home is the source of anarchy in the state, family discipline is the source of all good civil order, and therefore the goal of domestic education must be "a patient and perfect obedience." "If the child is *never* permitted to disobey, it will soon cease to think of it as possible. And it should *never* be permitted! . . . Only when living under law—only when walking in obedience, is child or man, family or State, happy and truly prosperous. Selfish passion every where is anarchy, begetting injustice, and bringing forth destruction." Sentimental novels, along with advice books for young women, child-rearing manuals, and religious literature of all sorts, helped to inculcate the notion that obedience was a domestic as well as a civic virtue, especially in the case of women. Beginning in the 1830s, as Nancy F. Cott has shown in *The Bonds of Womanhood: "Woman's Sphere" in New England, 1780–1835* (New Haven: Yale University Press, 1977), pp. 158–159, clergymen directed their sermons on the need for order in family and society especially at women, "vividly emphasizing the necessity for women to be subordinate to and dependent on their husbands."

30. Ann Douglas, *The Feminization of American Culture* (New York: Alfred A. Knopf, 1977), p. 11.

31. Tocqueville, II, pp. 210, 212, describes the process of moral education of American women in very much the same terms. "Americans," he says, "have

found out that in a democracy the independence of individuals cannot fail to be very great, youth premature, tastes ill-restrained, customs fleeting, public opinion often unsettled and powerless, paternal authority weak, and marital authority contested. Under these circumstances, believing that they had little chance of repressing in woman the most vehement passions of the human heart, they held that the surer way was to teach her the art of combating those passions for herself." Thus, Tocqueville continues, having cultivated an extraordinary "strength of character" and learned to "exercise a proper control over herself," the American woman "finds the energy necessary for . . . submission in the firmness of understanding and in the virile habits which her education has given her."

32. Harvey C. Minnich, ed. *Old Favorites from the McGuffey Readers* (new York: American Book Co., 1936), pp. 178–179, prints a poem, from the *Fourth Reader*, entitled "A Mother's Gift—The Bible." The first stanza reads as follows:

> *Remember, love, who gave thee this,*
> *When older days shall come,*
> *When she who had thine earliest kiss,*
> *Sleeps in her narrow home.*
> *Remember! 'twas a mother gave*
> *The gift to one she'd die to save!*

The Bible is the symbol of the mother in sentimental literature, taking her place, after she is dead, serving as a reminder of her teachings, and as a token of her love. To forget what the Bible says is to forget one's mother:

> *A parent's blessing on her son*
> *Goes with this holy thing;*
> *The love that would retain the one,*
> *Must to the other cling.*

33. For example, Douglas; Barbara Epstein, *The Politics of Domesticity* (Middletown, Conn.: Wesleyan University Press, 1981); Barbara Welter, *Dimity Convictions* (Athens, Ohio: Ohio University Press, 1976).

34. Epstein, p. 75. The original source is Irving's *Sketch Book*.

35. Epstein, p. 75.

36. Sandra Sizer, *Gospel Hymns and Social Religion* (Philadelphia: Temple University Press, 1978), p. 33, describes that relation as follows: "The secret of his saving power lies in a movement inward, not only toward shelter and refuge with Jesus and/or in heaven, but to a realm of intimacy. It is a sphere not only of passivity but of passion—the passion, the emotions, in nineteenth-century language the 'affections.' " Sizer's book is the best discussion I know of the relationship between the domestic ideal and evangelical Christianity. In summing up the relationship between the gospel hymns and popular fiction, p. 110, she writes:

> In short, the hymns incorporate the ordering of the world provided by the ideology of evangelical domesticity in the novels; the two rhetorics are parallel and very nearly identical. Jesus and heaven, so central in the hymns, are being understood in terms of domestic descriptions. The tender affections, the feminine virtues, the home-haven which gives protection and generates inward strength through intimacy—all become part of the hymns' picture of Jesus and his heavenly realm.

37. Reverend E. Peabody, "Importance of Trifles," in *The Little Republic, Original Articles by Various Hands*, ed. Mrs. Eliza T. P. Smith (New York: Wiley and Putnam, 1848), p. 120. The "importance of trifles" theme is ubiquitous in nineteenth-century inspirational literature. It is directly related to the Christian rhetoric of inversion ("The last shall be first"), to the cultivation of the practical virtues of honesty, industry, frugality ("A stitch in time saves nine"; "A penny saved is a penny earned"), and to the glorification of the mother's influence. In another essay in the same volume, "A Word to Mothers," pp. 210, 211–212, Thomas P. Smith writes: "Let us not forget that the greatest results of the mind are produced by small, but continued, patient effort." "As surely as a continued digging will wear away the mountain, so surely shall the persevering efforts of a Christian mother be crowned with success. . . . She is, through her children, casting pebbles into the bosom of society; but she cannot as easily watch the ripples made: no, they reach beyond the shore of mortal vision, and shall ripple on, in that sea that has neither shore nor bound, for weal or for woe, to them, and to the whole universal brotherhood of man."

38. Peabody, in *The Little Republic*, ed. Smith, pp. 124–125.

39. Lewis O. Saum, *The Popular Mood of Pre-Civil War America* (Westport, Conn.: Greenwood Press, 1980), p. 3.

40. Tocqueville, II, p. 225.

41. Herman Melville, *Moby-Dick or, The Whale*, ed., introd. Charles Feidelson, Jr. (New York: The Bobbs-Merrill Company, 1964), p. 247.

42. *Pilgrim's Progress* is Ellen's favorite book.

43. Charles Kingsley, *The Water-Babies* (London, 1903), p. 174, as cited by Foster, *Susan and Anna Warner*, p. 48.

44. American Home Missionary Society, *Fifteenth Report* (New York: William Osborn, 1842), p. 104.

NOTES TO CHAPTER VII

1. Carolyn Karcher first called my attention to the way literary anthologies reflect the shifting currents of social and political life by referring me to Bruce Franklin's helpful discussion of this phenomenon in *The Victim as Criminal and Artist: Literature from the American Prison* (New York: Oxford University Press, 1978), pp. xiii–xxii.

For another informative account of American literary anthologies and their relation to social and cultural issues, see Paul Lauter, "Race and Gender in the Shaping of the American Canon: A Case Study from the Twenties," *Feminist Studies*, 9, No. 3 (Fall 1983), pp. 432–463.

2. *Century Readings for a Course in American Literature*, ed. Fred Lewis Pattee, 1st ed. (New York: The Century Co., 1919); *Major Writers of America*, ed. Perry Miller et al. (New York: Harcourt, Brace & World, 1962), I.

3. *Masters of American Literature*, ed. Gordon N. Ray et al. (Boston: Houghton Mifflin, 1959); *Twelve American Writers*, ed. William M. Gibson and George Arms (New York: Macmillan, 1962); *Eight American Writers*, ed. Norman Foerster and Robert P. Falk (New York: W. W. Norton & Co., 1963).

4. *Twelve American Writers*, ed. Gibson, p. vii.

5. *Major American Writers*, ed. Howard Mumford Jones and Ernest Leisy (New York: Harcourt Brace and Co., 1935), p. v. Lauter points to the even more glaring contrast between the nine writers Foerster selected to represent American prose in 1916 in *The Chief American Prose Writers*, ed. Norman Foerster (Cambridge, Mass.: The Riverside Press, 1919), and the eight he chose in 1963 in *Eight American Writers*. On the two lists, only three names are the same.

6. The quote is from the preface to the 1974 Macmillan anthology, *Anthology of American Literature*, ed. George McMichael et al. (New York: Macmillan, 1974).

7. *Major Writers of America*, ed. Miller, pp. xix, xx.

8. *Century Readings*, ed. Pattee, p. v.

9. See, for example, *American Literature*, ed. Thomas H. Briggs et al. (Boston: Houghton Mifflin, 1933); *American Poetry and Prose*, ed. Robert Morss Lovett and Norman Foerster (Boston: Houghton Mifflin, 1934); *Major American Writers*, ed. Jones; *American Life in Literature*, ed. Jay Hubbell (New York: Harper and Brothers, 1936); and *A College Book of American Literature*, ed. Milton Ellis et al. (New York: American Book Company, 1939). The thirties also saw the appearance of new types of specialized anthologies such as *Proletarian Literature*, ed. Granville Hicks et al. (New York: International Publishers, 1935).

10. This was *American Literature*, ed. Briggs.

11. *American Literature*, ed. Briggs, p. iv.

12. *A College Book of American Literature*, ed. Ellis, p. v.

13. *American Life in Literature*, ed. Hubbell, p. xxiii.

14. *American Life in Literature*, ed. Hubbell, p. xxiii.

15. *Major Writers of America*, ed. Miller, p. xviii.

16. *Major Writers of America*, ed. Miller, p. xviii.

17. *Major Writers of America*, ed. Miller; *Masters of American Literature*, ed. Henry A. Pochman and Gay Wilson Allen (New York: Macmillan, 1949); *Masters of American Literature*, ed. Ray; *Twelve American Writers*, ed. Gibson and Arms; *American Heritage, An Anthology and Interpretive Survey of Our Literature*, ed. Leon Howard et al. (Boston: D. C. Heath & Co., 1955); *The Growth of American Literature, A Critical and Historical Survey*, ed. Edwin Cady et al. (New York: American Book Company, 1956); *The Norton Anthology of American Literature*, ed. Ronald Gottesman, Laurence B. Holland, David Kalstone, Francis Murphy, Hershel Parker, William H. Pritchard (New York: W. W. Norton & Co., 1979); *Anthology of American Literature*, ed. George McMichael et al., 2nd ed. (New York: Macmillan, 1980).

18. Barbara Herrnstein Smith, "Contingencies of Value," *Critical Inquiry*, 10, No. 1 (September 1983), pp. 1–35.

19. In 1958, eleven months after the launching of Sputnik, the President appointed a special assistant for science and technology, and the government passed the National Defense Education Act, which increased grants given to students of mathematics, the natural and social sciences, and modern languages. See Daniel Snowman, *America Since 1920* (New York: Harper & Row, 1968), p. 128.

20. Paul A. Carter, *Another Part of the Fifties* (New York: Columbia University Press, 1983), p. 169.

21. *Century Readings in American Literature*, ed. Fred Lewis Pattee, 4th ed. (New York: The Century Co., 1932), p. 343.

22. *Century Readings* (1932), ed. Pattee, pp. 343–344.

23. *The Norton Anthology of American Literature*, ed. Gottesman, p. 875.

24. *The Norton Anthology of American Literature*, ed. Gottesman, p. 876.

25. *The Norton Anthology of American Literature*, ed. Gottesman, p. 876.

26. Frederick Crews, *Sins of the Fathers: Hawthorne's Psychological Themes* (New York: Oxford University Press, 1966).

27. F. O. Matthiessen, *American Renaissance: Art and Expression in the Age of Emerson and Whitman* (New York: Oxford University Press, 1941), p. vii.

28. Matthiessen, p. xi, actually claims that "successive generations of common readers who make the decisions have agreed that the authors of the pre–Civil War era who bulk the largest in stature are the five who are my subject." But in the period Matthiessen delimits, 1850 to 1855, common readers were engrossed by the works of Susan Warner, Harriet Beecher Stowe, Fanny Fern, Grace Greenwood, Caroline Lee Hentz, Mary Jane Holmes, Augusta Jane Evans, Maria Cummins, D. G. Mitchell, T. S. Arthur, and Sylvanus Cobb, Jr. See James D. Hart, *The Popular Book: A History of America's Literary Taste* (Berkeley: University of California Press, 1950). With the exception of Emerson, none of the authors Matthiessen names was read by the common reader, nor did common readers have a hand in assuring their survival.

Matthiessen, who had been active in leftist politics during the thirties, needed to believe that the works he had chosen represented "all the people," at the same time that, because of his formalist critical commitments, he needed to believe that they met the "enduring requirements for great art." As Jonathan Arac has shown, in "F. O. Matthiessen, Authorizing an American Renaissance," *The American Renaissance Reconsidered,* Selected Papers from the English Institute, 1982–83, ed. Walter Benn Michaels and Donald E. Pease (Baltimore: The Johns Hopkins University Press, 1985), pp. 90–112, because of the policy of alliance-building adopted by the Popular Front in the late thirties, Matthiessen was able to combine his Christianity, his leftist politics, and his formalist critical allegiance through a strategy of "reconciliation" which emphasized the continuity of the present with the "great tradition" of American literature.

Index

DATE DUE

JUL 1 9 2012

SEP 3 0 1988	DEC 2 3 1996	
FEB 03 1989		
JUN 1 3 1989	JUN 2 5 1997	
JUN 0 8 1992	DEC 3 1 1997	
JUL 3 1 1992	DEC 0 5 1997	
DEC 1 9 1992	DEC 2	
APR 1 2 1993	DEC 0 2 2008	
MAR 1 3 1994		2000
DEC 2 7 1995	DEC 3 0	
10-4-95		
OCT 3 1 1995	MAY 2 8 2003	
DEC 1 2 199		